The Whole Heaven Catalog

Other Books by Marcia and Jack Kelly

Sanctuaries: A Guide to Lodgings in Monasteries, Abbeys, and Retreats
The Northeast
The West Coast and Southwest
The Complete United States

One Hundred Graces: Mealtime Blessings

By Marcia Kelly

Heavenly Feasts: Memorable Meals from Monasteries, Abbeys, and Retreats

The Whole Heaven Catalog

A RESOURCE GUIDE TO PRODUCTS,
SERVICES, ARTS, CRAFTS, AND FESTIVALS
OF RELIGIOUS, SPIRITUAL,
AND COOPERATIVE COMMUNITIES

Marcia and Jack Kelly

BELL TOWER/ONE SPIRIT   NEW YORK

A percentage of the authors' royalties from this book will go to a kindness and compassion scholarship at Martin Luther King High School in New York City and the Hanuman Foundation Ram Dass Fund, P.O. Box 478, Santa Fe, NM 87504.

For permissions, see page 284.

Published by Bell Tower, an imprint of Harmony Books, a division of Crown Publishers, Inc., 201 East 50th Street, New York, New York 10022. Member of the Crown Publishing Group, Random House, Inc., New York, Toronto, London, Sydney, Auckland
www.randomhouse.com
and
One Spirit
Resources for the Spirit, Mind, and Body

Bell Tower and colophon are trademarks of Crown Publishers, Inc.

Printed in the United States of America

Design by June Bennett-Tantillo

Library of Congress Cataloging-in-Publication Data
Kelly, Marcia.
The whole heaven catalog : a resource guide to products, services,
arts, crafts, and festivals of religious, spiritual, and cooperative
communities / Marcia and Jack Kelly.—1st ed.
Includes bibliographical references and indexes.
1. Religious communities—United States—Directories.
2. Collective settlements—United States—Directories.
3. Commercial products—United States—Directories.   4. Handicraft—
United States—Directories.   5. Festivals—United States—
Directories.   6. Retreats—United States—Directories.   I. Kelly,
Jack, 1934–   .   II. Title.
BL2525.K44   1998
291.6′5′02573—dc21   97-53283
CIP
ISBN 0-609-80120-1

10 9 8 7 6 5 4 3 2 1

First Edition

ACKNOWLEDGMENTS

❖

We learned a wonderful mealtime blessing at a New Year's retreat at Pendle Hill, the Quaker center in Wallingford, Pennsylvania:

Let us give thanks for unknown blessings already on the way.

We would like to give thanks for the many blessings that have already arrived:

+ For Toinette Lippe, our gifted Bell Tower editor.
+ For Robert Welsch, One Spirit Book Club's director, whose foresight and creativity inspired this book.
+ For Tom Simpson, our editorial assistant, whose intelligence, focus, hard work, excellent research, and attention to detail added an important dimension to this book.
+ For Judith Rosenberg, who gave us our first copy of *St. Benedict's Rule* and tirelessly translated international Internet messages for us, among other thoughtful and encouraging good deeds.
+ For Carole Kraus, a very good neighbor.
+ For Sister Donald Corcoran of Transfiguration Monastery in Windsor, New York, who brought us news of English nuns who made fishing flies, mead, and pewter—and, most intriguing of all, nuns who raise llamas in North Dakota!
+ For Brother Victor-Antoine d'Avila-Latourette of Our Lady of the Resurrection Monastery in La Grangeville, New York, who fed us heavenly feasts and was our French connection, along with Sister Thérèse Marie, of La Trappe de Chambarand, Roybon, France.
+ For Cassidy Marcus, a wonderful treasure in our family, and his mother Kristi, who led us to the invaluable *Communities Directory*.
+ For Geoph Kozeny, community founder and roving reporter for the *Communities Directory*, who kindly shared his time and knowledge via E-mail and telephone from wherever he happened to be, even a steaming bath!

Although we have specialized in visiting monasteries, abbeys, and retreats, we knew little about the world of intentional communities. The discovery of the Fellowship for Intentional

Community and their fabulous *Communities Directory* and *Communities Magazine* opened up a whole new world to us, of which we will give you a glimpse in this book. The directory lists 540 cooperative communities in North America and 70 on other continents. This made it easy for us to discover which communities had intriguing ways of making a living: from manufacturing sandals, tofu, and birdcall tapes to gathering wildflower seeds. The quarterly magazine supplements the directory with current information and happenings in North American communities.

Laird Schaub, the fellowship's secretary, writes, "We are excited to build this bridge to monastic orders, whose tradition of community living extends back for two millennia. Just as there are many spiritual disciplines, so are there many approaches to community living. By being more aware of what each is doing, there is more information and more choice. Cooperating, we give ourselves the best possible chance to make wise choices about how we live."

Communities Directory ($28)
Communities Magazine ($18 for 4 issues)
138-G Twin Oaks Rd.
Louisa, VA 23093
(540) 894-5126 / 894-4112 fax

A
C
K
N
O
W
L
E
D
G
M
E
N
T
S
◈

CONTENTS

❖

C
O
N
T
E
N
T
S

◈

INTRODUCTION

◆

During our travels to more than 250 places for our book series *Sanctuaries: A Guide to Lodgings in Monasteries, Abbeys, and Retreats,* we discovered that many of these religious communities had developed an ingenious number of ways to create income, using creativity, determination, and steadfastness to create products and services that would find a market in the outside world. These communities have the same need to support themselves as we do in the secular world, to pay for food, heat, lighting, clothing, insurance, and health care.

To identify the different products, arts, crafts, and services the communities have developed is the purpose of this book. Some ventures are as simple as making beautiful photographs, taken by a resident nun, into note cards that are sold in the monastery shop; others are complex businesses, like the 30,000 loaves of Monk's Bread made each week by the monks at the Abbey of the Genesee in Piffard, New York, and the great cheeses from three different communities: the Trappists at Abbey of Gethsemani in Kentucky, the Trappistine sisters at Our Lady of Angels Monastery in Virginia, and the New Skete monks in Cambridge, New York. The candies from Mount St. Mary's Abbey in Massachusetts were a delightful discovery when we first visited there in 1990, and we have continued to order them ever since. There are other candy makers with exceptional skills at Our Lady of the Mississippi in Iowa and at the Monastery of Our Lady of Consolation in Oregon. Whether one prefers butter-nut munch from Massachusetts, caramels from Iowa, or fudge from Oregon is a temptation to wrestle with alone or by family consensus. There are many other food products that can be ordered by mail, such as jellies and jams, fruitcakes, cheesecakes, and meats, to name a few. But food is only a part of the offerings. The monks at Mepkin Abbey in Moncks Corner, South Carolina, who make their living selling eggs, have invented a product from chicken droppings called Earth Healer, a premium garden compost; the Woodcrest Bruderhof community in Rifton, New York, makes furniture for the disabled and has an airplane for charter; there's even a community in France from which you can order Lourdes water via the Internet.

As the plan evolved for the products and services from the different religious communities, we discovered hundreds of other cooperative communities across the country with interesting businesses that would be useful to know about. Though some of these communities do not belong to a particular religious order, they all seem to have a spiritual base of commendable intents, from treating the environment with respect, to helping others, or simply trying hard to be the best people they can possibly be by living and working in harmony. An astonishing array of offerings are represented: computer services, marching bands, bed-and-breakfasts, motels, schools, training in organic farming, lawn services, kayaking, dog training, plant medicine, hammock weaving, and nut butters, among many other things. Often ideas developed spontaneously; for example, at the Abbey of the Genesee, the breadmaking business came from a monk, an ex–navy chef, who made great breads that guests always wanted to take home. Other communities benefited from a specialty of a temporary community member who taught the others a skill, and then moved on, leaving the gift behind. Tentmaking, ironworking, and a new candy recipe are examples of these gifts.

We visited the places we write about either in person or by telephone and followed up on suggestions from friends and acquaintances. It was remarkable how people came up with the most amazing nuggets of information, so that one thing kept leading to another.

In the end, this is a book that celebrates a part of our culture we rarely hear about, but is the source of a tremendous variety of products and services, arts and crafts, which we can all enjoy knowing about, purchasing for ourselves and others, or use as an inspiration for similar beginnings of our own. We've also tried to share a glimpse of lifestyles that are out of the ordinary, often not visible at all in our fast-paced world, but are abundant and thriving throughout the United States.

HOW TO USE THIS BOOK

◆

At the beginning of the book we have written the stories of the places and organized them by state, then alphabetically within each state. This is the section that will give a flavor of the community and its lifestyle and information about what it does to make a living. If there is something you might want to know more about, or something you might like to purchase, this is where you will find details of how to go about this. If there is a fax number or E-mail address, we've included them, as we have any Web-site information. If there is a catalog or gift shop, we have used the symbol 📖 or 🎁 to indicate this.

Getting in touch with the places directly is the best way to discover what is currently available. Sometimes policies change depending on the size of a crop, the current weather conditions, the number of community members available to make a certain product. Sometimes a decision is made to sell only through an outside dealer or distributor because handling orders from their farmhouse phone no longer works efficiently. Sometimes the specialist responsible for developing a product moves on to a sister community and takes the skill along, so the product can be found only at the new location. The Abbey of New Clairvaux in Vina, California, sells its prunes to Sunsweet, its walnuts to Diamond, but there have been so many individual requests that the abbey is considering bagging some for its own gift shop. At the Greyston Bakery in Yonkers, New York, most of the pies are sold directly to restaurants these days, but its cookies and pecan tarts are still sold to individuals. Unlike most mainstream businesses, many of the community businesses are much more flexible in their decision-making, so policies and products can change from day to day. Remember that these are all unique places; some are rustic farms, while others are sophisticated operations with full-color catalogs mailed on request. A phone call will add to your information about each place, and introduce you to a member of the community at the same time.

We have provided an index to all the products and services and events included in the book. Under each product you will find the name, city, and state of each place that makes a product, for easy reference back to the main section with the contact details. So there are two ways you can approach the book: Start at the beginning and read straight through, learning about each community and its products, or go directly to the alphabetical listing of all products and find the fudge you're seeking, for example, and the page with ordering information.

We have also listed special events, fairs, festivals, and ceremonies that are open to the public.

We have really enjoyed the adventure of learning about all the wonderful ways that communities have invented to help support themselves and the lifestyles they have chosen. We take great pleasure in introducing them to you as a way to bring attention to the products, services, and events they offer, and to enable each of us to participate in this good work that is going on quietly all around us. Please, dear reader, be gentle with these places because they usually have very few people handling requests, and many of them lead lives devoted to prayer rather than to commerce.

We look forward to hearing from you about places we have missed, products that should be included, information that has changed since publication. At the back of the book you will find a questionnaire with details of what we would like to know about a new monastery or community you would like to see included in the book. We hope there will be many future editions of *The Whole Heaven Catalog,* each one with wonderful new things for all of us to enjoy.

MARCIA AND JACK KELLY

Alabama

This community of Catholic Benedictine sisters came to northern Alabama in the late 1800s to found a school for German immigrants. They bought this property in 1902 and have built an impressive complex of buildings over the years, which they continue to use while adapting to the needs of today's society. They host seminars, retreats, and programs throughout the year, have apartments for the elderly, and host Elderhostels. The adaptation of this community is a reflection of the talents in the group—administrators, teachers, chaplains, nurses, a lawyer, and a legal secretary—educated and capable women who can adjust to current needs and have the ability to plan fulfilling lives through sharing their prayer and demonstrating the value of communal living while using their considerable talents. The apartments for the elderly are attractively designed and situated in a quiet spot behind the main building on the lush, campuslike 200-acre property. Retreatants and guests are housed in former school dormitories near the chapel and the dining room, where meals are taken with the sisters. An intriguing offering is the monastery's study tours to sacred places. Experienced and knowledgeable sister guides have led tours to the Middle East, and in 1998 they plan a pilgrimage to Spain.

We drove up the long drive through manicured lawns to an impressive brick building, a former school that now serves as offices and hospitality suites, with the church at the far end. We arrived in time for afternoon prayer, so we went in and joined the sisters in the lovely, tranquil chapel. Sharing the prayer services of communities was one of our great pleasures, and we seemed often

SACRED HEART MONASTERY

◆

**916 Convent Rd.
Cullman, AL 35055
(205) 734-8302**

STUDY TOURS TO SACRED PLACES

THEMATIC RETREATS

APARTMENTS FOR THE ELDERLY

SPIRITUAL PROGRAMS

ELDERHOSTELS

to arrive at prayer time. That always made it easier to find our contact, since the entire community comes together for services.

Our host showed us into the main building and took us to our room, then on a tour down the long, pristine hallways with their 20-foot-high ceilings, to the elegantly painted and decorated guest parlor with its comfortable chairs and couches. This was where parents were greeted when their daughters were brought to the boarding school. Although the school closed some years ago, this room is kept in perfect condition and used for special occasions. Next came the dining room, where the community was gathered for the evening meal. Our host charmed us with reminiscences of her time at the monastery. She had been the prioress for a number of years, and then handed over the mantle of leadership to a younger sister. As we ate, a number of the sisters kept dropping by our table, talked to us for a little while, and then left. We learned later that they had a mission: to evaluate this couple from New York who were doing a guidebook to retreat houses. Should they consider being part of it? Later that evening, the current prioress told us we had passed the test and they would love to be in our book. We had passed a test we didn't know we were taking. How gently they dealt with us.

The next day we toured the property and visited the guest houses. One tree-lined path led to a new building with a welcoming foyer, hallways leading off to apartments for elderly singles or couples, the whole place designed for efficiency and comfort, and watched over by these considerate sisters.

"**B**uild it and they will come." Long before this phrase, from the film *Field of Dreams,* was written, creative individuals and groups have been involved with projects that have permanence and an appeal to pilgrims and spiritual seekers, or just the curious. Every year, many do make their way to this quiet Catholic Benedictine abbey to spend time on the monastery grounds, where one of the resident monks labored for many years to create a grotto of miniature stone scenes of important biblical towns and areas. Visitors have benefited spiritually from using the quiet pathways and scenes as a meditative experience. Many stay at the St. Bernard Retreat House and join the monks in the chapel for their daily prayer schedule or take advantage of the regular retreats offered.

ST. BERNARD'S BENEDICTINE ABBEY

◆

1600 St. Bernard Dr. Cullman, AL 35055 (205) 734-3946

OUTDOOR GROTTO OF MINIATURE SPIRITUAL SCENES

RETREATS

A READER'S VERSION OF THE RULE OF SAINT BENEDICT IN INCLUSIVE LANGUAGE

The rule of Benedict is read in every monastery of the Order every day. Both Benedictine women and men, then, grow into monasticism listening to the Rule to learn its wisdom and taste its experiences. The problem is that the Rule as read in the original was written for Benedict's own communities of men. Consequently, the Benedictine woman hears only about the Abbot and the brethren rather than the Prioress or the sisters all her life. The images of Benedictine life, then, that the Rule conjures up are images of male Benedictine life. The language of the Rule itself, as a result, distances women from the experiences of their own monastic tradition.

This Reader's Version of the Rule is inclusive of both women and men and can be a contribution to the community model of the tradition itself and a key to its continued value for women in our time and culture. We offer this volume, therefore, not to change the Rule in any way but only to make it a richer reading experience for all of us.

◆

From the introduction by Sr. Joan Chittister, O.S.B., Mount St. Benedict, Erie, Pennsylvania

All the selections from St. Benedict's Rule in The Whole Heaven Catalog *(of which we will share 10 chapters from the total of 73) are from this version, which is available from Mount Saint Benedict Monastery, 6101 East Lake Rd., Erie, PA 16511. Reprinted with permission.*

VISITATION MONASTERY

◆

2300 Spring Hill Ave.
Mobile, AL 36607
(334) 473-2321

**DESERT EXPERIENCE
RETREATS FOR WOMEN**

**RETREATS FOR MEN AND
COUPLES**

An eight-foot-high wall surrounds almost two acres of lawn and stately trees and bushes, and offers privacy and solitude for those seeking a quiet retreat. This monastery was founded in 1832 when five sisters came south to Mobile to open a school at the request of the local bishop. The convent and 17-acre property have received awards from the Historic Preservation Society recognizing efforts to preserve and maintain the integrity of the monastery's century-old buildings, which add to the charm of this important Southern city. Retreats for women began in the 1950s and the program expanded for men and couples in the 1960s. Local laypeople are very helpful to the cloistered contemplative nuns who gather in the chapel five times a day for community prayer and for morning mass at 6:30. The sisters offer a "desert experience" of from two to eight days of silence and solitude for women to live with them and share their life of prayer.

We timed our Sunday arrival in Mobile so that we could have brunch at a well-known local restaurant, but it was closed, and we found downtown Mobile quietly slumbering, so we proceeded, hungrily, to the monastery. Our route took us past some elegant Southern mansions with spacious lawns to the church steeple and high walls that marked our destination. We entered a building at the side of the church and encountered a friendly woman who directed us through a door into a courtyard. There we glimpsed another door that led to the dining room, where retreatants talked quietly as they had their lunch. The buffet table was right in front of us, still stocked with salads and fried chicken and gravy, mashed potatoes, biscuits, and desserts. We helped ourselves to the offerings, and the Southern style and flavors of the meal were as good as any restaurant could have offered.

That evening we went to Vespers in the chapel, where the nuns sat in an alcove to the side of the altar and sang the evening prayers, completely focused on their song. We were the only others in the church, and we floated in that peaceful ocean all by ourselves.

Alaska

◆——◆——◆

The Shrine of St. Thérèse of Lisieux, known as "the little flower," is located on a small island in Lynn Canal, 24 miles north of Juneau, Alaska. It was inspired by Bishop Crimont, S.J., D.D., who was from St. Thérèse's native France and who knew members of her family. Knowing of her devotion to the missions, he placed the entire Alaskan mission under her protection, five years prior to her canonization, when she was declared queen and patroness of Alaska.

Father William G. LeVasseur, S.J., envisioned the Shrine of St. Thérèse as a place that would call people to a greater devotion to God. In the 1930s when this process began, there were no retreat houses in Alaska. Five acres in a forest reserve were secured, and by the summer of 1932 access was gained to the land from the main highway. The original estimate for building the retreat house and chapel was $3,000, not including furnishings. Since this was during the Depression, fund-raising was difficult and 500 letters a week were sent out requesting funds. The most common donations were twenty-five-cent and one-dollar donations. "We had a hundred-dollar truck, a wheelbarrow, a mortar box, a mortar hoe, a rope, and falls for hoisting stone, and a handmade skip," said D. P. "Doc" Holden, the volunteer construction foreman. "There were some bad times, but the work continued, and in time the chapel was completed." Finished, the chapel measures 63 by 28 feet, with a 28-foot-high Notre Dame tower, all made with local stone, carried by adult and children volunteers.

Today the Shrine of St. Thérèse encompasses 40 acres and includes the church, shrine, lodge, caretaker's house, and rock structures that surround new alabaster

SHRINE OF ST. THÉRÈSE

◆

**5933 Lund St.
Juneau, AK 99801
(907) 780-6112**

**SHRINE
CHRISTOTHERAPY
WEDDINGS
CAMP
RETREATS**

Stations of the Cross. The Shrine Causeway is a footpath providing access to Shrine Island overlooking Pearl Harbor, from which, on clear days, the craggy, snow-covered Chilkat Mountains are visible in the distance. Visitors find this a peaceful place to meditate as they wander the property. People from around the world visit the Shrine, finding it a place of refuge, prayer, and reflection. One visitor said, "I find this a spiritual meeting place in nature. Surrounded by water and sky, I feel the spirit of God."

Many people are drawn to the story of St. Thérèse, described in her autobiography, *The Story of a Soul.* Despite bouts of depression and self-doubt, she said that what matters in life is not our great deeds, but our great love. She believed that "opportunities for loving occur most often in the ordinary events of one's life, and through these happenings we are called to love others with God's help. No one has to earn God's love, God loves us first, and the purpose of life is to respond to this love."

The shrine runs a "Fun in the Sun" summer camp for diocese children, hosts community groups, including Alcoholics Anonymous, has family picnic grounds, offers retreats, and is the site of many weddings. In addition, a resident Christian counselor provides Christotherapy, a form of Christian counseling, healing, prayer, and spiritual direction. He writes, "During the group sessions I not only listen, share, and at times guide specifically, I pray with the seeker by joining hands and praying deeply for the enlightenment of the Holy Spirit. It is a Christ-approach to counseling. Christ often went away to pray for wisdom, to hear the guiding message of the Spirit of God. [The name Christotherapy refers to] the Christ and the healing that can come from invoking the Lord in Jesus' name. Christotherapy flows from Father Bernard Tyrrell, a priest who is a professor at Gonzaga University, a Jesuit college in Spokane, Washington."

Arizona

✦━━━◆━━━✦

When we got to Flagstaff, we were tempted to go north 90 miles to view the Grand Canyon, but a storm was coming and we were told that not only would the driving be tough, but we wouldn't be able to see anything anyway. So we headed south following a dramatic, narrow road, a series of switchbacks down and around, one sharp curve after another, a path cut out of the rocks, the tops of tall trees at eye level to begin with and then reaching their full height as we descended farther. We were bound for Sedona, tucked in the foothills of the Rocky Mountains, reportedly the site of an energy vortex. This has long been recognized by people with psychic powers who have settled here and given the town the reputation of being the home of 400 channels, although it has no TV station.

The man behind Arcosanti (an amalgam of *architecture* and *ecology)* is Paolo Soleri, an Italian-born architect, who had a vision of a way to use land for people rather than automobiles. His concept is to eliminate cars, which require streets and garages, so that individuals walk to meet their living needs. Committed to a mortgage-free development, Soleri charges helpers a modest fee for the experience of building the future in the company of the regular staff of 50. Arcosanti produces and sells beautiful-sounding bronze and ceramic wind bells that can be ordered by mail. Visitors can buy fresh baked goods at the café. From Interstate 17, the buildings look like a space village in the desert, sitting on a mesa above the Agua Fria river valley. Arcosanti is about 65 miles north of Phoenix.

ARCOSANTI

◆

**HC 74, Box 4136
Mayer, AZ 86333
(520) 632-7135
Web site:
www.arcosanti.org**

**BRONZE AND CERAMIC
WIND BELLS AND CHIMES**

**WORK INSTRUCTION IN
BUILDING FOR THE FUTURE**

BAKED GOODS

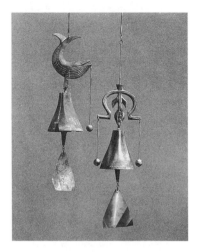

Wind bells (© COSANTI FOUNDATION, ARCOSANTI, MAYER)

During our tour of Arcosanti, we were privileged to meet Paolo Soleri, who bounded down from an elevated office where he was working and spent a few minutes with us. He was a thin, wiry man with sparkling eyes, handsome and full of energy. We then continued on with our guide and were shown a model for the completed Arcosanti, an ambitious and beautiful concept. Our guide told us that Soleri was once asked how much money it would take to complete the project. He is reported to have smiled and answered, "About the price of one attack bomber."

Blue Evening Star, a member of this community, developed her tentmaking skills out of necessity in 1976 when she needed a place to live. This skill is now the basis of Living Shelter Crafts, which uses three commercial sewing machines and 15 community members to make tipis and yurts. Her book, *Tipis and Yurts: Authentic Designs for Circular Shelters,* gives details on the tipi-making process. The community has published a book on its philosophy, *The Cosmic Family.* Its Community Healing Team uses psychospiritual counseling, personal transmissions, light body visualization, and tron therapy, a psychospiritual therapy that restores broken circuitry within the body, removes diseased cells, and is a touch therapy destined to replace surgery. Gabriel of Sedona & The Bright Morning Star Band, an eleven-piece group, plays original music called "CosmoPop," a blending of rhythm and blues, rock, jazz, and folk. They have just released a CD called *Holy City,* which was created with the hope of uniting all people spiritually.

In the mid-1930s, a small group of Benedictine sisters came from Clyde, Missouri, at the invitation of the local bishop, who said, "Nothing would please me more than to have a sanctuary of perpetual adoration in this rim of Christendom." The sisters had their own reasons for a new foundation in the Southwest, not the least of which was the climate for those who found the cold and damp of the Missouri winters difficult. By 1939 they had laid the cornerstone of their new monastery on the outskirts of town. The design was Spanish Renaissance with red tile roofs, patios, and seven arches along the side, surrounded by acres of grounds. When it was nearing completion, the architect suggested the entire structure be painted gray, but the prioress responded, "How can you suggest gray when there's so much joy inside!" The pale rose monastery is now a landmark in Tucson; in 1997 the *Arizona Daily Star* ranked it third on a long list of readers' favorite buildings. When the monastery was completed in 1943, it was surrounded by desert. Today the views are of buildings as far as the eye can see. Only the distant Catalina Mountains remain unchanged.

The 22 sisters who live here are primarily involved in publishing and vestment creation. They write, edit, and produce the bimonthly magazine *Spirit & Life,* which goes out to thousands of subscribers, as well as the newsletter *Harmony,* which appears three times a year. These publications offer gentle reminders of the spiritual nature of life and how to overcome or get through the feelings of futility. A recent issue quoted Dorothy Day: "Lay one brick at a time, take one step at a time, beg for an increase of love in our hearts that will vitalize and transform our individual actions. . . ." Other sisters make liturgical vestments such as albs, chasubles, stoles, and altar linens. Some vestments are made to order.

These sisters spend one hour a day in silent devotion to the Blessed Sacrament. The community has outreach programs to share their spirituality, such as a weekly contemplative prayer group that meets to practice centering prayer, and an oblate chapter of more than 80 members convenes regularly.

BENEDICTINE SISTERS OF PERPETUAL ADORATION

◆

**Benedictine Monastery
800 North Country Club Rd.
Tucson, AZ 85716
(520) 325-8444/
321-4358 fax**

MAGAZINE
NEWSLETTER
VESTMENTS
SPIRITUAL PROGRAMS

DESERT HOUSE
OF
PRAYER

◆

**Box 574
Cortaro, AZ 85652
(520) 744-3825**

**DESERT RETREAT EXPERIENCE
ON THE EDGE OF THE
SONORAN DESERT**

This retreat occupies 31 acres of primitive desert at the foot of Safford Peak in the Tucson Mountains. The purpose of the small community that lives here is to maintain a climate of quiet and solitude where one can get more deeply rooted in God through prayer.

There are twelve rooms with private baths for retreatants. The community meets three times a day in the chapel for mass, a prayer service, and a meditation session. There is a 6,000-volume library and hundreds of tapes, including a complete set of Thomas Merton's discussions, many of him addressing novices at the Abbey of Gethsemani in Trappist, Kentucky, where he was a monk. Surrounded by the stark beauty of the desert and aided by the spiritual atmosphere that is almost palpable, this place presents an opportunity to advance for those who are ready.

We were staying at Picture Rocks Retreat, on the edge of Saguaro National Monument–West, in the foothills of the Tucson Mountains, a delightful place named for the petroglyphs carved centuries ago by Hohokam Indians, when we heard of another retreat nearby that sounded intriguing. We arranged to visit, and that was how we found Desert House of Prayer. None of the buildings are visible from the road, and the hard-packed sand drive curves around desert bushes and leads to the chapel, a nondescript structure until you enter it. One wall is made entirely of glass, framing the desert landscape that stretches for miles before your eyes, the low scrub, rocks, and giant saguaro cacti, with the azure sky and the distant mountains completing the diorama. Our guide showed us beautifully designed hermitages a short distance from the main building, and we walked around the outdoor Stations of the Cross that curved out into the desert. As one visitor said, "The grace of this place is its silence."

Sedona is in the rugged foothills of the Rocky Mountains, a place where Native Americans have been coming for centuries to be refreshed and healed. John Paul Weber returned to his hometown to found the Healing Center in 1981. He built his center in the form of a group of geodesic domes arranged like a large daisy, with light, airy spaces, and he included a hot tub, sauna, flotation tank, and a meditation chamber. The place reflects "the need for nondenominational centers of light and love of all humanity to give grounding and remembrance of the divine presence." Weber has written several cookbooks, which are available for purchase, describing the fine cuisine he creates for his guests and retreatants. The Center offers personalized retreats tailored to the needs of individuals. Weber also leads tours to sacred places around the world, always returning to the magic of Sedona.

During our stay at the Healing Center, we were shown a spot in the meditation room that had especially powerful vibrations. The next morning, Jack went into the room and settled in lotus position on the designated spot. He had no sooner closed his eyes than the house cat came in, climbed onto his lap, and stayed there for his entire meditation. The cat had not approached him before, nor did it afterward. The meditation was serene and clear like the air in Wilson Canyon, where the sky is incredibly blue and the huge boulders and rock formations reflect the light in quiet majesty.

We later learned that the cat, Kunzang ("everything's all right") had been named and baptized by a Tibetan monk, and was drawn to those people who needed energy. He's very popular with visitors and many want to take him home, but he's content with his current place and practice.

The geometry of the daisy-shaped dome tends to magnify any processing individuals are going through during their meditation. Several have reported past-life experiences they never had before, and getting answers about what to do with their lives. Others with pain symptoms report that after a while their pain just went away.

HEALING THERAPIES

Design your own healing retreat from the following therapies:

BODYWORK
acupressure

massage

shiatsu

yoga

GENERAL HEALTH AND HEALTH ASSESSMENT
health and nutritutional counseling

t'ai chi

sound and color therapy

herbology

PSYCHOTHERAPY
hypnotherapy

neuro-linguistic programming

rebirthing

career counseling

SPIRITUAL/PSYCHIC COUNSELING
meditation

past life regression

psychic channeling

personal ceremony and ritual instructions

WE CAN ALSO REFER YOU TO:
guided vortex tours

jeep adventures in the desert

sweat lodges

geological tours

◆

Healing Center of Arizona, Sedona

In January 1991 we arrived here on Super Bowl Sunday afternoon for the celebration mass in honor of a young woman formally joining the community. It was an emotional and moving ceremony, and though we had only just arrived and knew no one, we felt a part of it. The chapel was filled with family and friends. The priest gave a homily and told how the young woman had been moved to leave her job as a supermarket cashier, and had found her way to Holy Trinity, where she quietly fitted in and did her work. Gradually the uncertainty of her parents and the community began to drop away and acceptance grew. After years of apprenticeship, she had decided this was the place for her, and she was welcomed with love and appreciation. "It turns out," the priest said with great emotion, "the gift is not that we took her in, but that she has brought to us the blessing of her joyfulness and grace which illuminates us all."

As we left the chapel, Jack noticed it was kickoff time. He fell in step with the crowd going to the refectory for dinner and asked a friendly-faced man, who turned out to be from Iowa, whether the monastery had a TV. "Oh no," the man answered, "they have no need for that." Just as Jack had suspected. "Why do you ask?" he said. Jack explained that the Super Bowl was about to begin, an event as important as the coronation of a pope. "If you like," the man replied, "you can watch it in my RV. I have a color TV hooked to a satellite dish." So Jack got to see the New York Giants prevail over the Buffalo Bills by the scantest of margins, from a monastery deep in Apache territory, fourteen miles north of Tombstone and 17 miles from the Cochise Stronghold.

This Catholic Benedictine monastery is a perfect example of evolving monastic traditions. The community is made up of priests, brothers, sisters, laypeople, and married couples, all of whom have different responsibilities such as tending the pecan orchards, cooking and cleaning, running the gift shop, art gallery, and Benedict's Closet thrift shop, and maintaining the grounds and caring for farm animals and resident peacocks. Thousands attend the spring and autumn festivals for the

food, music, and crafts, and bags of pecans are available in season. There is a separate house for private retreatants, but those who arrive in RVs can park in the back and contribute some muscle to keeping a 93-acre monastery-ranch functioning. The chapel is adobe, rounded, weathered, and seemingly built a long time ago—an ageless look, as though the first Spanish explorers had constructed it. There is a pond next to it, alive with ducks, an oasis in the desert for animals and people. The whole ranch has a casual, welcoming grace about it, and the surrounding desert stretches away to the distant mountains in Mexico.

OUR LADY OF SOLITUDE

◆

House of Prayer
P.O. Box 1140
Black Canyon, AZ 85324
(602) 374-9204

2-TO-4-WEEK DESERT
SPIRITUALITY LIVE-IN

2-TO-12-MONTH SABBATICAL
LIVE-IN AT CABINS IN A
DESERT SETTING

This 20-acre property is surrounded by state and federal land, perched on a mesa looking out to the vast expanse of the Sonoran Desert. Traffic noise is nonexistent, and the view of Black Canyon City serves to accentuate the separation from the trammel of life. There are six guest rooms with shared baths in the main house, and meals are provided. The chapel sits on a separate knoll, a very quiet building that has a picture window looking out over the valley below. Near the chapel are four hermitages set apart from one another, designed for basic comfort and privacy. It's hard to imagine a more fitting place for solitude and contemplation, offering the chance to know yourself, where the mystery of the desert can work its wonders.

SANTA RITA ABBEY

◆

HC 1, Box 929
Sonoita, AZ 85637
(520) 455-5595/
455-5770 fax

MAGAZINE
RETREATS

This Trappistine monastery publishes *Cistercian Studies Quarterly,* which contains articles and information about Catholic Trappist monks and sisters. Private retreatants can come to share the daily prayer.

As we drove through southern Arizona, signs announced that we were approaching the Painted Desert, and that we should not miss one of nature's grandest sights. We'd seen the same signs two years before and hadn't stopped then, and we didn't have time now. We were on a schedule, and that was that.

A gas stop was necessary, and as we pulled into the pumps, two boys walked by, one holding a cat by the scruff of the neck. "Where are you taking the kitten?" Marcia asked as she got out of the car, alarmed by the cavalier roughness of the boy. After a few minutes of discussion, Marcia had the cat in her arms, a trusting, long-haired beauty that weighed perhaps three pounds. When I returned to the car, we had a furry passenger drinking water from a bowl in the front seat.

As we pulled onto the highway, I asked, "Now what?" Before beginning this journey, we'd carefully arranged for our two cats to be taken care of, knowing that the rigors of our travels would be difficult with pets. It would be hard enough for just the two of us, and retreat houses don't want you to bring pets. "Now what?" I repeated. The cat was curled in Marcia's lap, purring contentedly. "Take the next exit," she said. And when I did, the sign announced, WELCOME TO THE PAINTED DESERT.

There was a cafeteria, and a good number of people were about. If you want to pass along a cat, you need people. Unfortunately, these people were travelers like ourselves, enamored of cats, but already well supplied at home.

One thing led to another. We got the little beauty a turkey sandwich (hold the mayo, lettuce, and bread). Then Marcia phoned the local telephone operator, who gave her the number of someone who might be helpful. When this woman heard the story, she said that she was just about to get a cat this very weekend for one of her children. The drop was easily arranged. We followed her directions: "Drive through the Painted Desert and I'll meet you at the other end, it's hardly out of your way." So if you want to be sure to see the Painted Desert, pick up a stray cat.

QUALIFICATIONS OF THE MONASTERY CELLARER

As cellarer of the monastery, there should be chosen from the community someone who is wise, mature in conduct, temperate, not an excessive eater, not proud, excitable, offensive, dilatory or wasteful, but God-fearing, and like a parent to the whole community. S/he will take care of everything, but will do nothing without an order from the prioress/abbot. Let her/him keep to those orders.

S/he should not annoy the members. If anyone happens to make an unreasonable demand, s/he should not reject her/him with disdain and cause distress, but reasonably and humbly deny the improper request. Let her/him keep watch over her/his own soul, ever mindful of that saying of the apostle: "They who serve well secure a good standing for themselves" (1 Tim. 3:13). S/he must show every care and concern for the sick, young, guests and the poor, knowing for certain that s/he will be held accountable for all of them on the day of judgment. S/he will regard all utensils and goods of the monastery as sacred vessels of the altar, aware that nothing is to be neglected. S/he should not be prone to greed, nor be wasteful and extravagant with the goods of the monastery, but should do everything with moderation and according to the prioress'/abbot's orders.

◆

Chapter 31, A Reader's Version of the Rule of Saint Benedict in Inclusive Language

Arkansas

Little Portion is a most unusual community, made up of celibate monks and nuns, families, and singles, and founded by a former rock star. Having experienced a religious conversion while traveling with the rock band Mason Proffitt in the late sixties, John Michael Talbot, whose grandfather was a Methodist preacher, bought 25 acres of land in the Ozarks, hoping to return one day and settle on the land. By the late seventies, after deep soul-searching and inspired by Saint Francis, John Michael clarified his vocation and decided he wanted to become a Catholic and to found an agrarian, self-supporting community.

He began to compose and record religious music, such as *The Lord's Supper* (1978), as he entered Catholicism. Profits from this music, the first of a Catholic artist to reach across all boundaries, were used to begin the community in 1983. The original 25 acres have grown to over 250 acres, including a ten-acre retreat center. The profits from his 30 albums, with over 4 million sold, support the building projects at Little Portion, such as the new dining room and meeting house, and an energy-efficient greenhouse. Otherwise the community members are responsible for supporting themselves, and they do so with a farm that supplies most of its own food, some of which is sold to visitors at their Little Portion General Store, along with baked goods and crafts such as prayer benches, candle holders, Bible stands, and Christian jewelry.

A typical day begins at 6:30 A.M. when the morning bell echoes through the mountains, ending the sacred silence that started at 10:00 P.M. the night before and calling the community to prayer. They take one meal a day together, and six hours a day are allotted to each adult for ministry or labor, study, prayer, and spiritual

LITTLE PORTION HERMITAGE

◆

**Rte. 7, Box 688
Eureka Springs, AR
72632
(501) 253-7718**

**RECORDINGS
VIDEOS
BOOKS
GENERAL STORE
CRAFTS
PRAYER BENCHES
JEWELRY
BIBLE STANDS
FARM
RETREATS**

direction. This time includes their outreach ministries at a local nursing home, the St. Vincent de Paul Thrift Store, and the Little Portion Clinic for the poor.

This is a quiet and purposefully Christian lifestyle of "progressive, conservative Catholics with the mission of living and spreading the good news of Jesus in a radical, gospel lifestyle. We're radical but not fanatical, communal but not cultish, and we have the checks and balances of the Catholic Church," says John Michael. Many people inquire about joining the community, and ten postulants are chosen to join each year, though only three or four stay on after the first year or two, the rest finding the life too difficult. It's a long way from the rock clubs of his youth for John Michael, but his ministry has reached people around the world, bringing them a message many yearn for.

SHILOH COMMUNITY

◆

P.O. Box 97
Sulphur Springs
AR 72768
(501) 298-3299 or 3297
298-3359 fax

BREAD
HEALTH FOOD STORE
RETREATS

Shiloh Community was founded in southwestern New York in 1942, and moved to Arkansas in 1968 to be in a more central location for its bakery distribution. Its communal lifestyle and spiritual focus is described by them as "an Esoteric Christianity that also integrates teachings from other disciplines." The community has been self-supporting from the beginning through farming, dairying, and flour milling, which progressed to its current successful and extensive bakery operation that uses only stone-ground whole-grain flours and natural sweeteners and oils in the baking of 25,000 loaves a week of Shiloh Farms Bread. The bread can be found in health food stores in the Midwestern and Eastern United States, or mailed directly via UPS. As the bread business unfolded, they were amazed to discover that it cost them less to ship their bread via UPS than to deliver it themselves.

As this long-standing community ages, it becomes apparent that it is a community and business run by senior citizens, perhaps a good model for others. The natural food bakery on the property welcomes visitors to sit and snack on breads and pastry, and people are invited to tour the bakery and dine with the community

SHILOH FARMS BREAD

Shiloh Farms offers an amazing variety of healthy and tasty bread:

Sprouted 5-Grain

Sprouted 5-Grain, no salt added

Sprouted 5-Grain, no salt or sweetener added

Sprouted 7-Grain

Sprouted 7-Grain, no salt added

Sprouted Multi-Grain Sandwich Loaf

Oat Bran

Spelt (no added vital wheat gluten)

Sprouted Egyptian Kamut

Wheat Bran

Homestyle (all-natural white bread)

Zesty Sprouted Wheat & Rye with Onions

5-Grain Hearth, unsliced

Butter Hearth, unsliced

Whole Wheat

Whole Wheat, no salt added

Whole Wheat Raisin

Whole Wheat Sunflower

Sprouted 10-Grain

Breads for Life Sprouted 7-Grain, with unbleached flour

◆

Shiloh Farms Pure and Natural Bread, Sulphur Springs, Arkansas
(501) 298-3299

SUBIACO ABBEY

◆

**Parish Dr.
Subiaco, AR 72865
(501) 934-4411**

FESTIVAL

PEANUT BRITTLE

RETREATS

by arrangement. Retreats are held in a hotel once popular because of the nearby sulphur springs spa that was built by the Kansas City Southern Railroad in 1890. Groups can arrange to hold their retreats there by calling Shiloh's retreat coordinator.

An annual November bazaar is held at this Catholic Benedictine abbey located in the Arkansas River valley, 58 miles east of Fort Smith. There is a gift shop and bookstore, and retreats are scheduled regularly at the Coury House, which has 35 double rooms. Abbey Brittle, a homemade peanut brittle made from an original recipe adopted for its rich, creamy taste, is available by mail.

THE SLEEPING ARRANGEMENTS OF MONASTICS

Members are to sleep in separate beds. They receive bedding as provided by the prioress/abbot, suitable to monastic life.

If possible, all are to sleep in one place, but should the size of the community preclude this, they will sleep in groups of ten or twenty under the watchful care of elders. A lamp must be kept burning in the room until morning.

They sleep clothed, and girded with belts or cords; but they should remove their knives, lest they accidentally cut themselves in their sleep. Thus the members will always be ready to arise without delay when the signal is given; each will hasten to arrive at the Opus Dei before the others, yet with all dignity and decorum. The younger members should not have their beds next to each other, but interspersed among those of the elders. On arising for the Opus Dei, they will quietly encourage each other, for the sleepy like to make excuses.

◆

Chapter 22, A Reader's Version of the Rule of Saint Benedict in Inclusive Language

California

◆ —— ◆ —— ◆

California, our most populous state, has everything you could ever want, an old-timer told us, "and if you can't find it, Hollywood will make it up for you." It is the only state that could theoretically exist by itself. It grows enough food, creates enough jobs, and has more religions than seeds in a sunflower.

We visited 50 different retreats from south to north, San Diego to Mount Shasta. We followed the coast highway, Route 1—that winding road which borders the Pacific, much of it two-lane—as far as we could. This is not a route one takes to get somewhere quickly; rather, it is one of the most dramatic driving experiences in this country or perhaps anywhere. The road was carved out at the edge of the seacoast, and in many places, during severe storms, parts of mountains tumble down to the sea, closing passage to cars for some time. In good weather, it is a memorable experience that should be planned carefully and executed with a reliable vehicle, a full gas tank, and good tires: the normal precautions for any trip, but especially this one.

ABBEY OF NEW CLAIRVAUX

◆

**Seventh & C Sts.
Vina, CA 96092
(916) 839-2434**

WALNUTS
PRUNES
RETREATS

In 1955, Trappist monks acquired 600 acres along Deer Creek in this rich farming region of the northern Sacramento Valley, where they planted orchards of prune and walnut trees. The prunes are sold to Sunsweet and the walnuts to Diamond, and the income from these crops supports the monastery. These farmer monks have the same duties as their neighbors, keeping the orchards neat, trees trimmed, and equipment running, but their lives are slightly different. When the chapel bells ring, they stop work and chant the canonical hours in the chapel. Guests and retreatants may join the monks at these services. People come here for a spiritual respite, but there are no organized retreats. Guest rooms are near the refectory, a short distance from the chapel. Of course, prunes are served every day and the cakes are always garnished with walnuts. They have a small gift shop that sells books and pottery made by one of the monks.

We arrived for Palm Sunday weekend at this Trappist monastery that was once owned by Leland Stanford when a large brick building next to the present monastery buildings was the largest winery in the country. Our room was centrally located, a short distance from the refectory where food is carried over from the monastery kitchen and meals are taken with other retreatants. This gave us a chance to meet two California men on retreat with their sons for this special weekend, a tradition they had followed for years. Both men had once been seminarians together, then had determined their lives would be better served in the secular world. They married lovely women, had children, lived in different parts of the state, and maintained their friendship by meeting here each year. This all came out at our shared meals, which became more like a family reunion than a quiet breaking of bread. When one of the men—a prominent lawyer—found out about our mission, he said he couldn't think of anything he'd rather do than work on a project like ours.

At another meal we met a mother, a father, and a young man who was there to enter the monastery. His handsome early-twenties face reflected that of his beautiful, dark-haired mother. He was clearly happy about his decision, while his mother, feigning happiness for him, could scarcely contain her sadness.

We spent the weekend there, a break from our travels, and especially enjoyed the walks during the evenings in the orchards where, as one guest observed, "it gets so quiet here at night, you can hear a prune drop."

This spiritual community is based on the teachings of Paramahansa Yogananda (author of *Autobiography of a Yogi*) and has several branches worldwide with approximately 500 members.

Ananda has 750 acres of woods and meadows in the Sierra Nevada foothills in northern California and is home to their "Education for Life" school for 60 children from kindergarten age through eighth grade, and a new high school/boarding school; both schools are open to those from within and outside the community. The schools concentrate on the physical, emotional, intellectual, and spiritual growth of the students, including values, conflict resolution, inner calm, and peace. Yoga postures and meditation instruction make up about 30 minutes of each day. A working garden is part of the schools' science curriculum; the children plant corn in the spring, harvest it in the fall, then make popcorn from the kernels. One of the teachers who was a carpenter worked with the children to build an outdoor classroom that is now used regularly. Visitors can also come to Ananda for yoga teacher training, vegetarian cooking classes, or self-designed retreats. The teachings they share stress voluntary cooperation, friendship, harmony, and a cheerful spirit of service to God. They seek a balance between spiritual guidance and self-motivation, and the freedom to learn at one's own pace. Month-long tours and spiritual pilgrimages to Indian shrines and ashrams are led by community members, as are tours to Assisi, Italy, where they also have a community.

ANANDA VILLAGE

◆

The Expanding Light Retreat
14618 Tyler Foote Rd.
Nevada City, CA 95959
(916) 478-7500/
292-9009 fax
(800) 346-5350 retreats
E-mail: ananda@oro.net
Web site:
www.ananda.org

GRADE SCHOOL

HIGH SCHOOL

PILGRIMAGES

YOGA TEACHER TRAINING

MEDITATION AND OTHER INSTRUCTION

RETREATS

C
A
L
I
F
O
R
N
I
A

◈

23

BLACK OAK RANCH

◆

**P.O. Box 1359
Laytonville, CA 95454
(707) 984-6507 summer
(510) 525-4304 winter**

**WAVY GRAVY'S
CAMP WINNARAINBOW
—A CIRCUS AND
PERFORMING-ARTS CAMP
WITH TIPIS, ALSO AVAILABLE
FOR RENTAL**

JERRY GARCIA TIES

**T-SHIRTS AND POSTERS
FROM ANNUAL PICNIC**

BOOKS ABOUT HOG FARM

WAVY GRAVY ICE CREAM

PIGNIC

B lack Oak Ranch, three and a half hours north of San Francisco, calls itself home to a long-standing extended family made up of Hog Farm members (a counterculture commune established in the 1960s) and others representing a wide and diverse range of ages and occupations. Camp Winnarainbow grew out of a child-care program that community member Hugh Romney, better known as the performer/clown Wavy Gravy, was running at a Sufi camp for adults in the seventies. He was joined by his friend Ron Singer, a circus arts performer, as well as members of Black Oak Ranch and, over the years, many others in building and running a circus and performing arts camp for children (with a week for adults). Many performing artists come back year after year to work with the children in circus and performing arts such as acting, juggling, clowning, mime, unicycling, stilt- and tightrope-walking, trapeze, poetry and songwriting, and other summer activities. If you ever wanted to join the circus, this is a joyful place to give it a try! Royalties from the sale of Jerry Garcia ties and from Ben and Jerry's Wavy Gravy ice cream go to the scholarship fund, so kids who can't afford to pay can come. The annual rock 'n' roll concert, The Pignic, takes place on Labor Day weekend.

The Blue Mountain Center of Meditation offers instruction and guidance in meditation and allied living skills following an Eight-Point Program developed by Sri Eknath Easwaran, the author of the immensely popular *Words to Live By* and many other books. The Eight-Point Program is a daily guide to renew commitments, find strength to face challenges, and draw inspiration from a living source. The Eight Points are meditation; use of a mantra; slowing down; one-pointed attention; training the senses; putting others first; seeking spiritual companionship; and reading the works of the great mystics.

Easwaran, born in India in 1910, came to the United States in 1960 and founded the Center in northern California in 1961. Part of the Center's activities is the management of Nilgiri Press, which publishes and sells by mail more than 20 books by Easwaran, as well as six issues a year of the *Blue Mountain Journal for Spiritual Living.* In a recent *Journal,* Easwaran counsels by quoting from the Bhagavad Gita: "There are two ways of living, two paths a human being can take in life: one leads to deep fulfillment, the other leads to superficial living and increasing alienation. If you live for yourself, just for your own pleasure and profit, that very way of living will make you lonely and unfulfilled. If you forget yourself in living for the happiness of all, you will be secure, happy, loving, and loved. Then the Lord says: You choose."

As *The Rubaiyat of Omar Khayyam* reminds us, "I myself am heaven and hell," Easwaran shows a pathway toward a fulfilling life, away from emptiness. He reminds us: "Whatever we are today is the result of what we have thought, spoken, and done in all the present moments before now—just as what we shall be tomorrow is the result of what we think, say, and do today. If we live right today, then tomorrow has to be right." Other books by Easwaran are *Meditation: A Simple Eight-Point Program for Translating Spiritual Ideals into Daily Life; The Unstruck Bell,* a simple but effective approach to keeping the mind steady in times of stress; *Dialogue with Death: A Journey Through Consciousness,* a practical exploration of the

BLUE MOUNTAIN CENTER OF MEDITATION

◆

**Box 256
Tomales, CA 94971
(707) 878-2369/
878-2375 fax
(800) 475-2369 orders**

PUBLISHING HOUSE

JOURNAL

CASSETTES AND VIDEOS OF SRI EKNATH EASWARAN'S TRANSLATIONS OF SPIRITUAL CLASSICS FROM EAST AND WEST

PROGRAMS

RETREATS

meaning of death; and *Gandhi the Man,* which focuses on Gandhi's transformation from an ineffective teenager to a creative force for peaceful but revolutionary change. Audio- and videocassettes by Easwaran are also available. In 1996, Blue Mountain purchased a permanent home for its meditation retreats in Tomales, California, and has developed a full retreat program.

CARMELITE HOUSE OF PRAYER

◆

**Oakville Corner Rd.
P.O. Box 347
Oakville, CA 94562
(707) 944-2454**

**SEPTEMBER BARBECUE
RETREATS**

Carmelite friars purchased this former mansion on 29 acres in the 1950s, and the small community that lives here offers rooms for retreatants. To maintain the sacred space, retreatants are requested to stay on the property, and the minimum stay is at least two nights.

There are twice-daily prayer services, and guests dine with the community at the evening meal. The word Carmel comes from the Hebrew *kerem-el,* meaning "vineyard of the Lord," so it is fitting that the main building sits on a knoll looking out over the vineyards of the lush Napa Valley. A benefit barbecue dinner is held every year on the Sunday after Labor Day, when the public can come for a tour and a good meal.

The California friends who told us about the Carmelites had wanted to stay there overnight since it is in the wine country, but when asked what their intent was, they had been turned down. Our intent was quite different, and we were put in the guesthouse located below the mansion, just at the edge of the grape arbors. Early the next morning we wandered in the vineyards, and were rewarded with the sight of a hot-air balloon floating toward us. Its passengers waved to us and we to them, ships passing in the soft morning light.

The annual barbecue, a fund-raising event, is the time to visit the splendid mansion. The community holds a raffle, tickets are sent out far and wide, and in

1997 the winner of the grand prize was a man who lived in New York City. He was notified the Monday after the drawing, and much to his astonishment, his $10 donation had multiplied 100 times. His name was Jack Kelly!

(JACK KELLY)

The center has a collection of 10,000 Buddha statues in its meditation hall and shrine rooms, ranging from tiny replicas that fit in the hand, to life-size stone and wood carvings, and huge, outdoor cast-metal images. When we asked if there really were 10,000 Buddhas, we were told, "There are more."

When Buddhism came to China from India, one of the most important tasks was to translate the Buddhist scriptures from Sanskrit into Chinese. Now almost the entire Buddhist Tripitaka, a canon of more than 1,000 texts, is available in the Chinese language. Today, this community's task is to translate the canon into English. The translators emphasize the principles of Buddhism in terms of actual practice rather than theory. More than 100 volumes are already available in English and can be ordered by mail. There is also a monthly journal of orthodox Buddhism called *Vajra Bodhi Sea*, which has been published since 1970. Each issue contains the center's most recent translations of the Buddhist canon. In addition to the selection of books on Buddhist theory at the excellent bookstore and gift shop, they offer a nine-volume set, *With One Heart Bowing to the City of 10,000 Buddhas,* comprising the journals of two American monks who made a pilgrimage of "Three Steps, One Bow" from Los Angeles to Talmage, a journey that took 17 months.

The entrance to the City of 10,000 Buddhas is an impressive gate that clearly indicates you have arrived somewhere special. A devout Chinese woman was our

(JACK KELLY)

guide. English was not her native tongue, but she led us throughout the network of rooms and wondrous statues, gesturing us on from one to the next until we got to her favorite, a seven-foot stone carving of the Buddha on a four-foot-high pedestal. She said she visited him every day and spent time rubbing his toe, which had a polished look. She demonstrated how she did it, because, as she pointed out, the results were evident: his toenail was growing!

This is a residential community that offers some events to the public, including daily meditation in the grand hall.

COMMUNITY OF MINDFUL LIVING

◆

P.O. Box 7355
Berkeley, CA 94797
(510) 525-0101/
525-7129 fax
(800) 863-5290 orders
E-mail:
parapress@aol.com
Web site:
www.parallax.org

PUBLISHING HOUSE
TAPES
BELLS
MEDITATION CUSHIONS
CARDS
T-SHIRTS
JOURNAL

The Community of Mindful Living's Parallax Press offers more than 100 books and tapes for mindful living, as well as bells, cushions, cards, T-shirts, a journal called *The Windbell,* and other items that encourage mindfulness in daily living. They are the publishers of the works of the Vietnamese Buddhist monk Thich Nhat Hanh, and the contact in the United States for his Plum Village Community in France. Although not a community in a formal sense, the spirit of sharing these important teachings, and the tie to Plum Village and retreats in France, makes this endeavor truly "right livelihood" and an important listing.

BEING PEACE

THICH NHAT HANH

R uth Denison was born in Germany. She survived World War II with much hardship, then came to the United States in the 1950s and settled in Los Angeles, where she married. In the sixties, she and her husband traveled throughout the Far East to experience different meditation practices. One of her early teachers encouraged Vipassana practice, and taught her *shikantaza*, "just sitting," which balanced her energy and helped her to concentrate. She offered her Los Angeles house as a place for spiritual teachers to hold classes. Her living room became a birthplace for spiritual investigation. She would return to Burma periodically to study with her teacher, U Ba Khim, who had founded an international meditation center. He gave transmission (permission to teach) to only five westerners, including one woman. Ruth was that woman, and remembers him touching the tip of her nose as she left, saying, "May this be your best friend." In the early seventies, she taught in Europe almost nonstop for four years. She kept Los Angeles as her home base, and in 1977 she bought a small cabin with five acres in the California high desert just north of Joshua Tree National Monument, loving the isolation and quiet. She intended to use it as a private sanctuary, as a place for rest and repair, but often invited students to spend time there, and in the 1980s a community began to form and facilities were added.

Ruth states that the longer she taught, the more she realized the difficulties meditators were having, especially those who did not have the cultural and religious background to simply sit and pay attention to their body-mind sensations. So she includes verbal support during quiet sitting practice as a reminder to return from daydreaming and pay mindful attention to the proper meditation object. Most of all, she says, "I encourage people to go into their difficulties to cope with the change that is taking place. . . . Our life is nothing but

DHAMMA DENA

◆

**HC 1, Box 250
Joshua Tree, CA 92252
(619) 362-4815**

**DESERT EXPERIENCE
RETREATS WITH A FOCUS ON
VIPASSANA MEDITATION**

change, and it is to this change that I bow deeply. I bow deeply to life itself." Remote and isolated, this is an excellent location for a desert retreat experience. The austere setting magnifies the rugged beauty of the distant mountains, and the sky colors and the star-filled night sky are breathtaking.

The road was flat, sandy, and desolate, a vast expanse of desert stretching away on either side. Distant mountains rimmed this lake of sand. For those seeking solitude with no distractions, we appeared to be in the right place. In order to appreciate the desert, you have to spend time in it and find out what it has to offer. Water, that commodity we take for granted in the East, is trucked in and treated as precious. The living conditions are spartan, the outhouse nearby. You are on another planet. The world you know disappears from view. You are left with yourself, with your meditation, your prayer. That is your salvation.

We met Ruth Denison and meditated with her group, and that was the first time we could remember someone giving verbal encouragement during sitting. She said, "Watch your breathing, become your breathing, sink into the silence of your breathing." We found it very helpful.

THE HOT SPRINGS AT ESALEN

We would like those people who are planning their first visit to Esalen to know that swimsuits are optional, and nudity common, in the hot springs, massage area, and swimming pool. We encourage each individual to choose what is most comfortable, whether wearing a swimsuit or not, and emphasize that the environment we strive for at Esalen is one of personal sanctuary and respect for the human body. In addition to around-the-clock availability for Esalen guests, the hot springs are open to the general public by reservation only from 1:00 A.M. to 3:00 A.M. There is a $10 fee. To make a reservation, please call (408) 667-3047.

salen is located on 27 acres of coastline on the ocean side of Route 1. The Santa Lucia Mountains give this region of California an almost overwhelming setting of ocean, jutting rocks, mountains, and sky. The views from the southern edge of the property are 20 miles of surf-banded seacoast. The institute was founded in 1962 by Michael Murphy, whose family owned the land, and his friend, the late Richard Price. Their vision was to develop an educational center devoted to the exploration of unrealized human capabilities.

Esalen has a full calendar of workshops devoted to, among other things, the arts and creativity, biofeedback, social responsibility, and spiritual and religious studies. An excellent catalog lists many more in the humanities and sciences that promote human values and potential. Esalen is a center for experimental education and does not offer cures or assurance of change, but gives individuals the chance to explore the world and themselves more deeply. The bookstore has an extensive catalog of books related to their workshops.

The Esalen Indians who once lived here were attracted to the region by the hot springs. The sulfur water, approaching 120 degrees, is piped into stone tubs built on the edge of a cliff wall. The views of sky and ocean on a clear night are like being at sea in the universe.

During our stay, Michael Murphy gave a lecture on his research that was later published as *The Future of the Body: Explorations into the Further Evolution of Human Nature.* It was a great opportunity to see this visionary man, handsome, articulate, and polished, working with a group to elicit insights into the outer edges of human awareness. Many interesting stories were shared of experiences beyond the ordinary realm of understanding, a new dimension that they had entered accidentally. Even though the stories varied, there was one common denominator: the experiences had all occurred while the narrator was helping another person.

ESALEN INSTITUTE

◆

Big Sur, CA 93920
(408) 667-3000/
667-2724 fax
(408) 667-3049 orders
Web site:
www.esalen org

MINERAL BATHS
SELF-REALIZATION COURSES
WORK/SCHOLAR PROGRAM

GREEN GULCH FARM

◆

**1601 Shoreline Hwy.
Muir Beach, CA 94965
(415) 383-3134/
383-3128 fax
E-mail: ggszc@
earthlink.net
Web site:
bodhi.zendo.com/~sfzc
and
www.zendo.com/~sfzc**

GARDEN PRODUCE

WREATHS

VINEGAR

LAVENDER

BOOKS

STATUES

MEDITATION CUSHIONS

TEA

WORKSHOPS

In Marin County, just 25 miles north of the Bay, the San Francisco Zen Center has an affiliated community of more than 50 adults and children who live there and maintain a farm on 115 acres. The acreage is part of 535 acres deeded by George Wheelright III to the Nature Conservancy to preserve the property in a natural condition and maintain plant and animal life. The Zen Center bought the property in the 1970s on condition that it be farmed in perpetuity and remain open to the public. Green Gulch Farm is a showcase of high-quality produce, herbs, and flowers, which are sold at the Embarcadero market in San Francisco on Saturdays. On Sunday mornings, there is meditation, a lecture, and then tea is served, and visitors can buy produce. In addition, the resident community has an active schedule of retreats, classes, and gardening workshops. There is a guest student program in which individuals can live with the community, participate in Zen practice, and contribute their efforts to farming and maintaining the property while attending lectures and discussions with teachers and practice leaders.

The Lindisfarne Guesthouse at Green Gulch is the first building you see as you drive into the property. Most of the buildings, hidden by tall trees, are snug in a canyon that flattens out as the land reaches toward the ocean. This is where the rainbow rows of lettuce and other farm produce are grown, carefully tended and nurtured for community use and to be sold at market.

We stayed in the handcrafted guesthouse, which has nails only in its interior Sheetrock walls. The two-story structure's rooms flow together toward the 30-foot atrium in the center, where guests can sit around the woodstove on chairs and sofas.

One evening we overheard a young woman guest with a slight European accent tell a man who was outside smoking that he shouldn't be so close to the house. He dutifully moved farther away without a word. The next morning at breakfast, we heard the companion of the young woman approach the same man and apologize to him for the rudeness of her friend. The man looked at her and smiled, nodding without a word. The scales were back in balance.

In the 1960s, Richard Alpert and Timothy Leary were bounced from their professional duties at Harvard University for experimenting with mind-altering drugs. Alpert traveled to India and met a remarkable man, Neem Karoli Baba, who became his guru. Alpert was anointed by Babaji, who touched his forehead lightly and smiled, giving him the Sanskrit name Ram Dass (Servant of God). He returned to the U. S. and published his first book, *Be Here Now,* which has been a beacon for thousands searching for spiritual direction. For more than 30 years, Ram Dass has written, lectured, answered questions, and devoted his life to helping others. He is a talented, articulate, charming man who can weave stories and entertain while imparting wisdom on life's perplexities, and this foundation's tape library is the main channel for obtaining his tapes. In the six-tape series *Tuning to the Wisdom of the Heart,* the second tape examines the way dharma manifests in our lives when our egos step aside. In the three-tape set *Journey into the Heart,* he says, "The quality of devotion is one of the hardest things to convey in the West, because words like *surrender* and *unconditional love* are so poorly understood." Ram Dass has shared his extraordinary teaching gifts through talks, meditations, songs, and retreats with groups large and small. This library covers everything from a heart-opening set of tapes of a day-long devotional and chanting program at the Spirit Rock Meditation Center in Woodacre, California, to talks on conscious aging, dying, golf, meditation, visualization, inner work, family, and relationships. Also available are books about his guru and Hindu folklore, including *The Monkey's Tale,* in which two children meet an amazing monkey in magical woods.

We met Ram Dass in 1988, when he spent time in New York City working with the homeless, advocating a compassionate approach in dealing with a growing social problem that was easily visible on the streets. He asked Marcia to organize a retreat in October for homeless people, those who worked with them, and leaders from several religious and spiritual traditions. More than 50 people came by car and bus to a monastery in Tuxedo

HANUMAN FOUNDATION

◆

**524 San Anselmo Ave.
#203
San Anselmo, CA 94960
(415) 453-5111/
454-4143 fax
(800) 248-1008 orders
Web site:
www.RamDassTapes.org**

TAPES FROM LECTURES AND EVENTS GIVEN BY RAM DASS ALONE AND WITH OTHERS, PLUS SELECTED BOOKS ABOUT NEEM KAROLI BABA AND HINDU FOLKLORE

CALIFORNIA

◈

Hanuman Foundation logo

Park, New York, to explore ways of supporting one another, including Paul Gorman, coauthor with Ram Dass of the book *How Can I Help?;* Toinette Lippe, who was the editor of that book and was to become our editor on the *Sanctuaries* series and this book too; Bob Thurman, the Columbia University professor who was the Dalai Lama's first American translator; Zen abbot Bernard Glassman, the founder of the Greyston Foundation and author of *Instructions to the Cook;* John Jiler, noted journalist whose book *Sleeping with the Mayor* dealt with the homeless encampment at City Hall during Ed Koch's administration; and Larry Locke, one of the main characters in Jiler's book, who shouldered the burden of leadership during those heady but troubled times. There were many others who shared a social concern for what was happening then, and gained new direction and energy from that retreat.

Ram Dass's presence was all-pervasive. He was soft-spoken and wise, a man from a privileged background who had experienced what seemed like a fall from grace that led him to a life of service. It was how he handled his own life and his articulation of it that attracted all of us.

On our return from a trip to the West Coast, we drove by San Anselmo, California, and spent an evening with him. He had a cottage for his own use on the property of a friend, and he put us up for the night. He told us of his boyhood, growing up living on a private golf course, his father a rich and powerful businessman. As he talked about his father, he rummaged in a box and pulled out a picture of him playing the piano. The picture was attached to a tape recorder. "Listen," he said softly, and turned it on. It was the clear voice of an older man singing a love song. "While he played and sang, my mother sat on the bench next to him. He played it for her."

On 1,160 acres in a remote mountain setting of northern California, Harbin Hot Springs is built around natural mineral hot springs known for their soothing and healing properties. Part of the Heart Consciousness Church, which espouses the holistic health movement, natural healing, and universal spirituality, the community living here maintains the baths and makes it possible for individuals to come for retreat and for groups to hold and attend workshops and education programs. There are a variety of bodywork techniques available, and Watsu, massage in warm water, was developed here. There is a four-week work-study program offered each month, where individuals pay a modest tuition and contribute 32 hours of work, depending on need, and study with other group members techniques of self-expression and clear communication.

The Harbin property has hiking trails of varying degrees of difficulty, some quite demanding, and the mountain air is pure and invigorating. The large hot-spring pool is inviting.

HARBIN HOT SPRINGS

**P.O. Box 782
Middletown, CA 95461
(707) 987-2477/
987-0616 fax
E-mail:
pubshhs@wco.com.
Web site:
www.harbin.org**

HOT SPRINGS

**MASSAGE IN WATER CALLED
*WATSU***

**COURSES IN MASSAGE
TECHNIQUES**

INSTRUCTION

RETREATS

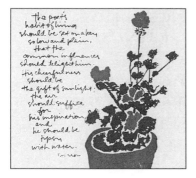

mary's geraniums, *Corita*, serigraph, 1980

Love, *Corita*, serigraph, c. 1976

crocuses for autumn, *Corita*, serigraph, 1980

IMMACULATE HEART COMMUNITY

◆

5515 Franklin Ave.
Los Angeles, CA 90028
(213) 466-2157

ORIGINAL DRAWINGS AND
REPRODUCTIONS
BY CORITA KENT

This community of Catholic sisters is made up of those who bravely stood their ground in the late 1960s when the Cardinal of Los Angeles issued a decree to the community requiring uniform dress and scheduled prayer. A majority of the sisters declared independence and became a "noncanonical community of religious persons." The artist Corita Kent was one of them, and the community has available for purchase a collection of her colorful serigraphs that deliver messages of hope and joy. Retreats are available at a large stone manor house that shares 26 acres with La Casa de Maria in Santa Barbara.

CANONICAL HOURS

The liturgy of the hours is the official daily prayer cycle of the Catholic Church, an adaptation of the liturgy of the synagogue, which has evolved over the centuries. The "hours" consist of Matins, Lauds, Terce, Sext, None, Vespers, and Compline. "Seven times a day I praise thee . . ." (Ps. 119:164).

The community members who live in the retreat house in Santa Barbara have a calling of hospitality and reach out to guests with warmth and compassion. They are always ready with a kind word, a sympathetic ear, a glass of orange juice fresh from their own grove, or chocolate-chip cookies right out of the oven. They create a center of quiet and safety in this beautiful house high in the Santa Barbara hills. We were fascinated to discover, while on a hike one day, that an exquisite and very expensive inn where we'd stayed some years ago (and said to be the place that John and Jacqueline Kennedy honeymooned) was on an adjoining property. We were happy to stay where we were, with the simple ecumenical service after a delicious homemade supper more fulfilling than a night on the town!

IMMACULATE HEART COMMUNITY CENTER FOR SPIRITUAL RENEWAL

◆

**888 San Ysidro Ln.
Santa Barbara, CA 93108
(805) 969-2474**

RETREATS

Located in a small farming town, this ten-acre retreat is named after the Egyptian goddess of nature and fertility and attempts to bridge the gap between ancient cultures and the New Age. The buildings are quaint and exotic, ranging from the temple to a semi-Victorian guesthouse, to other housing for visitors in a wine barrel, yurt, or tipi. Behind the residence of the proprietors, there are an aviary of peacocks, doves, and pheasants; cages with ocelots, servals, and bobcats; plus a corral with an emu and a llama. The animals contribute to the eclectic nature of the purpose of this oasis, which is to promote goddess consciousness and the feminine principle as a way to restore balance and harmony to the earth. There are workshops and programs throughout the year such as firewalking, visionary dance, alchemical hypnotherapy, and month-long training to become priests and priestesses of the Temple of Isis. The gift shop offers T-shirts, tote bags, mugs, and aprons with the image of the goddess, as well as sculptured altar artifacts depicting gods of ancient Egypt, and books and tapes such as the book *The Mysteries of Isis* by de Traci Regula, and Nancy Thompson's tape *Ritual Invoking the Goddess Isis.*

ISIS OASIS

◆

**20889 Geyserville Ave.
Geyserville, CA 95441
(707) 857-3524
(800) 679-RETREAT**

**CENTER FOR THE
GODDESS ISIS IN
THE UNITED STATES**

**EGYPTIAN TEMPLE FOR
CEREMONIES**

**EXOTIC ANIMALS AND BIRDS
ON DISPLAY**

RETREATS

KROTONA INSTITUTE OF THEOSOPHY

◆

**2 Krotona Hill
Ojai, CA 93023
(805) 646-2653**

**THEOSOPHICAL AND OCCULT
BOOKS AND RELATED
COURSES**

Theosophy (wisdom of God) is a body of ideas taken from religions and philosophies of India, China, Greece, and the Middle East, and from scientific discoveries past and present. It has three objectives: to form a nucleus of all persons without regard to race, creed, sex, caste, or color; to encourage the study of all religions, philosophy, and science; and to investigate the laws of nature and the latent power we all possess. Theosophy teaches that belief should be a result of individual study rather than acceptance of traditional dogma, and that every religion is an expression of divine wisdom to be practiced rather than preached. Programs and courses are offered here in the beautiful Ojai valley on the 118-acre setting of the Institute, where the bookstore is open daily, providing a full line of texts for those interested in Theosophy.

We approached Ojai from the east, out of a desert landscape, crossed the Topatopa Mountains, and got our first sight of the beautiful Ojai Valley from an elevation of about two thousand feet. Below us, the little town sat neat and orderly, a far-off suggestion of Shangri-la. We'd heard that this valley had been used as a backdrop in the 1930s during the filming of *Lost Horizon,* James Hilton's famous novel about a monastery secluded in mountains so remote that the outside world had no knowledge of it, and thus no influence on it. It was a place where people never aged, disputes and acrimony did not exist, and time was spent in the highest levels of intellectual pursuit.

Our visit to Krotona was a visit to the past. We remember being in the hushed library, the soft patina of the wooden shelves filled with books from the 1920s and 1930s, whose contents examined Theosophy and those who contributed to its development. Being there was like entering the novels of Raymond Chandler and Dashiell Hammett, both of whom vividly described California in the 1930s. Marcia's uncle, Henry Hotchner, had gone west many years before and had become a leader in Theosophy, and we found his name in the library's records.

The setting of this monastery on the Mexican border reminds some of the terrain of the moon: like a rock garden, surrounded by impressive mountains and amazing rock formations, but without a touch of green. The setting reflects the new territory of this eclectic community that combines rituals from Catholic, Jewish, and other faiths with New Age beliefs. Students are studying for friar status in the Paracelsian Order, or priest status in the Johannine Catholic Church and Temple of the Absolute Light. Membership in the monastery is necessary for permanent residence, but retreats can be extended for several years. The community publishes a journal called *The Philosopher's Stone.*

MADRE GRANDE MONASTERY OF THE PARACELSIAN ORDER

◆

**18372 Highway 94
Dulzura, CA 91917
(619) 468-3810**

JOURNAL
RETREATS
NEW AGE MONASTERY

COMMUNAL STUDIES ASSOCIATION

The mission of the Communal Studies Association is to provide a forum for the study of communal societies, past and present; to encourage and facilitate the preservation, restoration, and public interpretation of America's historic communal sites; and to communicate to the general public the successful ideas from, and lessons learned by, communal societies. The CSA sponsors a yearly conference, and publishes an annual journal and a semiannual newsletter with a calendar of events and listing of recently published books on communal life. Each year the CSA holds an annual conference in October at a different communal site, offering optional tours to allow direct experience of community intentional living.

◆

The Communal Studies Association can be reached at P.O. Box 122, Amana, IA 52203, (319) 622-6464; or E-mail csa@netins.net, or Web site www.well.com/user/cmty/csa.html.

MERCY CENTER

◆

**2300 Adeline Dr.
Burlingame, CA 94010
(415) 340-7474**

**TAIZÉ SINGING ON THE FIRST
FRIDAY OF EACH MONTH**

**ANNUAL TAIZÉ SUMMER
FESTIVAL**

RETREATS

In a southern suburb of San Francisco, the main building of Mercy Center is the motherhouse of the Catholic Sisters of Mercy. The 40 acres of grounds hold 500-year-old California oak trees and three meditation walks constructed by a chaplain who had spent 28 years in Japan. On the lower level of the main building, there is a meditation room reminiscent of a Buddhist temple, blending the spirituality of East and West. A bookstore, art exhibits, and fully developed retreat programs are available.

The center is also known as the place where the Taizé ecumenical religious community of France comes annually for a week of singing and prayer. Founded after World War II in Europe, Taizé is the name of the village in France where the community of 100 brothers resides. Since the 1950s, young adults have been gathering on the hillside of this little village, to meet one another, to pray, and to discover how they can become messengers of hope and reconciliation. Taizé prayer involves the repetition of simple biblical phrases. The experience of singing these phrases nourishes at a deep, nonverbal level. The services involve quiet chanting, a psalm, a reading, and silence, and provide time for individuals to speak of their own needs and those of the world.

We attended morning service in the chapel on the main level of this outstanding building, then later in the day went to the Buddhist room on the lower level for meditation—a combination of spiritual exercises that served us equally well. More and more, we saw and heard of examples of commingling different religious paths, which reminded us of Thomas Merton's statement, "I think we have to keep in mind the fact that Christianity and Buddhism, in their original purity, point beyond all divisions between this and that."

Founded in 1798 by Spanish Franciscan padres, the "King of the Missions" is an important reminder of California's history. The buildings and grounds have been carefully restored and the mission walls accentuated with flowering bushes. The annual summer Fiesta weekend is held in late July or early August, when many come for music, dancing, food, crafts, and the blessing of animals. A small museum recounts the history of the mission and the role that missions played in the development of California. There is a gift shop that sells objects of interest for those who visit. The primary purpose of the Franciscan community that lives here and maintains the property is to provide rooms and meals for visitors and retreatants. There is a full schedule of retreats and programs.

The Mission church has a rough elegance that gives the feeling of stepping back almost 200 years. The original decorations have been restored and perfectly accent the thick walls and wooden beams. We were told that the property was confiscated by Mexico in the 1830s, then returned to the Franciscans by President Lincoln in 1865. Restoration began in the late nineteenth century, and now the property has the feeling of an outdoor museum. We found it a pleasure and very restful to wander the brick walkways to the oldest giant pepper tree in California, planted in 1830, and admire the Spanish-style courtyards and well-tended lawns.

MISSION SAN LUIS REY

◆

**4050 Mission Ave.
San Luis Rey, CA 92068
(760) 757-3651/
757-4613 fax**

**SUMMER FIESTA
1798 MISSION AND MUSEUM
RETREATS**

MOUNT BALDY
ZEN CENTER

◆

P.O. Box 429
Mount Baldy, CA 91759
(909) 985-6410/
985-4870 fax
E-mail: mbzc@aol.com

BUDDHIST TRAINING
RETREATS

*S*ixty-five hundred feet up in the San Gabriel Mountains, this small community offers intensive Rinzai Zen training periods of three months in winter and summer. During the spring and fall, the schedule is less formal, but zazen periods are held morning and evening.

On the way here we drove 35 miles east from Los Angeles, which is at sea level, and the twists and turns of the road that led up into the mountains afforded great views to the west.

During our visit, an intensive training session was being held, and we watched as the students, all dressed in kimonos, quietly walked in single file along the stone-marked paths.

MOUNT CALVARY
MONASTERY

◆

P.O. Box 1296
Santa Barbara, CA 93102
(805) 962-9855/
962-4957 fax

GREETING CARDS
COFFEE
RETREATS

*I*n the foothills of the Santa Ynez Mountains, 1,250 feet up on a rocky ledge with breathtaking views of the Pacific, an Episcopalian monk found a building shell in 1947 and built this monastery. The monks have a bookstore and gift shop, and host retreats for those who want to share their isolation and quiet. One of the monks, Brother Roy Parker, has a catalog of greeting cards beautifully executed in calligraphy and brush art, with religious themes and celebrating the holidays. He also has a series of exquisite cards with quotes from Rumi, the great Sufi philosopher-poet.

We had great difficulty finding the monastery. Unmarked roads led off here and there, but one distinctly said ROAD CLOSED, and there was no one around to ask. The neighborhood was sparsely settled with large

C
A
L
I
F
O
R
N
I
A

◈

42

houses barricaded by walls and gates. So we had to go back down the hill, find a phone, and when we described our difficulty to the monk, he quickly figured it out: "Just go around the 'Road Closed' sign, and keep coming up the hill."

The monastery has white stucco walls with a red tile roof, and sits on a rock base with steep cliffs on either side overlooking Santa Barbara and the sea. The entrance is through a large foyer with polished wood floors, furnished with Spanish colonial antiques under beamed ceilings. One of the rooms in the front has windows with the ocean view, a comfortable place to sit and chat before the Great Silence after evening prayers.

We spent some pleasant time there with a retired monk who had served as a missionary in Africa. He related his adventures, and as he spoke excitedly, he seemed to be reliving what had happened, not looking at us but at his own movie screen, watching his adventures replay in the theatre of his mind.

A friendship with a local coffee roaster led to the development of Monks' Blend coffee, initially for monastery use. Guests liked it so much they wanted to be able to order it. Only the best-quality coffee is used, roasted fresh every week to monastery specifications, a blend of beans from Kenya, Costa Rica, Guatemala, and Sumatra. The flavor is superb. One of the monks remembers spending a good part of a day sipping half-cups of coffee until the taste was just right. The coffee, whole beans or ground, is available by mail order.

MOUNT MADONNA CENTER

◆

**445 Summit Rd.
Watsonville, CA 95076
(408) 847-0406/
847-2683 fax**

SCHOOL

BOOKS

TAPES

ADULT PROGRAMS

YOGA

RETREATS

FESTIVAL

The core component of this intentional community of more than 100 adults and children is the study and practice of yoga, which they believe is not a religion but a spiritual path. "We are concerned," a member said, "with what is basic, true, and timeless, not with separating ourselves from others. Yoga's basic disciplines are essentially the same as Catholicism, Buddhism, and other great spiritual paths."

Sri Rama Publishing creates spiritual books and tapes, the profits from which go to support their Shri Ram Orphanage in India. Many of the books are written by the community's spiritual leader, Baba Hari Dass, who has kept a vow of silence since 1952, communicating only by writing on a slate. The audiotapes are of the Mount Madonna Choir singing ancient and modern choral music. There are also kirtan recordings of sacred Sanskrit chantings and instrumentals, including *Horizons—Improvisations for Flute and Harp,* a soothing and energizing sound journey.

The property, comprising 355 acres of meadows and forests, sits on a sloping hilltop with a sweeping, panoramic view of Monterey Bay. Retreats and conferences on spiritual themes are held throughout the year, and the fully accredited school, from kindergarten through high school, has more than 100 students. In 1997 the community completed a 20,000-square-foot conference center with a large hall and 33 guest rooms around a courtyard that takes advantage of the view. The nearby lake has a swimming beach, and there are volleyball, basketball, and tennis courts as well as miles of hiking trails. Each spring the school stages a grand production of the ancient Indian epic play the *Ramayana,* with 200 children and elaborate costumes, including a 30-foot dragon.

Their spiritual leader, Baba Hari Dass, has dedicated his life to selfless service and embodied the discipline of Karma Yoga to find inner peace, and his influence seems quite tangible.

This monastery is located in a remote part of the Santa Lucia Mountains, 1,300 feet above the California coast, with sweeping views of the ocean. In the morning the mist often settles in the canyons to the south and over the sea before the sun burns it off, and it seems as though you are walking in the clouds. These vistas are what make this a most popular retreat, and the guest rooms are booked months ahead. There is a powerful meditation period following Vespers in the church rotunda. Since the 1950s, hermit monks have occupied this ridgetop, quietly going about their eremitical lives. During one visit here, we talked to a monk who mentioned that they receive the daily New York and Los Angeles papers. Somewhat surprised, we wondered why they would bother to read the newspapers. He replied, "So we know where to direct our prayers!" The gift shop and bookstore have an array of arts and crafts made by the monks, and some of the local artists of Big Sur exhibit here. The monks sell by mail order their well-known Hermitage Cakes, fruitcake, and date-nut cakes dipped in brandy.

Our friend Rosa Nash had been part of the Immaculate Heart Community in Los Angeles when she was a young woman in the 1960s, then left, married the poet and artist Bob Nash, and lived much of her adult life on top of a mountain in Big Sur. Health problems caused her to come down from the mountains and the last time we saw her, she was guestmaster at this monastery. She insisted that we come for a weekend, and that was our first visit to that isolated setting. It was one of the influences that led to our subsequent visits to more than 250 retreats.

We remember her careful planning of our time, bringing monks to visit with us, urging that we attend the prayer sessions, and making our stay a most pleasant and delightful memory. Little did she or we know that this was all part of a process being woven that would set a direction to our lives for years to come. Rosa died within a year of our visit.

NEW CAMALDOLI HERMITAGE

◆

Big Sur, CA 93920
(408) 667-2456 or
667-2341/667-0209 fax

CARDS
POTTERY
PAINTINGS
FRUITCAKE
RETREATS

"Coastline Big Sur" by Fr. Arthur Poulin

FRUITCAKE

The fruitcake has a history as long as its shelf life and as rich as its ingredients. The Romans enjoyed a type of fruitcake that included pomegranate seeds, pine nuts, and raisins mixed into barley mash. Fruitcake lovers of the Middle Ages sweetened the recipe a little with honey, spices, and preserved fruits; in fact, the Crusaders themselves (poised to discover the jellies and jams of the Middle East) found sustenance in fruitcake for their arduous journey to the Holy Land. In modern England it is still a custom for unmarried wedding guests to put a small, boxed slice of the cake, traditionally a dark fruitcake, under their pillow at night so they will dream of the person they will marry. Perhaps what drives modern spiritual communities to produce fruitcakes is a fascination with that which endures, but more likely it is the rich beauty of process and product that prods them in their work. Profit could be an incentive as well; Our Lady of Guadalupe Abbey in Lafayette, Oregon, earns $36,000 a year (10 percent of their expenses) selling fruitcakes; Holy Cross Abbey in Berryville, Virginia, produced 28,000 fruitcakes in 1994.

◆

For more information on "Fruitcake History and Facts," visit www.tesla.csuhayward.edu.

Tarthang Tulku was one of the first Tibetans to arrive in the United States, in the late 1960s. A brilliant scholar and teacher of the Nyingma or "Old Ones" school of Tibetan Buddhism, he emphasizes directing energy to contribute something of value, developing skills to improve the quality of life, and recognizing limiting patterns in action and learning to break them. When thousands of Tibetans fled their homeland and brought with them the precious texts of their lineage, Dharma Publishing was conceived as a means to preserve the ancient scriptures by translating them for the West. An outstanding four-color catalog lists these high-quality publications and reproductions of sacred art. In 1973, Tarthang Tulku was able to purchase an old fraternity house on the northern edge of the University of California at Berkeley. From the front of the building, San Francisco Bay appears like a mirage on the horizon.

Nyingma Institute is located near the crest of "Holy Hill," where every religious persuasion seems to have a building or an office. Berkeley is built on gently sloping terrain that joins the Pacific at San Francisco Bay, and is one of the great intellectual centers of the United States. It is the site of what is referred to as the brightest light in the University of California's education system, and vies for the annual title of the most balanced and distinguished university in this country. It is a fitting place for Tibetan culture to grow and be renewed in an atmosphere of high intellectual energy.

For twenty-five years the Nyingma Institute has pioneered day and evening classes as ways to communicate Tibetan tradition to the West. Courses include Buddhist psychology, Tibetan yoga and meditation, and Buddhist visionary teachings of time, space, and knowledge. There are 42 prayer wheels here that spin continuously. These revolving copper drums are etched with mantras and filled with mantras and prayers written on paper; as the drums spin, the prayers are sent forth into the world. These are the only electrically powered prayer wheels known. The dean of studies writes: "For over two thousand years Buddhists have been constructing and

**NYINGMA
INSTITUTE**

◆

**1815 Highland Pl.
Berkeley, CA 94709
(510) 843-6812/
486-1679 fax
E-mail: nyingma
–institute@nyingma.org**

**PUBLISHER OF TIBETAN
BOOKS AND ART PRINTS
TRAINING PROGRAMS
PRAYER WHEELS**

C
A
L
I
F
O
R
N
I
A

◈

Prayer wheel at Nyingma Institute.

setting in motion dharma wheels (also known as 'prayer wheels') containing sacred texts and mantras that convey the blessing of compassion and harmony. Tarthang Tulku brought knowledge of the intricate science of creating dharma wheels with him to the United States. For close to thirty years he has worked to create a series of dharma wheels for the West. Through his efforts, more than a thousand 400-pound dharma wheels now turn day and night, powered by electric motors. Today, as in ages past, dharma wheels are honored as symbols of enlightened knowledge, able to evoke the healing powers of the mind." There is even a dharma wheel in the Library of Congress now. The institute does not currently accept orders for dharma wheels since demand exceeds production.

The institute also sponsors a ten-day World Peace Ceremony in late January each year in Bodh Gaya, India, which 30,000 people attend. Chanting and meditation at the Berkeley center is timed to coincide with the ceremony.

GRACE

Now that I am about to eat, O Great Spirit, give my thanks to the beasts and birds whom you have provided for my hunger, and pray deliver my sorrow that living things must make a sacrifice for my comfort and well-being. Let the feather of corn spring up in its time and let it not wither but make full grains for the fires of our cooking pots, now that I am about to eat.

◆

A Native American mealtime blessing from the Lama Foundation,
San Cristobal, New Mexico, from 100 Graces: Mealtime Blessings

This community is patterned after those of Native Americans. After Robert Bly led an all-night drumming workshop here a few years ago, so the story goes, a few neighbors kept up by the noise pointed out a number of code violations and the community was shut down. Now located on a 40-acre ridge of semi-wilderness, they no longer bother the neighbors, and the Foundation has become an educational sanctuary for adults and children, a community devoted to sharing practices, personal stories, and visions of a more peaceful planet, while living and working together close to the earth.

Their New Visions of Education Program is being used in many California schools. It involves a group process called "council," which involves listening and speaking from the heart. Classes from these schools can come to the land for retreats to appreciate the earth, or for a ropes course, a sweat lodge, or rites of passage retreat. Visitors report that they have the best bathtub in the world, a claw-footed tub in the middle of the forest, heated by a Pahoma water heater mounted on a nearby tree. "You can luxuriate here for hours, looking through the branches to the stars."

OJAI FOUNDATION

◆

**9739 Ojai–
Santa
Paula Rd.
Ojai, CA 93023
(805) 646-8343**

**NEW VISIONS OF EDUCATION
PROGRAM**

Whenever we travel in this part of California, nostalgia and delight take over and we feel we are back in the fifties again. Perhaps only in this environment could such a place as Orr Hot Springs exist. Native Americans stopped here to rest while on trading expeditions, and agreed to coexist peacefully while using the waters.

As we sat relaxing in the large hot tub, big enough for 12, a man got into the far side and we began to chat. He was from Alaska, where he'd chosen to live many years ago. He was an independent carpenter who worked for six months during good weather, then packed his trailer and headed south, wandering the byways of California, living modestly and enjoying his

ORR HOT SPRINGS

◆

**13201 Orr Springs Rd.
Ukiah, CA 95482
(707) 462-6277**

**HOT SPRINGS RETREAT
WITH CLOTHING OPTIONAL
IN BATHING AREAS**

C
A
L
I
F
O
R
N
I
A

◈

lifestyle. His art was photography, and he'd taken many fine pictures. Occasionally he'd sell one, but selling wasn't important. What he'd discovered was that looking at the world as a place to photograph had raised his awareness enormously, and he was so grateful for that.

PRESENTATION CENTER

◆

**19480 Bear Creek Rd.
Los Gatos, CA 95030
(408) 354-2346**

PROGRAMS
RETREATS

The Old World charm of the Center is due partly to the Spanish-influenced architecture of early California. The Catholic Sisters of the Presentation acquired the property in 1956. In the spirit of Christian hospitality, they currently make their facilities available to any nonprofit group, religious or educational, and host a number of retreats for specific needs, such as weekends for Spanish-speaking men and women and Alcoholics Anonymous. The Montezuma Mountain School for Boys was located here from 1911 to 1955.

We stayed in one of the cottages, a self-contained unit where teachers lived when the boys' school was here. We took our meals in the main dining room, a short walk from our cozy house, and noticed a number of young couples sitting there together as a group. We found out that this was a retreat weekend for men and women preparing for marriage. Led by experienced counselors, Engaged Encounter takes young couples through some of the pitfalls every marriage encounters, showing them how to avoid trouble where possible and deal with it if it occurs. Some report a better understanding of the whole idea of marriage as well as the spiritual side of living with and caring for another person. A small percentage of these couples postpone their union or decide not to get married.

For many years, Brother Benno took a truck out to gather food and clothing and served meals to the hungry in what came to be called Brother Benno's Kitchen in Oceanside. In 1991, a group of laypeople opened the Brother Benno Center where, in addition to providing food and clothing, there are shower facilities, a mail and message center, an employment office, counseling, and literacy classes. The center is separate from the monastery, which is perched on a hilltop outside of town. The Catholic Benedictines who live here celebrate the canonical hours in the magnificent chapel, and though they hold no organized retreats, there is a separate guesthouse for those who wish to come for retreat. There is also a gift shop with books and religious articles.

We had arranged the meeting for the morning after our arrival, and sat waiting in the dining room. The 83-year-old abbot walked by us with a nod, then disappeared through the kitchen door. Minutes later he reappeared pushing a cart laden with boxes of food, fruits and breads protruding from them. He swept by us into the lounge. We could see him deliver the cart to a man who had been waiting nervously, hat in hand, sitting on a sofa. His face brightened as the abbot approached. The man took the cart and wheeled it away. The abbot then turned and came back to us. He sat down and apologized for keeping us waiting, explaining that the man was out of work and had a family to feed. "Now," he said, "what can I do for you?"

PRINCE OF PEACE ABBEY

◆

**650 Benet Hill Rd.
Oceanside, CA 92054
(619) 430-1305 or 1306
E-mail:
princeabbey@aol.com**

**BROTHER BENNO CENTER
FOR THE POOR**

RETREATS

QUAKER CENTER

◆

**Box 686
Ben Lomond, CA 95005
(408) 336-8333**

**ANNUAL "ART & THE SPIRIT"
FIVE-DAY WORKSHOP
AROUND JULY 4**

RETREATS

Quakerism was started more than 300 years ago in England with Christian roots, and today encompasses a diversity of beliefs. Quakers, or Friends, as they are also known, assemble in groups to worship silently until the spirit moves an individual to speak. They believe in "continuing revelation" and that God still speaks today. Thus, worship takes the form of quietly waiting for God's word. Though Quakers have no formal creed or doctrine, the "peace testimony" that violence in any form is wrong is universally Quaker. Since this retreat was donated to the Religious Society of Friends in the 1940s, many spiritual meetings have been held on these 80 sloping acres in the Santa Cruz Mountains. When we visited, the family who lived here had a pet rabbit for their children. They decided to turn the rabbit loose, back to nature, but the animal had no interest in leaving, and had become so trusting it would hop onto your shoe. Programs are held throughout the year, individuals are welcome, and around every Fourth of July weekend, a five-day workshop is offered, called "Art & the Spirit," oriented to Quaker spirituality.

We made the climb to the Casa de Luz Meetinghouse, which is on a high point overlooking the treetops to the San Lorenzo River valley. The Casa is an A-frame with a deck and windows that take advantage of the view, a secluded building in an isolated setting. Though parts of these mountains were clear-cut in the 1940s, nature has responded and replaced the trees. When she gave the property to the Religious Society of Friends, Lucille Manley stated, "It should be perpetually dedicated and used for the enjoyment, betterment, education, and welfare of mankind."

This Catholic Benedictine abbey is located in Antelope Valley in the foothills of the San Gabriel Mountains, known as the high desert of southern California. It was founded in the 1950s by monks exiled from China after the Communist takeover. Benefactors made it possible for the monks to acquire this property, and they set about making their monastery a house of prayer. They began welcoming guests, and supporting themselves by their own labor.

In the 1960s they began the manufacture of ceramic figures designed by the artist-monk Father Maur van Doorslaar. At first these were sold only on the grounds, but in recent years, owing to popular demand, they are sold by mail and in several hundred shops throughout the United States. An extensive color catalog displays the elegant figures that depict Christmas, the Old and New Testaments, Madonnas, the saints, and a variety of angels dedicated to a range of occupations and sports. There are special angels for babies, graduations, relatives, and even a Star of David Angel. The process of creating these works of art begins with a sketch, incising the design into plaster, then pressing the design into the clay and firing the clay to the bisque stage. The bisque is then glazed by hand with glazes mostly compounded by the monks, and the final firing transforms the bisque into stoneware of great brilliance and depth of color. Near porcelain quality is achieved, and each piece is unique in coloration.

The monks also host workshops and retreats throughout the year, and welcome visitors to the Chinese pagoda and tea garden, reminiscent of the monastery's Far Eastern heritage. The Fall Festival, a weekend celebration of musical events, fresh farm produce, and ethnic food, attracts thousands every year.

One of the monks has grown grass in a grove of Lombardy poplars, an unusual touch and quite a challenge in the desert. At the noon meal the monks, with great care and attention, serve each guest a bowl of soup, a gesture that shows how pleased they are that visitors make the effort to come.

ST. ANDREW'S ABBEY

◆

31001 N. Valyermo Rd.
Valyermo, CA 93563
(805) 944-2178
(805) 944-1047/
944-1076 fax: ceramics

CERAMIC ARTIFACTS WITH
RELIGIOUS THEMES

SEMINARS

WORKSHOPS

RETREATS

FALL FESTIVAL

CERAMICS

How our ceramics are made:

1. The artist-monk sketches an original design and traces it through carbon paper onto a plaster of Paris slab.

2. He then incises his design into the plaster.

3. Clay is pressed into the design mold with a rolling pin and then carefully separated from the mold. (The clay used is a blend of clays and grog [alcoholic liquor, especially rum diluted with water], which, upon firing, yields a most agreeable and natural earth tone and texture.)

4. The design is excised with a stylus and put on an absorbent batt [a mass of cotton fibers] to dry.

5. When thoroughly dry, the fragile pieces of clay are individually and gently placed into the kiln for the bisque firing. For 14 hours the temperature is slowly raised to 1750 degrees Fahrenheit.

6. The bisque is ready for glazing. In order to achieve a full range of natural desert tones, we use a combination of 16 glazes and slips—only five of which we do not compound ourselves. The glazes are applied by hand to the bisque with an ear syringe—a delicate and tedious task, all the more difficult because the glazes give no hint of their ultimate color. All is now ready for the final firing to 2350 degrees Fahrenheit, a temperature which transforms the bisque into stoneware, vitrifies [changes or makes into glass or a similar substance, especially through heat fusion] the glazes (binding them to the stoneware), and gives the glazes their brilliance and depth of color.

7. Stacking the kilns for a glaze firing is an art in itself. The enormous heat must circulate evenly, or all is lost. A successful glaze firing lends a near porcelain quality to the finished work. Yet, even now the finished artifact is subject to careful quality control. Although, by reason of the nature of its manufacture, each piece is unique in its coloration, each is examined for the quality required of a collectable bearing our name.

◆

Adapted from the catalog of St. Andrew's Abbey in Valyermo, California

Though Roman Catholic in its foundation and heritage, Santa Sabina Center is ecumenical in its philosophy and interfaith in its outreach. The staff hosts groups that come with a spiritual and/or educational purpose. The center offers its own monthly weekend retreats, days of prayer, and Thomas Merton reflection evenings, as well as private retreats. The whole building, including the cloister, occupies a quiet corner of the 100-acre campus of Dominican College, and is a replica of the motherhouse on Capitoline Hill in Rome. There is a bookstore, a library, an art/meditation space, a separate small hermitage, beautiful gardens, and extensive hiking trails. Visitors can take a fire-trail walk to a lookout called Rim of the World, which overlooks the entire San Francisco Bay, a panorama of city, bridges, and the ocean beyond.

The Center is an elegant building with many European monastic touches. The arched doorway leads into a dark-wood interior, through one tastefully decorated room after another. There is an inner courtyard of grass, flowers, an orange tree, and a murmuring fountain, completely set off from the world outside, a most inviting inner sanctum where quiet prevails. Thomas Merton wrote: "Actually, what matters about the monastery is precisely that it is radically different from the world. The apparent 'pointlessness' of the monastery in the eyes of the world is exactly what gives it a real reason for existing. In a world of noise, confusion, and conflict it is necessary there be a place of silence, inner discipline, and peace."

SANTA SABINA CENTER

◆

**25 Magnolia Ave.
San Rafael, CA 94901
(415) 457-7727/
457-2310 fax
E-mail:
sntasabina@aol.com**

CONFERENCES

WORKSHOPS (INCLUDING PAPERMAKING)

THOMAS MERTON CENTER

RETREATS

C
A
L
I
F
O
R
N
I
A

◆

SELF-REALIZATION FELLOWSHIP RETREAT

◆

**215 K St.
Encinitas, CA 92024
(760) 753-1811**

**TEACHINGS WITH RESIDENT
COMMUNITY**

GARDEN TOURS

RETREATS

BOOKS AND TAPES

In 1937, this 17-acre property and handsome house were given to Paramahansa Yogananda by a devotee. A year later, Yogananda turned it into an open house so that all could enjoy the views from the 400-foot bluff looking out to the Pacific, and the beauty and serenity of the grounds. He spent most of his remaining years here, and wrote the classic *Autobiography of a Yogi,* which tells of his own searchings.

A monastic community lives here and holds structured meditation and classes on the teachings of Yogananda primarily for Self-Realization Fellowship members. Retreatants are expected to observe silence. The grounds are meticulously maintained, ponds are filled with Japanese goldfish, and the sea can be viewed from benches along the blufftop.

This is a truly beautiful location kept scrupulously out of respect for Yogananda, who founded the Fellowship in 1920 and died in 1952. His private rooms are preserved as a shrine and can be visited on Sunday afternoons. Yogananda taught Kriya Yoga, considered akin to Raja Yoga, and reportedly was eager to reconcile Hinduism with Christianity. He once said: "Every person needs a retreat, a dynamo of silence, where one can go for the exclusive purpose of being recharged by the infinite."

There is a gift shop with books and tapes at the temple at 939 Second Street in Encinitas, a few blocks from the retreat. Services are held at the temple on Thursdays and Sundays, and it is open every day except Monday from noon to 4:00 P.M.

The Seva Foundation grew out of a project to eradicate smallpox in India. A group of friends from the World Health Organization enjoyed working together so much that after the smallpox project was complete, they decided to concentrate on eye programs for curable blindness, a huge problem in India and Nepal. They brought doctors in from around the world, trained local doctors, and built clinics and eye camps that now operate independently and complete more than 100,000 sight-restoring operations a year. Over the years, Seva board members have added projects of special interest to them, and out of this came their Gifts of Service catalog, which allows buyers to purchase sheep for Guatemalan widows, eye surgery for those with curable blindness, medical care for a Lakota Indian reservation, and food for the homeless, all part of Seva's programs of compassionate action.

You can choose a project that you want to support, or you can pick one as a gift for someone else. When you send in your contribution, say for a new room for the hospital in India, you can request that Seva send one of their special notes of thanks telling your friend that a donation has been made in their name by you, and giving them not only a photograph, but an explanation of how the money is being used and the difference it will make in the people's lives.

SEVA FOUNDATION

◆

**1786 5th St.
Berkeley, CA 94710
(510) 845-7382/
845-7410 fax
Web site: www.seva.org**

GIFTS OF
COMPASSIONATE ACTION

(RAMESHWAR DAS)   (RAMESHWAR DAS)

GIFTS OF SERVICE

The origin of the word *salvation* is the Latin *salvare,* which means not only "to save," as from danger or sin, but to be in a state of health and well-being. In this latter sense, the Seva Foundation (*seva* is Sanskrit for "service"), although not affiliated with any particular religion, is actively seeking the salvation of the world's suffering and oppressed. The Foundation's Gifts of Service program ministers to suffering peoples worldwide. Gifts are typically given in the name of a friend or as a memorial. Gifts range from $30 to $10,000 and go toward alleviating blindness in Tibet, Nepal, and India (the Affordable Eyesight Fund); encouraging self-sufficient, productive community life in Mexico and Guatemala (the Building Communities Fund); organizing retreats for Seva activists so that they can reflect upon their work and rejuvenate themselves for work to come (the Fund for Creativity and Renewal in Service); reintroducing traditional foods like dried meat and native corns to Native Americans in order to ward off the spread of diabetes (the Native American Fund); and maintaining the normal operating and program costs of the Foundation itself (the Sustaining Seva Fund).

Part of Seva's strength lies in its contributions to all levels of self-reliance. Gifts that many of us would never think to offer play integral roles in the program; for example, a typical gift to the Building Communities Fund is money to pay for enough gasoline to allow a Mexican seller of wooden tables and chairs to make one round trip to market. Other monies go toward publishing a Tibetan translation of a widely renowned eye surgery text. In the Seva catalog, the executive director expresses the mission and goal of the Seva Foundation: "Each gift that is described in these pages is a window into a world where human beings are engaged in a struggle for health, survival, and renewal of spirit. . . . Our goal is to help resource renewal from within—whether it is at the individual or community level. This is our understanding of self-reliance."

◆

For a Seva catalog, call (800) 223-7382 toll-free, or (510) 845-7382 in the Berkeley area, or visit
Seva's Web site: www.seva.org

This abbey was founded in the early 1970s as a training monastery for priests in the Serene Reflection Meditation tradition (called, in Chinese, Ts'ao-tung Chan, and in Japanese, Soto Zen). Shasta Abbey Press has published many books to support and encourage the growth of Buddhist dharma in the West, among which are those of the late founder, Rev. Master Jiyu-Kennett, an Englishwoman who studied Soto Zen in Japan and came to the United States following her master's wish that she transmit the teachings to the West. She commented on the differences between Buddhism and Christianity: "There is no saviour in Buddhism. You have to do it yourself. No one else will meditate for you. At the time of death you will judge yourself . . . the ability to die in peace means the ability to live in peace . . . we make our own hell. . . . Meditation has nothing whatever to do with self-improvement . . . its purpose is to become one with the Cosmic Buddha or have an experience of God." She wrote *Zen Is Eternal Life,* which is a manual for practicing Zen and a guide to the basic teachings of Buddhism.

Seminary training for the Buddhist priesthood begins with a lay residency for six months, followed by a period of postulancy for one to two years, then at least five years as a novice priest.

Shasta Abbey's catalog lists its books, cards, gongs and temple instruments, incense, jewelry, meditation cushions and benches, posters, scrolls, statues, rosaries, and video- and audiotapes. This is a complete provider for the Buddhist student. The Abbey also holds a variety of retreats for laypeople, and celebrates Buddhist festivals in a serene 16-acre setting of wooded land within a few miles of Mount Shasta. Guests are expected to stay on the grounds during their visit. One monk said, "There is always a schedule to follow. Be willing to stay where you are and concentrate while you're here." Unlike any other Buddhist abbey, the morning and evening office is sung in English in four-part harmony, like Gregorian chant, with organ accompaniment, thanks to their late abbess, a fine musician.

SHASTA ABBEY

◆

**P.O. Box 199
3724 Summit Dr.
Mount Shasta, CA 96067
(530) 926-6682
phone and fax
(800) 653-3315/
729-1195 fax
Web site:
www.OBCON.org**

**BUDDHIST BOOK PUBLISHING
AND TAPE PRODUCTION**

**TRAINING MONASTERY FOR
MEN AND WOMEN PRIESTS IN
SERENE REFLECTION
MEDITATION**

MEDITATION SUPPLIES

**FESTIVALS HONORING
BUDDHIST TRADITIONS**

RETREATS

SHENOA RETREAT CENTER

◆

P.O. Box 43
Philo, CA 95466
(707) 895-3156

WORKSHOPS
RETREATS

This community follows the traditions of preserving and sustaining the natural environment. A center for renewal, education and service, it is affiliated with the Findhorn Foundation in Scotland. Current programs emphasize the appreciation of learning to reflect the peace and healing power found in nature and to experience sustainable living choices.

The 160-acre property, which includes a one-acre organic garden and has open meadows and forests of redwood, fir, laurel, and oak, adjoins the Hendy Woods State Park, and is bounded by the Navarro River. One member says, "World transformation is something anyone can be involved in, anywhere. We need only to ask: Am I being a way? What am I doing to transform myself and my world?"

In the winter and early spring, the river rises and reclaims its territory and cars cannot cross. The only way in is via a swaying footbridge above rushing waters and you wonder, as you cross, if this is the Bridge of San Luis Rey.

Sikh Dharma began in India over 500 years ago and reaches out to people of all faiths and cultural backgrounds in an effort to see beyond differences and to work together for world peace and harmony. The Healthy, Happy, Holy Organization (3HO), founded in 1969 by Yogi Bhajan, is a nonprofit educational foundation dedicated to uplifting humanity through yoga, lifestyle guidelines on nutrition, health, interpersonal relations, childrearing, and human behavior. It promotes vegetarianism, Ayurvedic healing, abstinence from drugs, and meditation.

The Foundation has five centers in North America and, besides ongoing classes, hosts three worldwide yoga festivals, one at the winter solstice in Florida, one at the summer solstice in New Mexico, and one in France in July. They have a camp for women in New Mexico, several preschools using the Montessori and Waldorf techniques, and youth camps in New Mexico and upstate New York.

The community has also created 22 businesses to help support it. One thriving business, Yogi Tea, grew out of a community practice of serving their own tea blend after yoga classes. Now they market 40 different widely available healing teas—with flavors including Egyptian Licorice, Tahitian Vanilla, Green Tea with Kombucha, Stomach E-Z, Bedtime, Wake-Me-Up, and Lover's Tea—and distribute via catalog from New Mexico. The Golden Temple Bakery makes Rain Forest Cereals such as Blueberry, Strawberry, and Crisp and Crunchy Granola, Super Nutty Granola, Rain Forest Flakes, and Honey Nut Clusters. Wha Guru Chews come in three flavors: peanut cashew, sesame almond, and cashew almond. Herbal capsules, extracts, and oils are also offered, along with music CDs and tapes, and yoga videos and books. All these products appear in their Ancient Healing Ways catalog.

The largest 3HO company, Akal Security (Sanskrit for "liberation"), has 2,000 employees in several states, and a contract with the U.S. Marshal Service to provide guards for courtrooms. In addition it supplies guards for many corporations in New Mexico, California, Arizona, and Hawaii.

SIKH DHARMA/3HO FOUNDATION

◆

Guru Ram Das Ashram
1620 Preuss Rd.
Los Angeles, CA 90035
(310) 858-7691/
274-8085 fax: yoga
(505) 753-6341:
festivals/summer classes
(800) 359-2940:
catalog orders
E-mail: sikhnet.com
Web site:
www.yogitea.com

CAMPS
INTENSIVES
YOGA FESTIVALS
EDUCATION
TEA
CEREAL
CANDY
HERBAL PRODUCTS
MUSIC AND YOGA VIDEOS
BOOKS
SECURITY

CALIFORNIA

◈

Other companies, such as Herbal Gems, which will supply herbal programs and packages and hotline support, are just getting off the ground.

SONOMA MOUNTAIN ZEN CENTER

◆

6367 Sonoma Mountain Rd. Santa Rosa, CA 95404 (707) 545-8105

ZEN TRAINING AND RETREATS

In the early 1970s, Jakusho Kwong-roshi founded this center on 80 hilltop acres in a quiet section of Sonoma County. The community practices Soto Zen and offers a yearlong resident training program, month-long *ango* practice in July, and three-to-five-day retreats, as well as one-day sitting sessions and introductory weekends. Kwong-roshi, American born and very available to his students, describes Zen practice: "The more you practice, you realize it's not for gain but for gratitude. Gratitude becomes the biggest treasure, and practice is the way." During our visit here, aside from the quiet beauty of the location and friendliness of the community, the walking meditation, used to relax the body during sitting, was a powerful, memorable phase of the meditation period. It seemed to add a new dimension to our appreciation of the meditative process, undoubtedly engendered by the community's feelings of gratitude, which they were indirectly sharing with each other and with us in the magic and silence of the zendo.

People are beginning to realize that a balance between body, mind, and spirit is essential for a fulfilled life. To tune the body, we exercise at the gym, play sports, and eat properly; to balance the mind, we visit psychiatrists and psychologists, and read; for the spirit, we delve into the meaning of our lives, why we are here and what we should be doing about it. We often find an avenue to greater understanding of these complex issues through religion or some other spiritual pathway. Each of us knows what is best for ourselves, but the way may be hidden behind years of neglect and misleading habits. Once the emptiness becomes apparent, we may be ready to talk and listen. In the mid-1980s, a group of Catholic sisters discovered that San Diego was a very good place to begin a spiritual ministry. They discovered an amazing hunger for spirituality, and they are meeting that need by providing a place for workshops, counseling, and retreats. The sisters also have a two-year program for qualified individuals to train as spiritual directors. Spiritual direction is aiding an individual to see how God is calling or leading in specific situations.

SPIRITUAL MINISTRY CENTER

◆

4822 Del Mar Ave.
San Diego, CA 92107
(619) 224-9444

SPIRITUAL DIRECTION AND RENEWAL PROGRAMS

2-YEAR PROGRAM FOR SPIRITUAL DIRECTORS

WORKSHOPS

RETREATS

FROM A
CHURCH BULLETIN

Next Sunday a special collection will be taken to defray the cost of the new carpet. All those wishing to do something on the new carpet will come forward and get a piece of paper.

TASSAJARA ZEN MOUNTAIN CENTER

◆

**39171 Tassajara Rd.
Carmel Valley, CA 93924
(415) 431-3349
May–September
Web site: bodhi.zendo
.com/~sfzc**

ZEN TRAINING
HOT SPRINGS
YOGA INSTRUCTION
WORK PRACTICE PROGRAM
BOOKS
RETREATS

The San Francisco Zen Center, under the leadership of the late Shunryu Suzuki-roshi, established a monastic community here in 1966. During the winter months, the remote retreat is a place for intensive Zen training and is closed to visitors. Beginning in the spring and continuing through fall, there are a number of programs, workshops, and retreats that bring people back year after year, to the seclusion, quiet, and beauty of the mountains, the hot springs, and the ambience of a spiritual community. This is where Edward Espe Brown developed his famous cookbooks *The Tassajara Bread Book* and *Tassajara Cooking*. The food reflects the mindfulness of Zen as the staff prepares it and visitors consume it, contemplate its benefit, and thank the plants for giving their energy, then dedicate its consumption for the good of others. All breads and pastries are baked fresh daily, and most herbs used are grown in the garden. A complete catalog describes the retreats and workshops given from May to September.

Vedanta means the end (*anta*) of the Vedas (ancient Sanskrit texts), or the culmination of spiritual knowledge. The basic teaching of Vedanta is that the essence of all beings and things, from grass to God, is spiritual, infinite, and eternal, nonchanging and indivisible; that people in their true nature are divinely spiritual, one reality, one being. This retreat is affiliated with the Vedanta Society of Northern California in San Francisco. Day visitors are welcome from 10:00 A.M. to 5:00 P.M. There is an extensive library of books dealing with Indian and Hindu philosophy and texts by and about Vivekananda and Ramakrishna. Some books are for sale. Spiritual seekers of any religious persuasion are welcome to visit and use the library, but to stay overnight one must be interviewed by the swami on duty in San Francisco. Men and women stay in separate buildings. The 2,000-acre property of meadows and deciduous trees is filled with deer and surrounded by the 62,000-acre Point Reyes National Seashore.

When we pulled into the parking area, we saw a man leaning against a farm building, dressed in bib overalls and a floppy hat, and went over to him to get some directions. After we explained our purpose, he said he'd be happy to show us around. He took us on a complete tour of the two main buildings, and answered our many questions. We found out that he was the swami in charge, and remarked how fortunate we were to meet up with him as soon as we arrived. He smiled and said, "There are no coincidences."

VEDANTA RETREAT

◆

**P.O. Box 215
Olema, CA 94950
(415) 663-1258**

**BOOKS BY AND ABOUT
VIVEKANANDA AND
RAMAKRISHNA**

LIBRARY

**SEPARATE WOMEN'S AND
MEN'S RETREAT HOUSES**

C
A
L
I
F
O
R
N
I
A

◈

WELLSPRING RENEWAL CENTER

◆

**P.O. Box 332
Philo, CA 95466
(707) 895-3893**

COOKBOOK
PROGRAMS
RETREATS

The cooks at Wellspring are known for their skill in using their own produce, and have published a cookbook that tells almost all their secrets. The directors offer programs of renewal and refreshment along life's journey. Individuals can plan their own retreat and use the campground, tent cabins, or cabins with kerosene lamps and nearby bathhouse. The unique cottage, with a grass roof, is a sight to behold. When we were there, a huge community conference was being held, with everyone from the surrounding area invited to discuss the future of the area. Much lively political discussion ensued, followed by a feast of dishes brought to share. The joyful evening ended with the sounds of group drumming echoing out over the gardens and fields, a true sound of fellowship.

WHITE LOTUS FOUNDATION

◆

**2500 San Marcos Pass
Santa Barbara, CA 93105
(805) 964-1944/
964-9617 fax
(800) 544-FLOW:
yoga video**

YOGA TRAINING
VIDEO
RETREATS

Twice a year, Yogaraj Ganga White teaches an intensive 16-day yoga teacher-training course, open to all levels of students. This residential program is given at the Foundation's center, 1,600 feet above Santa Barbara. The course begins with the fundamentals of yoga practice and theory, and the noncompetitive nature of yoga allows each student to go at his or her own pace using the postures, breathing, and meditations. The sessions emphasize precision and alignment while moving gracefully from one posture to the next. White, who draws on the best from the leading yoga systems as well as his own 25 years of training experience, says, "We like our practice to be fun, energizing, and complete."

The large main building of the center is like a cave against the canyon wall, and offers views of the city, Channel Islands, and the mighty Pacific. White is the creator of "double yoga," a method by which two people practice together. "Everything we do here is meant to empower individuals . . . to awaken the fire of yoga within each student." Retreats are given at special times of the year, as is a select course for advanced teacher training.

CENTER FOR COMMUNAL STUDIES

The Center for Communal Studies is a clearinghouse for information, a research facility, and a sponsor of activities related to historic and contemporary intentional communities. Through its contacts with communal and utopian study organizations, historic communal sites, and current communities worldwide, the Center provides information and sponsorship for conferences, lectures, seminars, classes, internships, student exchange programs, grants, and scholarships, and is planning to offer a master's degree in communal studies. The Center maintains a register of communal scholars, historic site directors, and current communal leaders. A $250 Center for Communal Studies Prize is awarded each March to the undergraduate or graduate student who submits the best scholarly paper on a communal theme by the previous December 15. The Center's research and historic communal site capacities are enhanced by its special relationship with the famous Harmonist and Owenite village of New Harmony. The collections of Historic New Harmony, the 1838 Workingmen's Institute, and the Owen family provide unique study opportunities. The Center Lecture Series brings noted speakers to New Harmony. The director of the center and 16 other scholars have published *America's Communal Utopias* (University of North Carolina Press, 1997), a 537-page book of essays examining the beliefs and practices of communities as diverse as the Shakers and the Branch Davidians.

◆

For information, contact the Center for Communal Studies, School of Liberal Arts,
University of Southern Indiana, 8600 University Blvd., Evansville, IN 47712,
(812) 464-1727/1960 fax; E-mail dpitzer.ucs@smtp.usi.edu.

ZEN MOUNTAIN CENTER

◆

P.O. Box 43
Mountain Center
CA 92561
(909) 659-5272/
659-3275 fax
E-mail:
zmc@primenet.com
Web site:
www.zmc.org/zmc

ZEN TRAINING

POTTERY

CUSHIONS

RAKUSUS

ALTARS

JEWELRY

BOOKS

CARDS

RETREATS

Every summer the Center runs a 90-day intensive Zen *sesshin* training period, which is a time to refine and immerse oneself in the practice. The Center follows the lineage of Maezumi-roshi, and its daily schedule includes six to eight hours of zazen, formal meals, interviews with teachers, mindful work, and daily service. The center is on 160 acres of wilderness in the San Jacinto Mountains at 5,500 feet elevation, 120 miles east of Los Angeles. The facilities are solar-powered and the zendo's water comes from a deep mountain spring. The Pacific Coast Trail touches the edge of the property and affords the opportunity to hike to the top, where trams come up from Palm Springs, on the other side of the mountains. Throughout the year there are introductory Zen meditation sessions given each Sunday and various weekend retreats and workshops on such subjects as environmental studies and pottery. A full line of Buddhist supplies is available by mail order.

RAKUSUS

In Buddhist practice, *rakusus* (pronounced *rock*-soos) are robes worn by practitioners who have taken the vow of *jukai,* the vow to accomplish the Way. At Zen Mountain Center in Mountain Center, California, two years of practice, a prerequisite course (lasting about three months), and a vow to follow Buddhist precepts are required before *jukai* can be taken and the distinguishing rakusu worn. The rakusu represents a smaller version of the Buddha's robe (the *kesa).* Some say this smaller version was designed and worn during a period of Chinese persecution against Buddhists; in such times the rakusu could be worn inconspicuously under one's clothes. Currently, Zen Flesh Zen Robes, part of Zen Mountain Center, no longer produces its own hand-woven rakusus, but they continue to offer rakusu kits to qualified practitioners who wish to follow the tradition of sewing one's own.

◆

For a Zen Flesh Zen Robes catalog, which includes many Buddhist supplies in addition to rakusu kits,
phone (909) 659-5272.

Colorado

NADA HERMITAGE

◆

**Spiritual Life Institute
Crestone, CO 81131
(719) 256-4778/
256-4719 fax**

**PRIVATE RETREATS IN A
REMOTE DESERT LOCALE**

BOOKS

TAPES

CARDS

A youthful group of apostolic hermits lives in this remote section of southeastern Colorado, in the foothills of the Sangre de Cristo Mountains, on the gently sloping eastern edge of the San Juan Valley, the largest alpine valley in North America—the size of Delaware. The site looks west to the La Garita Mountains, 40 miles away. The adobe hermitages are artfully designed and heated by passive solar energy with woodstove backup. All living needs are provided, but each person sleeps when tired and eats when ready—alone. A monk is available for spiritual direction if requested. There are communal vespers each afternoon in the chapel. The weekends have a slightly different schedule, with mass on Sunday. This is a place of solitude and quiet and splendid views. The community moved here in the 1980s from Arizona, where their grounds were being encroached on by development. They received a parcel of a large ranch that was being divided and donated to religious groups who would live on and improve the land. The teachings and writings of Father William McNamara are the guiding force behind the community and his tapes and books are available, as are those of Mother Tessa Bielecki, a well-known writer and speaker.

Wilderness Dawn card by Betty Brown

They now have a hermitage in County Sligo, Ireland, and a retreat in Nova Scotia that has a reputation for being extremely isolated and rustic, a great relief after the experience in Arizona. Recently the adjoining property in Nova Scotia was sold to a large lumber company that threatens to clear-cut the surrounding territory. Much prayer and protest is called for to protect this lovely place.

This university is based on the vision of its Tibetan founder, Chögyam Trungpa, Rinpoche, a scholar, artist, and meditation master who was recognized as one of the foremost teachers of Buddhism in the West. Named after Naropa, a great eleventh-century Buddhist scholar, teacher, and practitioner renowned for bringing together scholarly wisdom with meditative insight, this college combines contemplative studies with traditional Western scholastic and artistic disciplines. Its goals are to deepen students' knowledge of themselves and their place in the contemporary world, "to develop and strengthen personal discipline within a specific field of study, to nurture the desire to contribute to the world with understanding and compassion. In this way students are prepared for the constant challenges and rapid change of modern society. Through contemplative disciplines such as sitting meditation, precision, openness, and kindness to oneself and others" are developed.

The Naropa Institute code of conduct offers guidelines for the entire community, including the following:

1. *Arouse respect for teachers, the wisdom of many traditions, and all who seek wisdom. Honor the process of learning.*

2. *Seek out and practice disciplines which benefit yourself and others.*

3. *Be true to your inspiration. Apply yourself whole-heartedly. Enjoy yourself. Don't be afraid to take a risk.*

**NAROPA
INSTITUTE**

◆

**2130 Arapahoe Ave.
Boulder, CO 80302
(800) 411-5229
(303) 546-3572/
546-5295 fax
Web site:
www.naropa.edu**

FULLY ACCREDITED COLLEGE

4. Assume responsibility for your state of mind and all of your actions.

5. Speak gently and thoughtfully.

6. Refrain from slander. Maintain your dignity.

7. Be generous to all without prejudice.

8. Do not waver in meeting your obligations.

Naropa offers a full range of degrees, from anthropology and art to Native American studies, and writing and poetics, led by such teachers as the poet Anne Waldman. The late Allen Ginsberg founded Naropa's Jack Kerouac School of Disembodied Poetics. Inspired by the tradition of Buddhist educational philosophy, contemplative education helps combine intellect and intuition, and encourages the deepening of confidence, wisdom, and the desire to work for the benefit of others.

ST. BENEDICT'S MONASTERY

◆

**1012 Monastery Rd.
Snowmass, CO 81654
(970) 927-3311/
927-3399 fax
(970) 927-1162: retreats
E-mail: retreat@rof.net
Web site:
www.snowmass.org**

COOKIES
BOOKS
RETREATS

When the monks began their cookie business some years ago, they called on a Zen master from New York, Bernard Tetsugen Glassman, whose Greyston Foundation founded and still runs the Greyston Bakery in Yonkers, and he helped them get started. Three delicious flavors come in one-and-a-half- or three-pound tins or boxes, but they are for sale only at their gift shop.

In the 1950s, the monks chose this locale for its solitude, seven miles from the nearest village at more than 8,000 feet above sea level in a valley where the snowcapped Rocky Mountains make you stand and stare. Three authors call this monastery home: Father Thomas Keating, known as the proponent of the increasingly popular centering prayer, who has written many valuable books on spirituality; Father Theophane Boyd, who wrote *Tales of a Magic Monastery,* a gem of parables that delight and provoke the reader; and Father

William Meninger, whose *The Temple of the Lord* is a meditation on understanding that our bodies are the temples of God. Their books are available in the gift shop, which has a good selection of other spiritually useful titles.

The new guesthouse has 12 double rooms, each with a private bathroom. Private retreatants are welcome at a once-a-month intensive retreat. There is also a six-month program for those interested in examining what it is like to be a monk, and in learning the discipline of St. Benedict through "the bells and the eyes of the brethren."

We never got used to the mountains of Colorado, but they are a most suitable place when you consider one monk's comment: "A monastery should be in a place hard to get to and difficult to leave." Driving west from Denver, we kept going higher and higher, to one pass at 11,000 feet, then gradually descended to 8,000 feet at Snowmass. Mountaintops loomed in the distance, awesome and dramatic.

We visited the Trappists in the winter, and parked in a courtyard plowed of the January snow. The night before we planned to leave, we got stuck, hopelessly mired in a drift. We entered a lighted barn nearby and found a lean, taciturn man working on a tractor, and told him of our dilemma. Without a word, he walked to the door and, taking a piece of chain, hooked up our car to a truck and pulled it out. When a financial reward was offered, he looked surprised, shook his head, and went back to his task. He never spoke, and we never saw him again.

The next morning, when we told the guestmaster of the incident, he laughed and explained, "He has no use for money. He's our resident hermit, lives alone up on the mountain." Then he added, "I wonder what he was doing in the shop so late."

"That's easy," we said. "He was waiting to pull us out."

SOUNDS TRUE

◆

P.O. Box 8010
Dept. W10
Boulder, CO 80306
(800) 333-9185/
(303) 449-9226 fax
E-mail:
soundstrue@aol.com

**AUDIOTAPES, VIDEOTAPES,
AND CDS OF SACRED MUSIC,
HEALING, AND AWAKENING**

Tami Simon started Sounds True in 1985 as a distributor of local conference recordings, and has built it into an extraordinary organization with values that reflect the products it sells. Founded on the principle of service, with the mission of disseminating spiritual wisdom and encouraging spiritual growth, Sounds True holds daily morning meditations in the office meditation room, has weekly walking meditation sessions, and offers company benefits that encourage employees to take meditation retreats. It offers more than 300 original transformational titles representing all spiritual paths, from such authors as Thich Nhat Hanh, Alice Walker, Stephen Levine, Clarissa Pinkola Estés, Thomas Keating, Huston Smith, and Jack Kornfield. Best-sellers have included *Soul Life* with Thomas Moore; Julia Cameron's *Reflections of the Artist's Way;* and *The New Physics of Healing* with Deepak Chopra. One offering, *Saints Alive,* is about several saints and how they can change your life.

Sounds True began selling music cassettes and CDs in 1995, and is the U.S. representative for the Irish monks from Glenstal Abbey chanting with Noirin Ni Riain; the monks of Keur Moussa Abbey in Senegal, West Africa; and music recorded in Thich Nhat Hanh's Plum Village in France. A new CD, *Women in Chant,* featuring 28 members of the Sisters of the Abbey of Regina Laudis, has generated orders from around the world. Their Mother Dolores was once the actress Dolores Hart, who left Hollywood to join the community.

VOICES FROM HEAVEN

Glenstal Abbey, in County Limerick, is regarded as one of the last great castles built in Ireland. Constructed during the years 1838–49 for the Barrington family, it contains priceless examples of nineteenth-century ornamental stone carving. The castle passed into the hands of monks devoted to the teachings of St. Benedict of Nursia (A.D. 480–547).

Before St. Benedict, the concept of Western monasticism did not exist. There were only monks who lived in solitude as hermits. St. Benedict introduced three concepts that all Benedictines follow to this day: First, he insisted the monks take a vow of Stability. (Until that time, many monks traveled continuously from monastery to monastery.) Second, he required his followers to spend time in daily reflection with the holy scriptures, in *lectio divina* (holy reading). Third, he believed monks needed guidance and discipline.

The Glenstal Abbey is a fruitful example of St. Benedict's vision come to pass. The 45 monks who live there are a diverse group. They pursue history, Celtic theology, and spirituality, poetry, forestry, and woodturning; they create church artworks, keep a herd of 100 dairy cows, and run a boys' secondary school.

Yet it is their music, performed as a choir in the abbey, which has brought worldwide attention to the Monks of Glenstal. Since 1979 they have produced a remarkable body of music, always recording live, and always with Noirin Ni Riain, a traditional Irish soprano with a voice of indescribable sweetness. Each day the monks sing the Divine Office and mass, and draw from traditional Gregorian chants for mass and Vespers. This daily practice in the original Latin forms gives the Glenstal works an authenticity that is rare among choral recordings of the medieval liturgy.

Brother Ciaran Forbes from Glenstal Abbey writes: "The recordings made with Noirin are pretty unique—a combination of a woman and monks! She also participates in our liturgical celebrations—so one up for the feminists penetrating this all-male bastion!"

◆

Sounds True, Boulder, Colorado

Connecticut

ABBEY OF REGINA LAUDIS

◆

273 Flanders Rd.
Bethlehem, CT 06751
(203) 266-7727
(203) 266-7637: gift shop

WOMEN IN CHANT CD
EIGHTEENTH-CENTURY
NEAPOLITAN CRÈCHE
HERBAL PRODUCTS
CHRISTMAS BOUTIQUE
RETREATS

Catholic Benedictines of the Strict Observance came from France in 1947 and settled here on 300 hilltop acres. The sisters gather seven times a day in the wood-paneled chapel to sing the hours of the Divine Office and the mass in Gregorian chant. *Women in Chant,* a CD of their beautiful singing, is available by mail (and also through Sounds True). A separate building houses an eighteenth-century Neapolitan crèche scene enclosed behind glass. The intricate figures depict various attitudes toward the infant Jesus, from devotion to indifference. The monastery is a working farm with dairy cows that provide fresh milk which the nuns make into butter and cheese. A variety of herbal vinegars and other products are made from garden produce. They also bake their own bread. Retreatants are doubly rewarded with the sisters' singing and the good food. A Christmas boutique, featuring many of the Abbey's own crafts and foods, is open each December.

KITCHEN SERVERS OF THE WEEK

The members should serve one another. Consequently, no one will be excused from kitchen service unless s/he is sick or engaged in some important business of the monastery, for such service increases reward and fosters love. Let those who are not strong have help so that they may serve without distress, and let everyone receive help as the size of the community or local conditions warrant. If the community is rather large, the cellarer should be excused from kitchen service, and, as we have said, those should also be excused who are engaged in important business. Let all the rest serve one another in love.

On Saturday the one who is completing her/his work will do the washing. S/he is to wash the towels which the members use to wipe their hands and feet. Both the one who is ending service and the one who is about to begin are to wash the feet of everyone. The utensils required for the kitchen service are to be washed and returned to the cellarer, who in turn issues them to the one beginning the next week. In this way the cellarer will know what s/he hands out and what s/he receives back.

An hour before mealtime, the kitchen workers of the week should each receive a drink and some bread over and above the regular portion, so that at mealtime, they may serve one another without grumbling or hardship. On solemn days, however, they should wait until after the dismissal.

On Sunday immediately after Lauds, those beginning as well as those completing their week of service should make a profound bow in the oratory before all and ask for their prayers. Let the servers completing her/his week recite this verse: "Blessed are you, O God, who have helped me and comforted me" (Dan. 3:52; Ps. 86:17). After this verse has been said three times, s/he receives a blessing. Then the one beginning her/his service follows and says: "O God, come to my assistance; O God, make haste to help me" (Ps. 70:2). And all repeat this verse three times. When s/he has received a blessing, s/he begins her/his service.

◆

Chapter 35, A Reader's Version of the Rule of Saint Benedict in Inclusive Language

BENEDICTINE GRANGE

◆

49 Dorethy Rd.
West Redding, CT 06896
(203) 938-3689

ST. BENEDICT'S GUILD

◆

22 Cannon Rd.
Wilton, CT 06897
(203) 762-3633
open daily
11:00 A.M.–5:00 P.M.,
Sunday 12:30–5:00 P.M.

FINE-ART GREETING CARDS
AND POSTCARDS

BOOKS, ART, TAPES, CDS,
SACRED ARTIFACTS, AND
ETHNIC CRAFTS FROM THIRD
WORLD COUNTRIES

The founder of the Grange, Father John Giuliani, a Roman Catholic priest, is an extraordinary artist who has studied the techniques of Byzantine iconography and applied them in a most unusual way. He observed that painters from different countries always portrayed Christ and his mother as though they had been born in that country. For example, Sienese artists painted Mary and Jesus as Italians. Since Father John is an American, he felt it was most appropriate to paint the Holy Family as Native Americans, and so he portrays the Virgin as an Apache woman or the infant Jesus as a Navajo papoose, and so on. Every detail of their costume is authentic, and the stylized icons, painted with tempera on wood, are breathtakingly beautiful. Not everyone can afford an original, and so high-quality reproductions have been made in the form of greeting cards. Still, the colors are so jewellike that people often find it hard to part with even the cards.

Father John founded the Benedictine Grange about twenty years ago, borrowing the name from granaries used by early Benedictine monks for shelter and prayer after their work in the fields. Today the chapel, a pre–Civil War barn that was dismantled and reassembled, is a place of worship, and every Sunday at 10:30 A.M., hundreds gather for mass to the accompaniment of guitars and specially composed music. The Grange is associated with St. Benedict's Guild, a shop at the old Cannondale railroad station nearby that sells art, books, recordings of music by Schola (the musicians of the Benedictine Grange), sacred artifacts, and ethnic crafts from the Third World.

Navajo Christ Child and Blessed Kateri Tekakwitha by Fr. John B. Giuliani

I n 1958 the priests and brothers of the Catholic Montfort Missionaries built a grotto on this 170-acre property of woods and fields, and modeled it after Our
Lady of Lourdes in France. They named it Lourdes of
Litchfield, and the 35 acres of shrine grounds are open
year-round. Pilgrimage programs and devotion services
are held here outside from early May to mid-October,
and thousands come each year. The great stone mansion,
once a seminary, provides a regular program of retreats.

T he nuns of Villa Maria trace their lineage to a group
of Polish Bernardine Franciscan sisters who came
to the United States in 1894 to teach Polish immigrants. One way people help support their modest needs
is to buy the Pot o' Gold calendar. The sisters also sell
cards and provide rooms for retreats in a beautiful Geor-
gian-style mansion on 18 acres of landscaped grounds.

**MONTFORT
RETREAT CENTER**

◆

**P.O. Box 667
Litchfield, CT 06759
(860) 567-8434**

GROTTO
PILGRIMAGE PROGRAMS
RETREATS

**VILLA MARIA
RETREAT HOUSE**

◆

**159 Sky Meadow Dr.
Stamford, CT 06903
(203) 322-0107**

CALENDAR/CARDS
RETREATS

C
O
N
N
E
C
T
I
C
U
T

◈

WISDOM HOUSE

◆

**229 East Litchfield Rd.
Litchfield, CT 06759
(860) 567-3163/
567-3166 fax
Web site:
www.litchfieldct
.com/clt/wisdhse.html**

LABYRINTH
BOOKS
CASSETTES
POSTERS
T-SHIRTS
SWEATSHIRTS
CARDS
TOTE BAGS
RETREATS

The original farmhouse was built in the 1800s, and the large brick building that houses 100 retreatants, built in 1953, was once used as the Seat of Wisdom College for the Daughters of Wisdom, an order of Catholic nuns founded in France. The 58 acres, once a working farm, and the adjoining state forest make this a paradise for walkers. In the summer of 1997 the actor Richard Gere stayed at Wisdom House and called it "a truly wonderful place for a retreat."

Inspired by a labyrinth elsewhere, the community decided that Wisdom House should have one of its own, and on June 8, 1997, it was formally dedicated. Designed by Barbara Putnam, a local architect, and built of bricks and stone by volunteers, this labyrinth is a meditative walking path. "This design, found on ancient Cretan coins, is a single path, seven circles wide, or 48 feet wide, which winds first in one direction, then in another, culminating in a center where one can sit, rest, and reflect. In some medieval cathedrals a variation on this form was paved into the floor tiles. When the Crusades were raging in the Holy Land, pilgrims adopted the labyrinths at the great cathedrals as pilgrimage sites . . . and their journey through the labyrinth was a holy one. One of the most famous labyrinths is on the floor of Chartres Cathedral. Members of the Labyrinth Project in New Canaan, Connecticut, have painted the pattern of the Chartres labyrinth on a canvas which can be unfolded indoors for pilgrims to walk as part of their journey to the spirit center of their own lives."

Labyrinth and Tree of Life designs appear on T-shirts and tote bags.

Delaware

This community of 500 residents, founded in 1900 on the principles of single-tax economics and William Morris's Arts and Crafts philosophy, is home to more than 40 artists and craftspeople. The village, on 162 wooded acres, welcomes people of all beliefs, creeds, and cultures. On Labor Day Saturday, for more than 50 years, the annual Arden Fair has taken place. Seven to eight thousand adults and children attend, providing funds for the Gild Hall (sic), the meeting place for a number of the "gilds" in the village. Originally conceived as a farewell to summer, the fair includes craft booths, demonstrations of craftwork, a garden booth, a book stall, folk-dancing demonstrations, an art exhibit, music, toys, games, rides, food, and drink.

The current "gilds" include the Ardensingers, dedicated to the production of at least six Gilbert and Sullivan operettas each year; the Dinner Gild, which schedules volunteer crews to cook town dinners on Saturday evenings for members and nonmembers upon reservation (these are served at 6:00 P.M. from October through June); the Folk Gild, which operates weekly folk and square dance sessions year-round on Wednesday evenings and contra dancing on the first Sunday afternoon of each month; the Gardeners Gild, which hosts guest speakers whose members share plants and gardening information; the Library Gild, which operates the public library in the Gild Hall; and the Swim Gild, which operates the swimming pool for members. The current Gild Hall began as a well-built barn on the original farm property, was remodeled as a clubhouse in 1908–9, and has been expanded several times over the years.

The Arden Book states, "Many of the day-to-day tasks of running the village are handled by elected com-

ARDEN VILLAGE

◆

**The Highway
Wilmington, DE 19810
(302) 475-3912**

ARDEN FAIR

**SPRING HOUSE AND GARDEN
TOUR**

**GILBERT & SULLIVAN FIRST
TWO WEEKENDS IN MAY**

**SHAKESPEARE
JUNE/JULY**

**CRAFT SHOW
THANKSGIVING SUNDAY**

mittees of residents who check the roads for potholes, prepare the budget, keep the playgrounds in shape, and serve the community in many other ways. Arden has had a town meeting since its earliest days, when, according to village folklore, even babes in arms were considered voters. Oratory flourished, tempers exploded, sometimes to fisticuffs, and land value was argued endlessly." Because the early town meetings had no legal standing or power, eventually incorporation produced the present Town Assembly, which takes place four times a year. Every Arden resident over 18 years of age who has lived in the village for 16 months is eligible to vote in town elections, and everyone is encouraged to participate in the decision making.

An article about Arden in the May 1992 *Smithsonian* magazine quotes a visitor to the village in 1915, and says that this old spirit is still intact: "Arden is the capital of the state of Uncritical Friendliness; it belongs to the federation of Mutual Helpfulness, under a constitution of Equal Opportunity. It is far removed from the world we know."

District of Columbia

This Carpatho-Russian Orthodox monastic community operates the Icon and Book Service in Washington, D.C., which carries an extensive list of Orthodox-oriented books on theology, history, the lives of the saints, biblical and Celtic studies, children and family, and cookbooks.

Facing East: A Pilgrim's Journey into the Mysteries of Orthdoxy, by Frederica Mathewes-Green, tells how she and her family, searching for a more authentic faith and a closer connection to God, found their true spiritual home in the Eastern Orthodox tradition and she tells how her family and fellow parishioners have satisfaction and joy in their newfound church. The service has a very good CD and cassette selection of Orthodox hymns and chants for special occasions. It also offers beautifully printed icon cards from small to large scenes and portraits of Jesus, Mary, the Resurrection, the Mystical Supper, and more. There are a few rooms for retreatants.

MONASTERY OF THE HOLY CROSS

◆

**1302 Quincy St., N.E.
Washington, DC 20017
(202) 832-8519:
monastery
(202) 526-6061/526-3316
fax: book service
(800) 275-4566 (outside
area codes 301 and 202)**

BOOKS
TAPES AND CDS
CARDS
RETREATS

Florida

◆———◆———◆

FALKYNOR FARM

◆

4950 SW 70th Ave.
Davie, FL 33314
(954) 581-4950/
791-8904 fax
E-mail:
michaelblate@webtv.net

BOOKS
TAPES
CLASSES

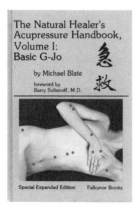

Falkynor Farm consists of three generations of a family of devotees of the Indian guru Sathya Sai Baba. They follow the pathway of Vedanta and its science of yoga. The farm has become a center of activities relating to Sai Baba, Vedanta, the study of the Bhagavad Gita, and related areas of interest. There are weekly bhajan (sacred Sanskrit chanting) sessions followed by a Vedanta discussion group each Thursday evening from 7:00 to 9:00 P.M.

The farm itself is both a plant nursery and an organic farm that produces pineapples, macadamia nuts, and a variety of other tropical fruit. On occasion, it has extra fruit to sell.

Also housed at Falkynor Farm is the G-Jo Institute, an educational organization devoted exclusively to sharing "self-health" information and techniques. Formally established in 1976, the Institute teaches classes both locally and throughout the world by means of publications and videotapes on how to heal yourself or your loved ones using free (or very low-cost), simple, and effective techniques. Books like the two-volume *Natural Healer's Acupressure Handbook: Basic G-Jo,* and *Cooking Naturally for Pleasure and Health* are their mainstay and specialty.

Our first retreat was taken in the early 1980s at Dai Bosatsu Zendo, New York, with Eido Tai Shimano Roshi. We were greeted by one of the monks, who introduced himself as Zenrin and was working on some Chinese and Japanese translations. We puzzled together over how to use American technology to produce both English and Chinese characters on a page.

The result of that work is now complete, with English translations and editing by Zenrin Chido Robert E. Lewis, now at the Jacksonville Zen Sangha, which offers regular zazen. *The Book of the Zen Grove,* phrases for Zen practice, Shibayama Zenkei Roshi's *Zenrin Kushu,* has never before been translated into any European language. As Eido Roshi says in his introduction, "This book is unprecedented. . . . Each phrase of the *Zenrin Kushu,* whether it is long or short, is the expression of enlightenment itself. It is beyond space and time and culture and language. As Buddhism moves to the West, it is natural to have an English version. In this sense the book is not a mere translation, but a newly created, newly compiled, twentieth-century *Zenrin Kushu.*" Eido Roshi was surprised to learn that a westerner not only knew of the existence of the *Zenrin Kushu,* but was translating it. Known as "capping phrases" or *jakugo,* these phrases are brought by the student to the master after solving the koan, or riddle, the master has given the student. They are taken from already existing text and summarize the student's new understanding. The following is one such *jakugo:*

A single wisp of white cloud
Across the ravine's mouth

How many homing birds
Will the darkness mislead from their nests?

One seeking outside with his eye of wisdom unopened will
probably end up without a place to come back to.

**JACKSONVILLE
ZEN SANGHA**

◆

**7405 Arlington
Expressway
Jacksonville, FL 32211
(904) 721-1050**

THE BOOK OF THE ZEN GROVE
ZAZEN

KARMA THEGSUM CHOLING TAMPA

◆

**c/o Jill McCann
820 S. MacDill Ave.
(mail only)
Tampa, FL 33609
(813) 870-2904/961-0559
E-mail: ktcjill@juno.com**

**BOOKS
BUDDHIST SUPPLIES
TIBETAN-LANGUAGE CLASSES**

This center was founded in 1982 for the practice of Tibetan Buddhism in the Karma Kagyu tradition. It offers more than 100 Tibetan Buddhist books and transcripts of talks by notable Buddhist teachers. It also sells five kinds of Tibetan incense, hand-made malas of semiprecious stones, Tibetan-style silk brocade mala bags, silk kathas (blessing scarves), porcelain bowls and vases for shrines, deity art prints, and Tibetan postcards. CDs and tapes of the Jataka Tales and Tibetan children's stories are also available. The group meets regularly for teachings and meditation. Classes in Tibetan language are given by native Tibetans.

THE DAILY MANUAL LABOR

Idleness is the enemy of the soul. Therefore, the community should have specified periods for manual labor as well as for prayerful reading.

We believe that the times for both may be arranged as follows: From Easter to the first of October, they will spend their mornings after Prime until about the fourth hour at whatever work needs to be done. From the fourth hour until the time of Sext, they will devote themselves to reading. But after Sext and their meal, they may rest on their beds in complete silence; should anyone wish to read privately, let her/him do so, but without disturbing the others. They should say None a little early, about midway through the eighth hour, and then until Vespers they are to return to whatever work is necessary. They must not become distressed if local conditions or their poverty should force them to do the harvesting themselves. When they live by the labor of their hands, as our ancestors and the apostles did, then they are really monastics. Yet, all things are to be done with moderation on account of the faint-hearted.

◆

Chapter 48, A Reader's Version of the Rule of Saint Benedict in Inclusive Language

Brother Paul, a monk born in Brooklyn, is an accomplished artist in oils, sculpture, and stained glass. His studio is on the grounds of this Catholic Benedictine abbey and college, and his art is available in the gift shop. There is a separate guesthouse for the abbey's retreat program and rooms are available next door with the nuns at Holy Name Monastery. In the center of the grounds, surrounded by gardens, is a beautiful aviary filled with exotic birds. A happy tradition at the abbey church is to invite all who attend the noon mass to join the brethren for lunch. The grounds are next to Lake Jovita, a charming, out-of-the-way place where peace and serenity come with the meals.

ST. LEO ABBEY

◆

**P.O. Box 2369
St. Leo, FL 33574
(352) 588-8638: gift shop
(352) 588-2009:
retreat center**

**AVIARY
ARTWORK
RETREATS**

This Unitarian Universalist Association–affiliated camp and conference center is available for groups and individuals for retreats, seminars, workshops, weddings, summer camps, Bible camps, and just rest and relaxation. Situated on 13 acres in central Florida and surrounded by rolling hills near orange groves and lakes, the Pines supports itself through programs like weekends, Elderhostels, canoe and bicycle hostels, and overnight stays. During the winter months, canoe trips are offered on three local rivers, including the Chassahowitzka River, over five days. The bicycle hostel uses the Withlacoochee State Trail for its three-day trips. The memorial garden, near the peace chapel, is available for people who wish to be remembered or to remember others with memorial stones for names and year of birth and death. Ashes may be scattered in the area.

UU IN THE PINES

◆

**7029 Cedar Lane
Brooksville, FL 34601
(352) 796-4457**

**RETREATS
CANOE AND BICYCLE HOSTEL
TRIPS
MEMORIAL GARDEN**

THE READER FOR THE WEEK

Reading will always accompany the meals. The reader should not be the one who just happens to pick up the book, but someone who will read for a whole week, beginning on Sunday. After Mass and Communion, let the incoming reader ask all to pray for her/him so that God may shield her/him from the spirit of vanity. Let her/him begin this verse in the oratory: "O God, open my lips, and my mouth shall proclaim your praise" (Ps. 51:17), and let all say it three times. When s/he has received a blessing, s/he will begin her/his week of reading.

Let there be complete silence. No whispering, no speaking—only the reader's voice should be heard there. The members should by turn serve one another's needs as they eat and drink, so that no one need ask for anything. If, however, anything is required, it should be requested by an audible signal of some kind rather than by speech. No one should presume to ask a question about the reading or about anything else, "lest occasion be given [to the devil]" (Eph. 4:27; 1 Tim. 5:14). The prioress/abbot, however, may wish to say a few words of instruction.

Because of Communion and because the fast may be too hard for her/him to bear, the one who is reader for the week is to receive some diluted wine before s/he begins to read. Afterward s/he will take her/his meal with the weekly kitchen servers and the attendants.

Members will read and sing, not according to rank, but according to their ability to benefit their hearers.

◆

Chapter 38, A Reader's Version of the Rule of Saint Benedict in Inclusive Language

Georgia

◆——————◆——————◆

The Abbey sells a huge selection of religious articles, including statues, medals, bread from their bakery, and books. One of the largest rosary collections we have ever seen is here, from small to wall-size. The Abbey store, which is a separate building, has a mail-order catalog. Nearby is another building that houses bonsai plants, pots, tools, and books—the largest collection in the United States—and serves a nationwide audience with an extensive catalog. The bonsai trees must be purchased at the shop, but the huge pot selection is available by mail.

Their stained-glass business began in 1952 as the monks were finishing their own church and still needed windows. The abbot general was on his tour of monasteries, and had just returned from a very hot and humid visit to South Africa, when he stopped by to see how the construction was proceeding. He recommended using colored glass to control the strong Georgia heat, and the monks developed a simple design and colored glass to do just that. The windows are so beautiful that requests came from all over for their craftspeople to make windows for others, and they complied.

They use Blenko Glass from Milton, West Virginia, the same glass they used for their chapel. In the early days they contacted many companies, but Blenko was the only one to respond, and they have continued to work together over the years. Today, five monks with backgrounds in art and architecture craft windows for churches, residences, hospital chapels, and mausoleums, among other uses. They have designed and made fantastic and intricate windows for churches as far afield as Arizona, including one from the story of Susannah in the Book of Daniel for a church in Louisiana.

ABBEY OF OUR LADY OF THE HOLY SPIRIT

◆

**2625 Hwy. 212 SW
Conyers, GA 30208
(800) 592-5023:
abbey store
(770) 760-0959:
guesthouse
(770) 918-9661/760-0989
fax: bonsai store
E-mail: Abbeystore@ga
.monks.org
E-mail: bonsai.monk@ga
.monks.org
Web site: www.ga
.monks.org**

RELIGIOUS ARTICLES AND BOOKS

STAINED GLASS

BONSAI PLANTS, BOOKS, AND TOOLS

BREAD

RETREATS

In his book *The Waters of Siloe,* Thomas Merton described the beginnings of the Abbey when Trappist monks from Gethsemani traveled from Kentucky by train to rural Georgia in 1944 and lived, for a while, in a converted barn with cows and chickens and "competed with a sharecropper's cabin as far as discomfort was concerned." Retreatants are now housed in a comfortable guest wing next to the Abbey church where the monks chant the canonical hours daily.

FOUR WINDS VILLAGE

◆

Great Spirit Retreat
P.O. Box 112
Tiger, GA 30576
(706) 782-6939/
782-1964 fax

BOOK PUBLISHING
JOURNAL
INDIAN MUSEUM
SPIRITUAL RETREAT
SEMINAR STUDIES
PEACE CHAMBER
QUARTERLY EQUINOX
SERVICES

This forming community looks forward to joining others to practice love, peace, and service, and to providing good role models for children. They are students of *Oahspe,* a book of revelations about earth, sky, and spirit for the new age of spiritual wisdom. They call it a New Age bible, based on worship of the Creator only, and it contains a religious history of the world beginning 8,900 years ago with Zarathustra. They also publish the journal *Four Winds Village News.* Angel guidance was given through clairvoyant John Newbrough, visited by angels in 1882. "The Angel Intelligence calls us the Lighthouse of Enlightenment," says their current president, Virginia Howard, who has written a book titled *The Messenger,* which they publish. Visitors are welcome at the community center, chapel, mobile homes, and campground on 80 acres in the northeast Georgia mountains.

This Christian service organization, founded in 1942, is committed to compassionate living, racial reconciliation, nonviolence, and environmental awareness. Its very successful enterprise is a peanut/pecan mail-order business to which they've added candy bars, varieties of chocolate and carob pecan bark and crunch, Miss Ruth's pecan pie, granola, and fruitcake, which, along with farming and gardening, supports it. The community also sells Christian books and tapes.

Since its founding, its members have been committed to creating low-cost housing and community development. Because they had no racial barriers, they were boycotted locally and forced to build their mail-order business in order to survive. They have one-to-three-month volunteer sessions that involve studying Christian life and faith for those who come for work/study experience, and a one-year intern program. "Snowbirds" are retired visitors who come to help in the fall and winter with the farm, the pecan plant, bakery, shipping room, and office. Koinonia is nondenominational and was founded as a "demonstration plot for the Kingdom of God."

KOINONIA PARTNERS

◆

1324 Georgia Hwy. 49 South
Americus, GA 31709
(912) 924-0391/
924-6504 fax
(800) 569-4128 orders
Web site: www
.koinoniapartners.org

PEANUTS
PECANS
CANDY
PIES
GRANOLA
FRUITCAKE
BOOKS
TAPES
WORK/STUDY

FROM A
CHURCH BULLETIN

Thursday night
—potluck supper.
Prayer and medication
to follow.

Hawaii

KAI MANA

◆

**P.O. Box 612
Kilauea, HI 96754
(808) 828-1280/
828-6670 fax
(800) 837-1782**

WORKSHOPS

S hakti Gawain, the author of *Creative Visualization,* gives one-week workshops four times a year in this tropical paradise. The setting is secluded, with ocean views. She discusses the art of using mental energy to transform and improve health, beauty, prosperity, loving relationships, and how to turn positive ideas and concepts into reality.

KALANI HONUA OCEANSIDE ECO-RESORT

◆

**RR 2, Box 4500
Pahoa-Kehena Beach
HI 96778
(808) 965-7828/
965-9613 fax
(800) 800-6886
E-mail: kh@ILHawaii.net
Web site: www.randm
.com/kh.html**

**DANCE FESTIVAL

YOGA AND MEDITATION
INSTRUCTION

RETREATS**

T his is a not-for-profit educational resort within Hawaii's largest conservation area. An annual summer dance festival takes place in July or August, exploring the movements of the hula and ballet, among others. Yoga and meditation instruction are available, as well as retreats for men, women, and couples.

Idaho

◆————◆————◆

This community began in 1882 when three nuns from a Swiss order founded in the twelfth century were sent to the United States to found a new community. They immediately began to serve the needs of the Northwest pioneers and eventually settled on a wooded butte overlooking Camas Prairie, building an impressive monastery of blue porphyry with red-domed twin bell towers.

Today the community is made up of 90 Benedictine sisters, 35 of whom live away from the monastery while working at jobs in other communities to help support the monastery. Sister Elisa lives in Los Angeles, working with street gangs—she keeps a posterboard in her office with pictures of teenagers she has known who were killed in gang violence. Sister Bernadine works on skid row in Seattle, ministering to the down and out. Sister Bernadette helps students in a migrant village with a tutoring program; others work in health care or education.

Those at the monastery are busy, too, with St. Gertrude's Museum, which holds relics of Idaho history and receives 6,000 visitors a year. "Blackened bake pans, hauled clear across the country in covered wagons, hand-made lace, a Madonna and Child from the Philippines made in the 1700s, hand-carved from ivory with silk clothing and flowers embroidered in golden thread" are all part of the collection. Another fascinating display is of jewelry made from human hair. "During the 1800s hair was often saved and woven into elaborate designs. Such jewelry also served as reminders of the dead, since in those days photographs weren't common," says one of the staff members. The museum also houses an extensive Asian collection donated by the art collector Samuel

MONASTERY OF ST. GERTRUDE

◆

**HC 3 Box 121
Cottonwood, ID 83522
(208) 962-3224
1 (900)-U-THIRST
daily Gospel reflection
ministry, $1.99 per call
Web site:
www.rc.net/boise
/st_gertrude/thirst.html**

MUSEUM

FOREST MANAGEMENT

900 NUMBER DAILY REFLECTION

BOOK

RETREAT MINISTRY

Emmanuel in honor of his wife Winifred, a piano prodigy whose fingers were insured at the age of 16 for $1 million.

The community is also involved in management of the monastery's forest. The "chief forester" is Sister Carol Ann, who has a 30-year plan in place. "Instead of a habit, she dons a hard hat, wears an orange cruiser's vest, talks logger jargon like she's reciting Bible verses, and manages almost 1,000 acres of wooded ground adjacent to the convent. She and the other nuns decided that stewarding the forests around the convent should be akin to nurturing yet another gift from God. Some 38,000 board feet worth of Ponderosa pine trees were recently harvested under the sister's direction and more logging is planned on a long-range, sustainable rotation."

An innovative new business to help support the monastery has just been started by Sister Judith, allowing her to leave her full-time college teaching job and come home to the monastery. She proposed to the sisters last winter that St. Gertrude's offer a daily Gospel-based, inspirational message via a 900 telephone line. Thirty-five calls a day, at $1.99 apiece, would cover the $625-a-month cost of operating the line and give the monastery a profit of 90 cents a call. "There's a spiritual need in our society for such a thing," says Sister Judith, "so a call to 1-(900) U-Thirst (1-900-884-4778) will help fill that need." They've named it "From the Monastery Well," and report that the early response has been gratifying. And last but not least, Sister Lucille has just published a 300-page book called *On the Way: The Journey of the Idaho Benedictine Sisters,* which chronicles the lives and works of the Benedictine Sisters from 1882 to 1983, and is available at the monastery bookstore and St. Gertrude's Museum.

Illinois

◆ ── ◆ ── ◆

This extremely active community of 500 people, part of the Evangelical Covenant Church, welcomes visitors who write or call beforehand. Though getting through may be a problem, once you do, you learn that the community had its roots in the Jesus Movement of the late sixties, when many of its members were "social rejects in search of something worth living for." Community living evolved as the practical expression of Christianity in their everyday lives. Today this thriving community supports Cornerstone Community Outreach, transitional housing for homeless women and children; Leland House, which has 20 apartments for poor families; Friendly Towers housing for low-income elderly, which includes three meals a day, housekeeping and doctor services, Bible studies, and other activities; Cornerstone Family Center, a walk-in center providing help with family issues; and neighborhood outreaches to kids and the cold and hungry via street evangelism and services. Their music ministries include the Resurrection Band; Grace & Glory, their gospel choir; and the Crossing, Crashdog, Seeds, and Sheesh, their folk, punk, folk/rock, and alternative rock groups, respectively; Mere

JESUS PEOPLE U.S.A. EVANGELICAL COVENANT CHURCH

◆

920 W. Wilson Ave.
Chicago, IL 60640
(773) 561-2450/
989-2076 fax
E-mail:
eric@jpusal.chi.il.us
Web site:
www.mcs.net/~jpusa

PUBLISHING
CORNERSTONE MAGAZINE
CORNERSTONE FESTIVAL
SEVERAL BANDS
HOMELESS SHELTER
FOOD STORE
WOOD DESIGN
SHEET METAL
ROOFING SUPPLY
ELECTRICAL WORK
HOUSING FOR LOW-INCOME ELDERLY
LOW-INCOME HOUSING FOR THE POOR
RECORD COMPANY

RECORDING STUDIO
CUSTOM T-SHIRT SCREENING
BOOKS
MUSIC

Bons Comics, written from a Christian worldview; Cornerstone Festival, a five-day-long music festival on the July Fourth weekend attended by 30,000 people at Cornerstone Farm near Bushnell, Illinois. Businesses include Lakefront Roofing Supply, Creative Wood Design, J.P. Electric, Tone Zone Recording Studio, Grrr Records, Belly Acres, and custom T-shirt screening.

MONASTERY OF THE HOLY CROSS

◆

3111 S. Aberdeen St.
Chicago, IL 60608
(773) 927-7424/
927-5734 fax
E-mail: monkhcj@ais.net

GIFT BASKETS
COOKIES
CAKES
CANDIES
PRESERVES
RICE AND BEANS
INCENSE
FURNITURE POLISH
TOILETRIES
COMPUTER SERVICES
RETREATS

This relatively new monastery was founded in 1991 on the South Side of Chicago by Catholic priests who are Monks of the Holy Cross of Jerusalem. They buy products from monasteries throughout the United States and resell them in gift baskets. Delectables such as jellies, candy, and cookies are available in small baskets, fruit or date-nut cakes, assorted jellies, and other fine foods come in a large basket, and an extra-large size includes the above items plus assorted candies, an icon, toilet water, furniture polish, and more food. They see this as a way to support other monasteries while creating income for themselves. In addition, the monks do computer outservicing for churches and law firms.

This small community leased a church that had been closed by the Chicago archdiocese. Their order has five characteristics: they are city dwellers, earn wages, rent their housing, have no walled enclosure, and are part of the local church. They open their church for prayer in the morning, at noon, and for evening Eucharist to make it possible for neighbors to join them. They have a few rooms for individuals desiring the city-quiet of the monastery.

COMPUTER SERVICES

The monastic tradition has in many ways embraced a union of the spiritual and the intellectual. Many scholars have European monasteries to thank for the preservation of classical manuscripts through the tumultuous Middle Ages. Now, as the latest technological revolution sets in, some American monastic communities are helping to preserve records of important literature. Monks at Holy Cross Abbey in Berryville, Virginia, and at the Monastery of the Holy Cross in Chicago, Illinois, have in the past few years begun to hire out their services to small data-services firms, and much of their business comes from university libraries struggling to incorporate catalog information into updated computer systems. This service to the larger community helps to cover community expenses, and the monks make sure not to take on more work than they can handle. By developing and offering their computer expertise to others, these monks have provided yet another example of how some religious communities engage directly with "the world" without compromising their spiritual, otherworldly commitment.

PLOW CREEK
FELLOWSHIP

◆

Rte. 2, Box 2-A
Tiskilwa, IL 61368
(815) 646-4730

GARDEN FARM
HOSPITALITY

A Christian congregation founded in 1971 and affiliated with the Mennonite Church, this community helps support itself with a garden farm. In the spring and fall, hundreds of customers come to pick their own strawberries, blueberries, raspberries, pumpkins, squash, and seedless watermelons. They have Sunday-morning worship and two communal meals a week. Other group projects include an "Overground Railroad" to house refugees. They have a ministry of hospitality and a retreat cabin for those in need of rest and solitude.

REBA PLACE
FELLOWSHIP

◆

Shalom Mission
Communities
726 Seward #2
Evanston, IL 60202
(847) 475-8715

APARTMENTS
REFUGEE WORK
PEACE WITNESS PROGRAM

This is a Christian lay community associated with the Mennonite Church and the Church of the Brethren and established in 1957. The Fellowship has about 40 residences for families and singles, with vegetarian food. In his book *Fire, Salt, and Peace,* community member David Janzen describes life at Reba Place Fellowship and other intentional Christian communities in North America. Reba Place Fellowship owns a dozen houses and over a hundred apartment units that help support the community and provide housing for guests and those in need. They practice income sharing; those who work in the outside community put their wages into the common fund. The Fellowship provides housing for the homeless, works with refugees from Cambodia and Central America, and has a peace witness program, all in a multiracial setting. Though their intention was to provide housing for their own community, not to start a business, the housing shortage in Evanston provided them with a perpetual waiting list. "As we have tried to care about our neighborhood, its houses and its people, it seems that God has taken care of our own needs as well," says David Janzen in his book.

◈

These Sisters of St. Joseph have created a mail-order business to support their missions and ministries throughout the world. Using the illustrative art of Mary Southard, they sell a daily planner with space to record thoughts, impressions, and personal reflections. They also have her lovely, Chagall-like paintings as cards for special occasions, a nature series, and prayer and verse cards such as one that quotes Emily Dickinson's "Hope": "Hope is the thing with feathers that perches in the soul, and sings the tune without the words and never stops—at all."

Religious sculptures of Jesus in bronze and Mother Mary in plaster and stone finish are beautifully executed. There are audiocassettes by Kathy Sherman with companion books that tell the stories behind the songs and invite readers to reflect on their personal journeys.

(MARY SOUTHARD, C.S.J.)

SISTERS OF ST. JOSEPH OF LA GRANGE

◆

Department M
1515 W. Ogden Ave.
La Grange Park, IL 60526
(800) 354-3504/
(888) 354-3504 free fax

CALENDAR PLANNER
CARDS
RELIGIOUS SCULPTURE
ART PRINTS
AUDIOCASSETTES

This nonprofit religious organization provides teachings on gnostic freemasonry, Theosophy, and other esoteric philosophies. *The Ultimate Frontier* was their founding tract. Although today not everyone who lives in the village follows the original philosophical approach, the community is a model for its use of solar and wind power, its cable television/radio capability, its water and waste-water plant—all technologies that are "a means for survival at the turn of the century." The first straw-bale house built in Illinois is in Stelle. Many who live there follow the founding values of personal responsibility, lifelong education, positive attitude, and cooperation. Because they were unable to get the telephone service they wanted, they were inventive enough to create their own.

THE STELLE GROUP

◆

127 Sun St.
Stelle, IL 60919
(815) 256-2200/
256-2299 fax

BOOKS
RARE ESOTERIC REPRINTS
INDEPENDENT BUSINESSES,
INCLUDING SOLAR
PRODUCTS

ILLINOIS

RARE ESOTERIC REPRINTS

Freemasonry • Alchemy • Ancient Civilizations • Architecture • Astrology • Astronomy • Baconian • Bible Study • Biography • Boehme • Comparative Religions • Divination • Eastern Thought • Egyptology • Esotericism • Gnosticism • Health • Hermeticism • Knights Templar • Magic • Mathematics • Metaphysical • Mystery Schools • Mysticism • Mythology • Numerology • Occult Sciences • Psalmistry • Philosophy • Prince Hall Masonry • Psychology • Pyramids • Qabalah • Religions • Rituals Series • Rosicrucianism • Spiritual • Symbolism • Tarot • Theosophy

◆

The Stelle Group, Stelle, Illinois
(815) 256-2200/2299 fax

VIVEKANANDA VEDANTA SOCIETY

◆

5423 S. Hyde Park Blvd.
Chicago, IL 60615
(312) 363-0027

TEMPLE
GUESTHOUSE
RETREATS
BOOKSHOP
LIBRARY

Swami Vivekananda was the first Hindu monk to bring the message of Vedanta to the West, at the first Parliament of Religions in Chicago in 1893. This center was founded in 1930, with headquarters in Belur Math, India. The center, and its affiliated monastery in Fennville, Michigan, have bookstores and libraries that are open daily and contain books on Eastern and Western religion and culture. The residential communities are made up of celibate adults who share a willingness to work and an acceptance of the paths of others.

The Cenacle Sisters have more than one dozen centers in the United States where retreats, programs, counseling, and days of prayer are held regularly. They reach out to men and women who desire to nurture their inner lives and seek a deeper spiritual connection. Their expertise is in spiritual counseling that helps individuals to discern how God is calling or leading in specific situations.

WARRENVILLE CENACLE RETREAT HOUSE AND SPIRITUALITY CENTER

◆

P.O. Box 797
Warrenville, IL 60555
(630) 393-1231
(312) 528-6300/
528-2456 fax
(800) 240-6702

SPIRITUAL COUNSELING

RETREATS

THE ARTISANS OF THE MONASTERY

If there are artisans in the monastery, they are to practice their craft with all humility, but only with the prioress's/abbot's permission. If one of them becomes puffed up by skillfulness in her/his craft, and feels that s/he is conferring something on the monastery, s/he is to be removed from practicing his/her craft and not allowed to resume it unless, after manifesting her/his humility, s/he is so ordered by the prioress/abbot.

Whenever products of these artisans are sold, those responsible for the sale must not dare to practice any fraud. Let them always remember Ananias and Sapphira, who incurred bodily death (Acts 5:1–11), lest they and all who perpetrate fraud in monastery affairs suffer spiritual death.

The evil of avarice must have no part in establishing prices, which should, therefore, always be a little lower than people outside the monastery are able to set, "so that in all things God may be glorified" (1 Pet. 4:11).

◆

Chapter 57, A Reader's Version of the Rule of Saint Benedict in Inclusive Language (Mount St. Benedict in Erie, Pennsylvania, runs an artisans' shop called Chapter 57.)

Indiana

MONASTERY THE IMMACULATE CONCEPTION

◆

802 E. Tenth St.
Ferdinand, IN 47532
(812) 367-1411/
367-2313 fax
(800) 738-9999
E-mail:
osbnuns@psci.net

GIRLS' PREP SCHOOL
SPECIAL EVENTS
HAND-PAINTED EGGS
BREAD
COOKIES
WORKSHOPS
PROGRAMS AND RETREATS
TOURS DAILY EXCEPT
MONDAY

In 1997 the Catholic Benedictine sisters celebrated their 130th anniversary in this location. The main occupation of the 240 resident sisters is to educate more than 100 girls who attend their prep school.

The alumni hold an annual reunion, and every five years the sisters have a summer social to celebrate their continuity here. There are Jubilees each year to honor sisters celebrating their anniversaries in the order, and the public is invited to attend. The upscale gift shop features items handcrafted by the sisters, and by artisans from Peru and Guatemala. A local reporter described the art in the shop thus: "There ain't no junk here." Freshly baked bread and cookies are always available. Five new monasteries have been founded from this one in other parts of the Midwest, North Carolina, and California. The sisters are thriving and growing, and seventeen novices have entered the order since 1995.

(SISTER KATHRYN KANE)

The sisters are open-minded about their religious lifestyle, and hold workshops, seminars, and retreats on various spiritual topics, some of which make it possible for women to learn what it is to have a vocation, how to approach it, and to see the benefits. "This is a monastery," one sister explained, "not a mortuary."

LETTER FROM MONASTERY
THE IMMACULATE CONCEPTION

Did I say that our gift shop is (fittingly) named "For Heaven's Sake"? (A succinct mission statement!) I believe you mentioned your book will include products as well as services and events. I think of the variety of handcrafted (and reasonably priced) items from the sisters: sculpture, pottery, paintings, prints, baskets, stained-glass objects, rosaries, intricately decorated eggs (Ukrainian-style), wooden objects, quilts, paper angel Christmas tree toppers, greeting cards. Items from artisans in Peru and Guatemala (where the community has missions) include colorful embroidery, weaving, and pottery. There are bread and cookies, of course, and a recent addition, salsa. Plus all the items supplied by outside vendors.

But I don't want to sound as if I'm just doing marketing here! When people visit, they sense a special (and surprising) dimension to the gift shop that can't be communicated in an inventory list. Maybe it's the peacefulness of the place—soft music playing (often the sisters' own recordings) and the smell of incense and candles. It's probably also the care that the sisters have put into their handcrafted pieces. And it's the kind staff, who often do some important "ministry of listening" with customers.

◆

Karen Katafiasz for the Sisters of St. Benedict, Ferdinand, Indiana

PADANARAM SETTLEMENT

◆

RR 1, Box 478
Williams, IN 47470
(812) 388-5571 or 5599
E-mail:
padanarm@tima.com
Web site:
www.kiva.net
/~padanarm

FOREST PRODUCTS

COMPOST

SCHOOL

BOOKS

NEWSLETTER

**SPRING AND FALL
CONVENTIONS**

ORGANIC PRODUCE

HERBAL PRODUCTS

BAKERY

This spiritually oriented community is not associated with any one group, but members are working on an international communal utopia, building close ties with like-minded communities. It holds spring and autumn spiritual conventions and an open house in mid-October. Write or call ahead if you would like to visit. The Settlement has a thriving forest-products business, utilizing the entire tree—bark mulch, garden blend compost, sawdust, lumber, and veneer—which serves both the general public and corporations. In addition, it operates schools for community members, craft shops, and a community kitchen. Its certified organic produce and herbal products are sold at local farmer's markets and by mail order. The bakery specializes in a variety of baked goods and breads (they're known for their "veggie bread"), which they sell locally. The newsletter, *Millennial Chronicles,* is available on request, as are a few books written by members of the community. "Wisdom is our leader, truth is our guide" is their motto on the *Chronicles.*

FROM A
CHURCH BULLETIN

The associate minister unveiled the church's new tithing campaign slogan last Sunday: "I upped my pledge. Up yours."

CANNING RECORDS FOR 1996

Our organic gardens and orchards provide fresh produce and fruit that is consumed through-out the summer. We have over 600 trees. We had 50 gallons of strawberries, which delighted the children as well as the adults. In canning we use quarts and half-gallon jars, since our extended family is so large.

Tomatoes: over 1,600 half-gallons

Jams & jellies: 100 quarts (includes strawberry, apple, grape, blackberry, and herbal jelly)

Pickles: 325 half-gallons (dill, bread-and-butter, sweet, relish, green tomato pickles with cayennes)

Squash: 75 baskets

Peppers: 7 half-gallons (cayenne, super chiles, green chiles, Hungarian wax, and salsa with peppers)

Pickled beets: 27 half-gallons

Sauerkraut: 200 gallons canned

Juice: 55 half-gallons grape juice and 349 half-gallons apple juice

Green beans: 28 gallons frozen

Four crates of cayenne were dried for the table. Herbs also for cooking, teas, and medicinal use.

◆

Millennial Chronicles, A Journal Outreach for Communities, *Issue 7 (1996)*,
Padanaram Settlement, Williams, Indiana

HERBAL COSMETICS

In community, there is emphasis on being original and creative. Someone is always trying something new! One area I'd always been intrigued with was making my own cosmetics. I had collected books for years, but the idea never came to fruition until I became interested in growing herbs. I started with four hexagon-shaped herb gardens, planted organic herbs of all kinds, and wildcrafted herbs from the woods. I gathered, dried, and stored them in jars.

Cosmetic recipes found in my books called for peppermint, thyme, calendula (pot marigold), comfrey, chamomile, scented geraniums, elderflowers, and other herbs. Our grandmothers and great-grandmothers before us had passed them from generation to generation in the form of cold creams, salves, vinegar rinses, shampoos, and toilet waters. I was hooked! Why couldn't I do the same? I realized by this time that many harmful ingredients were in the cosmetics on my shelves.

I purchased equipment—mortar and pestle, spice grinders, enamel or glass pans, measuring spoons and cups for cosmetics only. I yard-saled for unique bottles and containers. Friends saved jars for me. I found cocoa butter, lanolin, coconut oil, and nut oils at health-food stores. I read labels—only the finest, purest would do!

I spent many hours experimenting—making teas, infusions, decoctions, oils, and tinctures. Lip balms, hand creams, face masks, shampoos, and deodorants appeared—it was endless. It was much like cooking sauces and puddings. Some of my experiments looked like goosh, brown mud, or failed candy, but I kept trying. Without preservatives and dyes, cosmetics do not look the same, but many were pleasing to the eye and smelled wonderful.

Over time I improved on the recipes or made original concoctions of my own. It wasn't long until my friends began asking for something for chapped lips or fever blisters, a cream for chapped faces from riding horses in the wind, or lotion for gardeners' hands—not to speak of the teenagers who wanted lip balm and perfumes.

Today I have a small herbal cosmetics business. I sell by mail as well as provide products to several local health-food stores. All of our gardens are certified organic. I do workshops teaching the art of making herbal cosmetics. My line of products is expanding to include massage and body oils as well as makeup and beauty aids. Numerous people throughout the world share my philosophy of herbs for health. Taking it one step further, we should be concerned not only with what we put into our bodies, but what we put *on* our bodies.

◆

Rachel Summerton, Padanaram Settlement, Williams, Indiana

This is one of the oldest and largest Catholic Benedictine monasteries in the Midwest. St. Meinrad's College and School of Theology prepares students for the priesthood, lay ministry, and Christian service. Many of the 140 monks who live here teach at the seminary. The monks from St. Meinrad's have founded five other monasteries in the United States, in Arkansas, Louisiana, Illinois, South Dakota, and California. They also own and operate Abbey Press, which makes and sells religious and inspirational cards and gifts nationwide from an extensive catalog. They work hard at personalizing their products, offering to put any name you request on Bibles, cards, framed prints, and other collectibles for baptisms, First Communions, ordinations, and marriages. In addition, they have a department called One Caring Place that offers products dealing with death, grief, pastoral care, and counseling. They have sold 50 million booklets of their 250 titles.

This is a beautiful setting in southern Indiana, and the 2,000-acre monastery property has a Romanesque church built in 1907 as a focal point, a short distance from the guesthouse, which has a full program of retreats.

ST. MEINRAD ARCHABBEY

◆

St. Meinrad, IN 47577
(812) 357-6585
(800) 581-6905:
guesthouse
(800) 962-4760/
(812) 357-8260 fax:
Abbey Press

SEMINARY

RELIGIOUS GREETING CARDS

RETREATS

PERSONALIZED RELIGIOUS AND INSPIRATIONAL PRODUCTS, INCLUDING ROSARIES, AND DEATH, GRIEF, AND PASTORAL CARE PRODUCTS

(SISTER GREGORY EMS)

Iowa

◆——◆——◆

ION EXCHANGE VILLAGE

◆

**1878 Old Mission Dr.
Harpers Ferry, IA 52146
(319) 535-7231/
535-7362 fax
E-mail:
hbright@means.net
Web site:
www.ionxchange
.com**

**NATIVE WILDFLOWER SEEDS
NATIVE WILD GRASSES
RELATED BOOKS**

Howard and Donna Bright own 280 acres in a remote Iowa valley on the Yellow River, six miles upstream from the Mississippi River. Their purpose is to take enough time someday from their thriving wildflower seed business to form a community that will provide a safe, secure, natural setting for raising children and conserving natural resources. They are committed to their "Good Life Principles":

1. Emotional, physical, and mental security
2. Gaining knowledge for self-enhancement
3. Recognizing and enjoying beauty
4. Being courageous
5. Seeking a balance in life, assuring temperance
6. Caring for self and others
7. Loving and being loved
8. Sharing
9. Pleasure
10. Fairness
11. Trustworthiness
12. Making sense of the day

The Brights currently offer over 200 species of seeds and over 100 species of plugs (seeds already started), which they sell by mail order or by appointment. In season, they employ 20 people full-time and in the winter they have a staff of ten. Harvesting is done mainly by hand, and then the seeds are dried and cleaned. The Brights lease native prairie, own native wetlands, and have extensive greenhouses. So far they've sold mainly in the Midwest, to places like departments of transportation, fish and wildlife services, and major corporations, but a recent article in a Boston paper about their joe-pye weed brought much interest from the East. Foxglove, beardtongue, heart-leaf alexander, ox-eye sunflower, and prairie blazingstar are just a few of the seeds they have available.

WILDFLOWER SEEDS

Another season of planting, sowing, weeding, and collecting has been recorded in the annals of Ion Exchange. Four summer interns arrived in the spring with smiles on their faces and visions of dancing through sunlit prairies abounding with thousands of wildflowers blowing in the gentle breeze while their long white gowns made them appear as angels. They all left this fall with calluses on their hands and their clothes permanently stained and torn with hours of sweat and toil. A few new wrinkles from the sun and the etching scars of reality modified their spring vision and replaced it with real memories. It was work but it was fun. Knowledge that can be gained nowhere else now resides in the minds of these individuals. Will they return to Ion? Ion Exchange now offers over 200 species of seeds and over 100 species of plugs (fully rooted plants that can be put directly into the ground) and potted plants, including

Tall Green Milkweed	Sky Blue Aster
Sweet Flag	Bog Birch
Red Baneberry	Partridge Pea
Giant Yellow Hyssop	Marsh Marigold
Water Plantain	Tall Bellflower
Wild Garlic	Sweet Joe Pye
Leadplant	Midland Shooting Star
False Indigo	Sweet Everlasting
Angelica	Cow Parsnip
Columbine	

◆

Ion Exchange, Native Seed and Plant Nursery, Harpers Ferry, Iowa

MAHARISHI INTERNATIONAL UNIVERSITY

◆

**N. Main St., Rte. 1
Fairfield, IA 52556
(515) 472-7000/
472-1189 fax**

UNIVERSITY

**TRANSCENDENTAL
MEDITATION TEACHING**

This university, fully accredited through the Ph.D. level, offers courses in management, neuroscience of physics, human consciousness, physiology and molecular and cell biology, science of creative intelligence, psychology, fine arts, engineering, math, physics, and professional writing, among others. It is the centerpiece of the worldwide Transcendental Meditation (TM) movement. It has a faculty and staff of 600, and 1,200 students. Members who move into the community buy their own homes and meditate together in large domes. The University's aim is to have 7,000 meditators living in one place on each continent to create a spiritual coherence that will provide the basis for world peace. There are now over 3 million TM meditators worldwide. Because many of their members are entrepreneurs, the local economy is booming. Long-range plans include developing an electric car system and pursuing their aim of high-tech, environmentally friendly businesses.

Some years ago we read about a study at Harvard that showed meditation was very helpful in lowering blood pressure. Thinking it was safer for our mother to meditate than to take blood-pressure medication, we searched out a TM teacher in Buffalo, seventy miles away. He agreed to drive to her small town each day until she completed the course, and we arranged for it to happen over the Christmas holidays, when we would all be there. A calm young man arrived each day and explained the simple technique to us all, and then we tried it. It seemed very restful. We all remember that young man with pleasure, so bright, cheerful, and thoughtful—somehow, without our seeing him, he was able to slip a tiny package for each of us under the tree, which we discovered and opened with delight on Christmas morning! And everyone's blood pressure is normal!

This abbey is the only Trappist monastery in the United States solely dependent on farming for its livelihood. Its residents raise 1,100 acres of corn and 700 acres of soybeans. In the early nineties they set aside 250 acres for cereal grain, soybeans, corn, alfalfa, and sunflowers, which are certified organic, stating, "We commit ourselves to sustainable agriculture that will protect the ecological health of our environment. . . . We realize our land provides sustenance not only for ourselves but for the generations who will succeed us." They have a 1,000-acre forest where, since the 1950s, they have planted 30,000 trees, such as black walnut, oak, white and red pine, and European larch. These trees are maturing, and the lumber is being sold to commercial users. Monks came here from Ireland in the mid-1800s and found the gently rolling hills of eastern Iowa suitable for their serene lifestyle. In 1999 they will celebrate their 150th anniversary in Peosta. There is a guest wing attached to the impressive stone church where the monks sing the canonical hours daily, and one floor is set aside for men interested in experiencing the daily life of a contemplative monk. Regular retreat programs are offered throughout the year.

NEW MELLERAY ABBEY

◆

**6500 Melleray Circle
Peosta, IA 52068
(319) 588-2319**

SOYBEANS
CORN
ORGANIC CROPS
TIMBER
VOCATION DISCERNMENT
RETREATS

OUR LADY OF THE MISSISSIPPI ABBEY

◆

**8400 Abbey Hill
Dubuque, IA 52003
(319) 582-2595/
582-5511 fax**

CANDY

ART CARDS

ICONS

WEAVING

SOAP

BEEF CATTLE

HAY

FIELD CROPS

RETREATS

ver the years, these Catholic Trappistine sisters developed several varieties of candy and have created a delectable line of caramels. The most popular is a chocolate-coated caramel, the recipe for which was taught them by a Dominican sister. They also produce caramels of vanilla flavor, honey, and chocolate best described as "like a Tootsie Roll." In addition they offer fudge, penuche, munch, and green and chocolate Swiss mints. The 28 women in the community use their talents in many ways: one paints icons on commission, others create art cards, another makes soap, and they all work very hard from September to December bringing in the hay, or gathering the oats or barley or corn—whatever their farm committee had decided to raise that year—and preparing the beef cattle for market. The sisters also accept women who would like to experience their prayer and work life for periods of one to three months. A few rooms are available for retreatants.

Sister Columba Guare

Kansas

In 1863 seven sisters, half the community of the Benedictine Sisters of St. Cloud, Minnesota, came to Atchison to teach children of German immigrants at the request of the bishops who wanted to found a Catholic school in every parish. The sisters traveled by stagecoach, train, and riverboat, coming by way of Chicago, Hannibal, and St. Joseph, Missouri.

Today, in addition to classroom teaching, the 235 sisters who make up this community provide spiritual leadership in liturgy, prayer, sacramental preparation, counseling, social service, peace and justice, hospital chaplaincy, health services, and care of the aging. They have missionaries in Brazil and faculty at Bethlehem University in the Holy Land.

The Mount Conservatory of Music currently has 210 students and offers beginning and advanced lessons in piano, organ, harp, violin, voice, woodwinds, brass, guitar, hand bells, and music theory.

Two of the sisters who recently returned from fifteen years in Brazil have opened a tea room and gift shop where homemade pies and breads are available in addition to tea, coffee, and "surprises." The gift shop features crafts, needlework, pottery, and items from their Peruvian collection—wood carvings, musical instruments, ceramics, tapestries, paintings, and other artifacts. Other sisters specialize in carpentry, plants, and editing.

The printery produces notecards and Christmas cards designed by the sisters and an annual Lenten journal entitled *How Are Your House Plants Doing?* The Sophia Center offers retreats and workshops on monastic life, spirituality for the "golden years," centering prayer, and is a resource center including lecturers for scholars, schools, churches, and monasteries.

MOUNT ST. SCHOLASTICA

◆

**801 S. 8th St.
Atchison, KS 66002
(913) 367-6110/
367-3866 fax**

**CRAFTS
PRINTING
CARPENTRY
EDITING
PLANTS
TEA ROOM
COMMUNITY CENTER
MUSIC SCHOOL
CONFERENCE CENTER
THRIFT SHOP
WORKSHOPS
PILGRIMAGES
SPECIAL EVENTS
RETREATS**

A Kansas Thomas Merton Conference is held each November. A Celtic pilgrimage to the holy sites of Ireland offers pilgrims a balance of journey, instruction, worship, and prayerful solitude. In addition, the third weekend of November brings a craft and bread sale; the second Sunday of July, a chicken dinner in aid of the Mount Community Center and its day care, preschool, tutoring, music conservatory, and Helping Hand thrift store; and January, a barbershop chorus celebration and benefit.

SHANTIVANAM HOUSE OF PRAYER

◆

22019 Meagher Rd.
Easton, KS 66020
(913) 773-8255
(800) 659-3227/
726-9033 fax: Forest of
Peace Publishing

BOOKS
TAPES
SACRED ART
CROSSES
ICONS
CARDS
RETREATS

A community of laypeople was founded here in the 1970s by a Catholic priest, Father Edward Hays, to provide a place for solitude and prayer. The community started the Forest of Peace Publishing program, which sells supplies for pilgrims, such as books on spiritual thought, tapes for prayer and reflection, beautifully crafted crosses, icons, images, and cards. One of the books, *The Conspiracy of Compassion,* by Joseph Nassal, looks at the original meaning of the word *conspire,* which is "to breathe together" and be a co-conspirator in the story of salvation. The author reminds us that both Hebrew and Christian scriptures are full of stories about God's sacred breath, and by connecting to this sacred breathing, the conspiracy of compassion is born. According to one reviewer, Father Edward Hays is America's best theological storyteller. His book *The Gospel of Gabriel* describes the humanity of Jesus, struggling in time of prayer, delighting in dancing and feasting, calling disciples who are women as well as men, sinners as well as saints.

The community, which lives on 120 acres of rolling timberland 14 miles west of Leavenworth, and has rooms, cabins, and hermitages for retreat, suggests that visitors design their own programs for reflection.

Kentucky

P ort Salut cheese was originally developed by a Trappist monastery in France, which shared the recipe with Canadian brethren who, in turn, passed it on to the monks here, who have been making it in mild, aged, and smoked flavors since the 1950s. They sell more than 100,000 pounds of it annually. For 20 years, chef Henry Haller served the cheese at the White House, calling it "the best in the U.S." The monks also make a fruitcake with candied fruits marinated in burgundy. After the cakes are baked, Kentucky bourbon is added to mellow the flavor. In a taste test of mail-order fruitcakes, the judges at *Newsday* ranked it number one, describing it as "just like my grandmother's." Kentucky bourbon is also used in their fudge, a relatively new and popular confection. One of the monks says, "You can't eat it and drive!"

This is where Thomas Merton lived and wrote for much of his life, and he slyly referred to it as "a monastery tied to a cheese factory." But he also praised the underlying value here, where men and women are welcome to visit and stay in the newly renovated guesthouse and be willing "to entertain silence in the heart and listen for the voice of God . . . to pray for your own discovery." Merton's books are in every bookstore, his writings form the basis of a wide range of programs, his quotes are used by a Sufi retreat house, and a room is named for him in a Northwest monastery. If anyone has ever had a true sense of basic spirituality, seeing the similarity in all religions, and overcoming the divisiveness that some religious leaders thrive on, it was Merton. His message of unity and love was given in such a compelling style that people who read him transcend religious dogma and can identify with his thinking and add clarity to their own.

ABBEY OF GETHSEMANI

◆

3642 Monks Rd.
Trappist, KY 40051
(502) 549-4133: retreats
(502) 549-3117/
549-4124 fax:
food orders
Web site:
www.monks.org

CHEESE
FRUITCAKE
FUDGE
RETREATS

Louisiana

NEW ORLEANS ZEN TEMPLE

◆

**748 Camp St.
New Orleans, LA 70130
(504) 523-1213/
523-7024 fax
E-mail: aza@gnofn.org
Web site:
home.gnofn.org
/~aza**

BOOKS
ZAZEN SUPPLIES
TAPES
INCENSE
PAINTINGS
RESTAURANT
ART GALLERY
RETREATS

The temple carries a full line of books by the late Taisen Deshimaru, the teacher of the founder of this Zen temple in the warehouse district of the Big Easy. Deshimaru's *Sit* is a critical comparison of Soto and Rinzai Zen practice, and his *Way of True Zen* captures the essentials of his teaching. Also available are books by Kosho Uchiyama, such as *Opening the Hand of Thought*, which is an introduction to the meaning of zazen, and his *From the Zen Kitchen to Enlightenment,* which is a translation and commentary on Dogen's classic *Instructions to the Cook.* The temple also has John Stevens's translation of *Japanese Soto Zen Philosophy*, one of the few complete translations available. There is a wide range of zazen supplies such as zafus, hand cushions, kimonos, and work clothes, a tape of Deshimaru chanting the traditional daily ceremony in his Paris sangha, as well as a good selection of incense and burners. Beautiful paintings by Elizabeth Polchow Livingston, wife of the resident teacher Robert Livingston Roshi, and calligraphy by Kazuaki Tanahashi are for sale.

The temple owns and manages the Zen Temple Bar & Grill, staffed by sangha members, which is on the street level of their building. They offer simple, natural, carefully prepared foods in an art gallery setting.

ARTIST'S STATEMENT

Painting for me is a form of practice. Like zazen, it is something to be done on a regular basis, hopefully every day and with a *mushutoku* attitude, which means an attitude of no goal or no profit. For me, in my painting, this means I don't plan a painting out. It takes form and flows from moment to moment on an intuitive and spontaneous level. As a large-scale work progresses I do need to engage my critical faculties, but these decisions are based on intuitive observations involving color and balance. Also with the attitude of painting as practice I am liberated from any ideas of creating a masterpiece and the pressures that that way of thinking can create. Doing zazen regularly helps me to be more spontaneous in my work.

My imagery is based on the observations of nature. It is abstract. I work in several different modes, ranging from a primitive form of geometric abstraction to what a friend calls "botanical expressionism." In the latter the picture plane is crammed with flowing vortices of tropical landscape elements. Color plays an important role in both these types of images as it does in my third mode, which I think consists of an unconscious attempt to synthesize the other contrasting styles. In these, plant forms and geometric shapes are arranged in a geometric and/or faceted framework. My palette usually is dominated by various shades of greens and earth tones. I work in a variety of media: watercolor crayon, oil pastel, acrylic, and oil paint. The scale ranges from four by six inches to eight by nine feet. Prices range from $30 for a small print to $2,000 for a large oil painting. Viewing of work can be arranged by appointment by calling the New Orleans Zen Temple.

◆

Elizabeth Polchow Livingston

ST. JOSEPH ABBEY

◆

**River Rd.
St. Benedict, LA 70457
(504) 892-1800/
892-3473 fax**

SEMINARY
RETREATS

The primary mission of this Catholic Benedictine abbey is St. Joseph Seminary College, an accredited four-year school that trains men for the priesthood. Graduate courses in theology and related subjects are also available for non-seminarian men and women.

A seminarian we met was helpful to us, and we talked a little about how he happened to enter the seminary. He confessed to having been a wild college student, but felt drawn to a life of discipline and service. He wasn't sure whether he would become a priest or a brother, only time would tell, but he did know he was no longer frantic, anxious, competitive, or indulgent. He certainly seemed content to us.

There are outstanding murals in the Abbey church and other buildings painted by the Benedictine monk Dom Gregory de Wit, and completed in 1946. Retreats are held in a separate building near the church. The monastery has 1,200 acres just across Lake Pontchartrain from New Orleans, part of the Mississippi Delta with old-growth trees, swamps, marshes, and bayous. Walker Percy, the noted writer who lived in nearby Covington and was an oblate to the monastery, is buried on the grounds.

FROM A
CHURCH BULLETIN

Don't let worry
kill you. Let the
church help.

CHASUBLES

The chasuble is the outermost garment worn by a Catholic priest when celebrating mass. In the early centuries of the Church, the garment was made by cutting a hole (for the head) in a large square or circular piece of cloth. Inevitably, restricted arm movement (which made preparing and offering the sacraments difficult at best) led to modifications that allowed for the present free motion of the arms. The chasuble presently worn in Rome is cut from a piece of cloth roughly 46 by 30 inches. The garment requires a priestly blessing before it can be worn, and it is heavily symbolic, representing all-covering charity and the yoke of Christ.

Sister Elizabeth Wagner at Hermitage Arts in Thorndike, Maine, describes her work producing chasubles and stoles as "a way to earn a living in solitude." When asked whether the beautiful array of colors in her chasubles is in any way nontraditional, she replied that she wasn't sure about the history, but in general she aims toward "what works as liturgical art." For 16 years, producing stoles and chasubles has been Sister Elizabeth's major means of support.

◆

For a catalog of Hermitage Arts stoles and chasubles, call (207) 568-3731. Osage Monastery in Sand Springs, Oklahoma, also makes religious garments to order, as does St. Joseph's Abbey in Spencer, Mass. And Pax Christi in Erie, Pennsylvania, offers stoles and scarves through Common Threads, a knitting project for disadvantaged women of inner-city Erie. According to their catalog, Common Threads "works to break the cycle of injustice and poverty by enabling women to improve their economic situations."

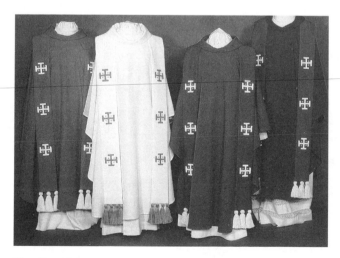

Hermitage Arts

Maine

◆ ◆ ◆

HERMITAGE ARTS

◆

RR 1, Box 398
Thorndike, ME 04986
(207) 568-3731/
568-3612 fax

CHASUBLES
STOLES
GOURMET FOOD PRODUCTS
HERMITAGE RETREAT

Transfiguration Hermitage is a small community of Catholic hermit sisters who live in rural Maine and create exquisite handwoven and appliquéd vestments. Their chasubles and stoles come in a number of colors and designs, and their coronation chasubles, of textured polyester with satin lining, are suitable for the highest celebrations such as Christmas, Easter, or the installation of a new pope, male or female. This resourceful community also makes and sells herbal vinegars, salsas, oriental foods, pesto, jams, jellies, and cakes and bakery products to order. There is one hermitage retreat for individuals seeking solitude and quiet on 90 acres that look west to spectacular sunsets over the mountains.

NOTRE DAME SPIRITUAL CENTER

◆

Alfred, ME 04002
(207) 324-6160/324-6612
(Mon–Fri 9 A.M. to 4 P.M.)

MAPLE SYRUP FESTIVAL
APPLES
BAKED PRODUCTS
FIREWOOD
INDOOR ICE-SKATING RINK
RETREATS

Maple Syrup Sunday is held each year on the last Sunday in March, after the community's maple syrup is processed. The Brothers of Christian Instruction, a Catholic teaching order, acquired these 400 acres of former Shaker community land in 1930 and used it for education until 1980, when they opened the center for conferences and retreats. The 3,000 apple trees give a bountiful harvest in the fall, and are sold in the Apple Store along with fresh baked products and firewood. An indoor ice-skating rink, on natural ice inside a Shaker barn, is open from Christmas to mid-March, depending on temperature. Retreats and conferences are scheduled throughout the year.

Maryland

These Episcopal sisters have an extensive catalog of fine note cards for all occasions, as well as holy cards, postcards, and bookmarks. They sell their own books and tote bags to support the Joseph Richey Hospice House, where, since 1990, they have cared for more than 700 terminally ill people who have died in loving and comfortable surroundings. One of their books, *Beakless Bluebirds and Featherless Penguins,* by Sister Barbara Ann, is the touching and funny story of the rescue of two Eastern bluebird babies who were attacked by a predator and saved by the sisters, who used an eye-dropper to feed them. The birds recovered and lived for the next seven years in the convent, and brought much joy to this compassionate community. The sisters' journal, *New Every Morning,* is illustrated with beautiful photographs, and their cookbook, *Nun Like It,* may explain the excellent food and baked goods we had while visiting. Retreats are available for men in the monastery, women in the convent, and couples in the guesthouse.

ALL SAINTS EPISCOPAL CONVENT

◆

**P.O. Box 3127
Catonsville, MD 21228
(410) 747-4104**

BOXED ILLUSTRATED NOTE CARDS

BOOKS

TOTE BAGS

JOURNAL

HOSPICE

RETREATS

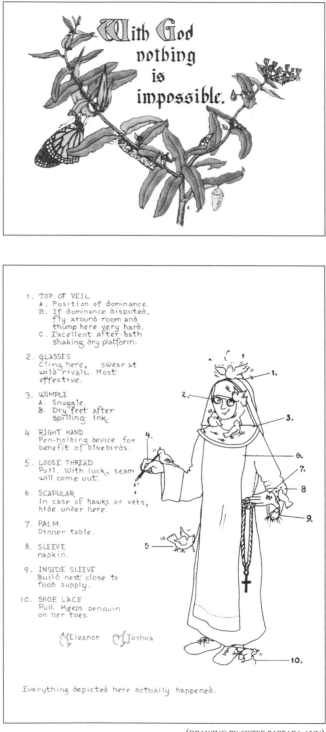

(DRAWING BY SISTER BARBARA ANN)

BEAKLESS BLUEBIRDS

Here are a few excerpts from a fascinating tale of two gravely injured bluebirds and how the sisters of an Episcopal convent raised them within its confines.

MAY 24

In an attempt to maintain detachment and avoid emotional involvement, I have not named the birds. However, the junior sisters have worked so hard and been such dependable babysitters that I have asked them to be godmothers . . . as for their future, if the rehabilitation permit is not granted, we will have to hand them over to whomsoever the government requires. "Never!" declares Sister Emily Ann passionately. "Suppose they never got beaks and they don't learn to feed themselves, the government might have them killed. We're the only people with time enough to feed them every twenty minutes, and someone is always here. We'll go into hiding with them first!" So much for maintaining objectivity.

MAY 25

At night the birds sleep in their nest on my pillow, for Eleanor (now named) continues to have seizures or nightmares. When I awaken, the first thing I see is two sets of bright eyes regarding me over the edge of the nest, but they do not begin clamoring for food until the rising bell goes off. I reach to the chair where there is a supply of live worms (no refrigeration necessary) and feed them.

MAY 27

The little birds are nearly two weeks old now. Wing and tail feathers have opened and Rachel is getting bluer and bluer. She is almost certainly a male. Sister Emily Ann admits that she has always wanted to name a little boy Joshua, so Eleanor and Joshua it is.

FEBRUARY 6

Since Joshua cannot see straight ahead, food placed directly in front of his mouth is ignored. We wave the worms or meat around a bit, he gets a fix, opens his mouth, and we shove down the meal. The quickest and simplest way is to pass the food vertically, then horizontally, in front of his eyes. I had not realized how this appeared to the uninitiated until, as I feed Josh, one guest remarks to a new visitor: "Joshua is my favorite bird because he is so religious. Watch," she goes on, "he won't eat until they make the sign of the cross with his food!"

◆

From Beakless Bluebirds and Featherless Penguins *by Sister Barbara Ann,*
Scriptorium Publications, All Saints' Convent, Catonsville, Maryland

TARA
ENTERPRISES

◆

**18400 River Rd.
Poolesville, MD 20837
(800) 775-8272/
(301) 972-8822 fax**

TIBETAN BUDDHIST FINE ART
BOOKS
TAPES
BUMPER STICKERS
SUNCATCHERS
PRAYER BEADS
CARDS

This is the seat of Tibetan Palyul lineage in the West, and the community offers products and gifts designed to promote peace and kindness in the world. The Buddhist statues, carvings, reliefs, and plates are exceptionally fine, and some are considered collectibles. There are also books and tapes by founder Jetsunma Ahkon Lhamo, who was born in Brooklyn of Jewish/Italian parents and started a prayer and meditation center in Washington, D.C., in 1981. The supreme head of the Nyingma School of Tibetan Buddhism declared her teachings to be pure teachings of Buddhism, and in 1988 he identified Jetsunma as a reincarnate lama and lineage holder. The title of Jetsunma indicates that in her previous incarnation she attained enlightenment. The bumper sticker "Practice random acts of kindness and senseless acts of beauty" is available here, as well as suncatchers, laminated bookmarks with Buddhist designs, and prayer beads.

Massachusetts

This unique ecumenical community has 12 clergy from five mainline denominations, including Presbyterian, Episcopal, and Congregational, in a neighborhood on Cape Cod Bay in Orleans. Its 330 members all have their own livelihoods. Spiritually, all things are held in common. Some homeowners share large homes with others, which allows much helpful support between generations. A monastic community houses 60 sisters and 25 brothers who are supported by their church through tithing.

A Christian ecumenical publishing house reissues old classics with a contemporary slant; Paraclete Press (Holy Spirit) produces sacred sheet music and sells Gregorian chant recordings and manuals; a television studio called Paraclete Video Productions does promotional videos for corporations; and a tape called "How to Deal with Pregnancy Loss" has been widely distributed. The mission of the community is the transformation of individual lives through a way of life centered on

COMMUNITY OF JESUS

◆

**5 Bay View Dr., Box 1094
Orleans, MA 02653
(508) 255-1094 or
255-6204/255-9490 fax**

PUBLISHING HOUSE

TV STUDIO

CHOIR

THEATRE

BANDS

LAWN SERVICE

CONSTRUCTION COMPANY

COURSES

FESTIVALS

CALENDAR OF EVENTS

OCTOBER
3 Dinner Theatre, *The Murder Room*, 6:30 PM
5 Theatre Matinee, *The Murder Room*, 3 PM
6 Adult Workshops and Courses, 7:30 PM
10 Dinner Theatre, *The Murder Room*, 6:30 PM
11 Dinner Theatre, *The Murder Room*, 6:30 PM
12 Theatre Matinee, *The Murder Room*, 3 PM
13 Adult Workshops and Courses, 7:30 PM
20 Adult Workshops and Courses, 7:30 PM
24 Gloriæ Dei Chamber Ensemble Concert, 7:30 PM
27 Adult Workshops and Courses, 7:30 PM

NOVEMBER
3 Adult Workshops and Courses, 7:30 PM
10 Adult Workshops and Courses, 7:30 PM
27 Thanksgiving Service,
Chapel of the Holy Paraclete, 10 AM
30 Advent Service of Lessons and Carols, 4 PM
Handbell Prelude, 3:30 PM

DECEMBER
6 Christmas Village Festival
Gloriæ Dei Brass and Gloriæ Dei Ringers
Christmas Concert, 8 PM
7 Christmas Village Festival
A Christmas Garland, 4:30 PM

JANUARY
16 Dinner Theatre, *Cocktail Party*, 6:30 PM
17 Dinner Theatre, *Cocktail Party*, 6:30 PM
18 Theatre Matinee, *Cocktail Party*, 3 PM
23 Dinner Theatre, *Cocktail Party*, 6:30 PM
24 Dinner Theatre, *Cocktail Party*, 6:30 PM
25 Theatre Matinee, *Cocktail Party*, 3 PM
30 Gloriæ Dei Chamber Ensemble Concert, 7:30 PM

FEBRUARY
1 Community of Jesus Orchestra Concert, 4 PM

MARCH
29 Gloriæ Dei Brass and Gloriæ Dei Ringers
Concert, 4 PM

God. The missionary outreach traveling choir meets daily and does one to two tours a year. As part of this mission they have a theater, and a Sousa band.

There is also a lawn service, and a privately run construction company specializing in home repair and construction. They hold a Fourth of July celebration. At a Christmas Village, which offers house tours open to the public, five or six houses are highly decorated in the style of a foreign country; baked goods from that country are sold, as well as native crafts. There is a full calendar of events year-round, including harborside teas, a gigantic yard sale, dinners and concerts, theater, a concert series, and courses in such subjects as cake decorating, calligraphy, flower arranging, upholstery, furniture repair, and watercolor. Visitors are welcome to join the activities.

COWLEY PUBLICATIONS

◆

**28 Temple Place
Boston, MA 02111
(800) 225-1534
(617) 423-2427/2354 fax
E-mail:
cowley@cowley.org
Web site:
www.cowley.org/~cowley**

BOOKS
MUSIC
TEACHING SERIES
CD

Cowley Publications is a nonprofit ministry of the Society of St. John the Evangelist, an Anglican religious order for men in the Episcopal Church, with a monastery located in Cambridge, Massachusetts. Formed in the mid-1970s by the superior of the order, who is now the bishop of Massachusetts, Cowley Publications was originally housed in the monastery itself. It now has office space in the Cathedral of St. Paul in Boston, publishes 15 books a year, and has approximately 100 backlist titles in print.

Emerging from the Society's tradition of prayer, theological reflection, and diversity of mission, the press is centered in the rich heritage of the Anglican communion. Cowley seeks to provide books and music, for the ongoing theological exploration and spiritual development of the Episcopal Church. It is dedicated to developing a new generation of theological writers, encouraging them to produce timely, creative, and stimulating books, and making them widely available to both clergy and laypersons. The Cowley and Cathedral Bookstore at the Cathedral is one of the ways it does this.

◈

In an introduction to Cowley's new catalog, the director says that the idea for a series of books that helps Episcopalians explore the Christian faith in a lively way and that helps them understand their own distinct tradition of Anglicanism is far from new. This fall it is offering a new church's teaching series that comes out of informal conversations of scholars and pastors meeting together and includes two volumes each for the Bible, history, theology, spirituality, worship, and ethics.

Other titles include *The Rule of the Society of Saint John the Evangelist, Singing the Daily Office, Christian Households: The Sanctification of Nearness, Spiritual Theology: The Theology of Yesterday for Spiritual Help Today, No Moment Too Small: Rhythm of Silence, Prayer, and Holy Reading,* and *New Wine: The Story of Women Transforming Leadership and Power in the Episcopal Church.*

This Catholic Benedictine monastery has a large gift shop with religious items for every occasion, and a 40-page catalog of books. The book selection runs the gamut of Catholic writers, thinkers, and doers, including Mother Teresa, Saint Augustine, Thomas Keating, Henri Nouwen, Cardinal Bernardin, and Thomas Merton. The catalog also has tapes and CDs such as *Catholic Classics* in two volumes. Private retreats are available for men and women in guesthouses on 60 acres of elegant New England countryside.

GLASTONBURY ABBEY

◆

**16 Hull St.
Hingham, MA 02043
(617) 749-2155**

BOOKS

TAPES & CDS

RETREATS

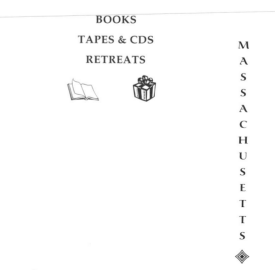

M
A
S
S
A
C
H
U
S
E
T
T
S

◈

HEARTHSTONE VILLAGE/SIRIUS CONFERENCE CENTER/THE ARK

◆

**91 Baker Rd.
Amherst, MA 01072
(413) 259-1251
(9:00 A.M.–1:00 P.M. EST)
Sirius
(413) 259-1701
(Mon.–Fri.,
9:00 A.M.–5:00 P.M.)
Hearthstone
E-mail: sirius
@siriuscommunity.org
Web site: www
.siriuscommunity.org**

BULK FOOD STORE

ALTERNATIVE INSULATION BUSINESS

RETREAT AND CONFERENCE CENTER

This is a community of friends who live on and around Baker Road in Shutesbury, Massachusetts. They live independently, call the "neighborhood" they have created Hearthstone Village, but sponsor the Sirius Community, a retreat and conference center open to the public on 93 acres of forest with nature trails.

The Ark, next door to Sirius, is a household of up to 20 people who share the work of "keeping home," allowing them to pursue alternative ways of making a living. One member runs an alternative insulation business using recycled materials, and several are alternative health practitioners and trainers. They also operate a neighborhood bulk food store to serve their own community. Village meetings are held four times a year, and the major holidays are celebrated together.

Sirius believes that planetary healing begins with personal transformation and expansion of consciousness, requires attunement to the local spirit of place and a global awareness, and manifests itself in each detail and action of daily life. Sirius was started in 1978 by former members of the Findhorn Community in Scotland, and named after the star that is known as the source of love and wisdom for our planet. Its members strive to live and work in such a way as to create a sustainable abundance to pass on to future generations.

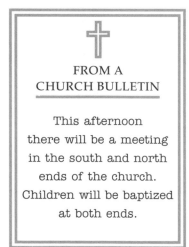

FROM A
CHURCH BULLETIN

This afternoon
there will be a meeting
in the south and north
ends of the church.
Children will be baptized
at both ends.

RECYCLING

The earth is the LORD's and the fulness thereof,
The world and those who dwell therein;
For he has founded it upon the seas,
And established it upon the rivers.

Psalm 24:1–2 (RSV)

The tone, the emotional charge of awe, found in this Psalm is largely absent from modern attitudes toward creation. More than gratitude for an invaluable gift, legal obligation and fear of diminishing landfill space motivate many recent efforts to recycle. Those who are deeply concerned about the earth are trying to correct the widespread myopia that leads only to cosmetic efforts to restore creation. Edith Stein, author of *The Environmental Sourcebook,* begs us to look to the source of the problem. She writes, "There are four ways to deal with solid waste: dump it, burn it, convert it into something that can be used again, or don't make it. . . . [S]ource reduction must be our real goal." Such communities as Ganas in Staten Island, New York, are tackling the problem of waste with creative energy. Ganas's three retail stores restore, repackage, and recycle all sorts of unwanted items. The religious communities of this country often embody the perceptive, enlightened gratitude for the beauty of the earth that makes recycling an ongoing expression of thanks rather than mere compliance with a law or adherence to a fad.

◆

For more on environmental efforts, agencies, and legislation, see Edith C. Stein's The Environmental Sourcebook, New York: Lyons and Burford, 1992.

INSIGHT MEDITATION SOCIETY

◆

**1230 Pleasant St.
Barre, MA 01005
(978) 355-4378/
355-6398 fax: retreats
(800) 969-7333/
(413) 772-5599 fax:
Dharma Seed Tape
Library
Web site:
www.dharma.org**

BOOKS

TAPES

CORRESPONDENCE COURSE

RETREATS

The Dharma Seed Tape Library is the publishing and distribution outlet for books and tapes on meditative instruction, guidance, and inspiration by teachers who give retreats at IMS. Recognizing that life is a constantly changing process, the teachers seek to help others accept pleasure and pain, fear and joy, and all aspects of life with balance and equanimity. There are more than twenty authors listed in their current brochure. Joseph Goldstein's *The Art & Science of Meditation* is a beautifully written discussion of the art of mindfulness, which leads to a deep investigation of our mind/body reality. Sharon Salzberg's *Delusion* helps us to understand that what we know is little, and what we presume is much. Goldstein and Salzberg, cofounders of IMS, have developed a 12-lesson correspondence course that helps students to see past the illusion of obstacles and work toward an awakened mind-state, a freedom worth achieving.

In *That's Funny, You Don't Look Buddhist*, Sylvia Boorstein discusses being a faithful Jew and a passionate Buddhist, a crossing of traditions that is becoming better understood. Retreats are held regularly in the Vipassana Buddhist tradition, which seeks to free the mind from self-centeredness, negativity, and confusion. IMS is particularly well known for its three-month silent retreat for 100 people, which is usually fully booked months in advance.

Join the IMS Staff

• Deepen Spiritual Investigation
  • Explore Service as Spiritual Practice

IMS Offers: A supportive Practice environment, daily sitting time, access to retreats, room, board, health insurance, stipend.

IMS Asks: Vipassana retreat experience, commitment to
daily meditation, adherence to the five precepts, a dedication to service, ability to live and work harmoniously with others, an 18 month commitment.

If you have office skills, cooking experience, computer skills and/or a maintenance background, please consider applying.

Ongoing
Vacancies

Call or write for more information
Insight Meditation Society, Personnel Coordinator, 1230 Pleasant St., Barre, MA 01005
tel. 978/355-4378 X19, fax 978/355-6398

Kripalu is the largest center for yoga and holistic health in the United States. Founded on the yogic philosophy that physical health is the foundation of mental and spiritual development, the programs, workshops, and training reflect this concern for a balanced body, mind, and spirit. A very professional catalog describes the programs succinctly as well as profiling the teachers. The main program categories are yoga from beginner to advanced, including teacher training; self-discovery through inner quest, writing, and relationships; spiritual attunement or choosing a spiritual practice; health and well-being and how to deal with stress, sexuality, and new medicines; bodywork, including a month-long certification program and energy balancing and sensory perception.

In a former 600-room Jesuit seminary adjacent to Tanglewood, Kripalu is meeting the spiritual needs of the whole person, recognizing that maintaining health through exercise, proper diet, and focus through meditation has a far more compelling and fulfilling place in an evolving society than do fire and brimstone or guilt and fear.

KRIPALU CENTER FOR YOGA AND HEALTH

◆

**P.O. Box 793
Lenox, MA 01240
(800) 741-7353
(413) 448-3400/
448-3196 fax
E-mail: bhavani
@kripalu.org
Web site:
www.kripalu.org**

**WORKSHOPS
YOGA TRAINING
MASSAGE
RETREATS**

THE MYSTICAL PATH OF YOGA

The ancient scriptures declare that before the first person was born, God established a path by which liberation from suffering could be obtained. This program, geared toward spiritual seekers who have practiced yoga asanas or meditation for at least one year, will approach yoga through the doorway of the mystical experience, learning practices that lead to spiritual attunement and to deep healing and satisfaction. The program includes

+ meditation techniques from different Eastern yoga traditions
+ exploration of the "biological supports" of spiritual practice
+ study of selected yogic scriptures and symbols
+ guided asana sessions focusing on the deeper aspects of Kripalu Yoga
+ dialogue about individual yoga practices

◆

Description of course with Michael Carroll (Yoganand), Kripalu Center Catalog, Lenox, Massachusetts

MOUNT ST. MARY'S ABBEY

◆

**300 Arnold St.
Wrentham, MA 02093
(508) 528-1282/
528-1409 fax**

CANDY

CARDS

BOOKS

AUDIO

HEIFERS

RETREATS

Since the 1950s, these Catholic Trappistine sisters have been making "divine" candy: butter nut munch, chocolate-coated caramels, almond bark, penuche, and fudge sold by mail order in various assortments and gift boxes. The butter nut munch begins with a crisp toffee center made of pure butter, sugar, dairy cream, and finely ground almonds. The toffee is covered with chocolate and sprinkled with imported roasted filberts. The combination of flavors is as good as they come. The secret ingredient may well be the care and love the sisters impart.

The Abbey also sells a few books by Miriam Pollard, O.C.S.O. One of them, *The Listening God,* helps the reader to find God in everything from fog to wolfhounds to the music of Benny Goodman. There is an audiotape of the 50-sister community singing the daily office. Some of the prayers are brief, the sisters say, but just right for placing us in the presence of God, and a reminder of why we are here.

The sisters have recently begun to raise heifers, an enterprise that has led to no end of adventures. Apparently the creatures know the best times to carry out their escape plan. One Sunday they waited until their keepers were at mass, broke out of the pasture, and cavorted down the road, heading for Boston.

Private retreatants can stay in their guesthouse.

CANDY

Early references to candy-making date from the fourteenth century, when the wide cultivation of sugarcane made refined sugar plentiful, and addiction to candy began to grow. For hundreds of years, only hand methods were used, so quantities were limited until the eighteenth century, when machinery for candy-making was developed. Today there are endless choices for the consumer. And it is an ideal occupation for those concerned with attention to detail and concern for quality.

Chocolate candies are the most popular. Almost half of all candy made each year has chocolate on it or in it. But the United States is not even in the top ten in chocolate consumption per capita, since Europeans, especially the Dutch, Danes, and Swiss, consume from 50 to 100 percent more chocolate than do Americans. No doubt this is due to our passion for careful eating, watching and measuring every calorie we take in. But there has been a scientific breakthrough, known only to a few, that is certain to increase the consumption of chocolate in the United States. The discovery is that any candy, cookie, or cake that is made with or covered by chocolate should be broken and held up *so the calories can fall out.* This renders the food calorie-free.

Here are some choices of excellent chocolate with geographic diversity: butter-nut munch from the Trappistine sisters at Mount St. Mary's Abbey, Wrentham, Massachusetts; chocolate-coated caramels from Our Lady of the Mississippi Abbey, Dubuque, Iowa; and chocolate fudge and truffles from Brigittine monks at the Monastery of Our Lady of Consolation in Amity, Oregon. These could all be described as sinfully delicious.

◆

Mount St. Mary's Abbey (508) 528–1282, Our Lady of the Mississippi Abbey (319) 582–2595,
Monastery of Our Lady of Consolation (503) 835–8080.

ROWE CAMP & CONFERENCE CENTER

◆

**Kings Hwy. Rd., Box 273
Rowe, MA 01367
(413) 339-4216/
339-5728 fax
E-mail:
RoweCenter@aol.com**

**CAMPS FOR ALL AGES
EDUCATIONAL PROGRAMS**

Affiliated with the Unitarian Universalist Association, Rowe Camp & Conference Center was started in 1924. Its aim is to provide a warm, noncompetitive environment in which people can experience community, creativity, learning, and joy, as well as personal and spiritual growth. It is an organization of mainly volunteers who want to enrich and enhance their own lives and those of others. Teachers such as Joanna Macy, Grandfather Wallace Black Elk, and Starhawk offer courses in such subjects as Ayurvedic Health, Healing, Fitness; Celebrating Lesbian Relationships; Jazz as a Model of Our Work for a Just Society; Men and War; How to Awaken Your Inner Storyteller; Women, Mysticism, and Judaism; and Singing in the African American Tradition.

SACRED HEART RETREAT HOUSE

◆

**Route 1A, Box 567
Ipswich, MA 01938
(508) 356-3838**

**FESTIVAL
RETREATS**

Each autumn, the local Lions Club holds its Oktoberfest on the 80 acres of lawns and fields of this retreat facility run by the Catholic Salesians of St. John Bosco, the patron saint of youth. There are rooms for conferences, retreatants, and a separate building primarily used for youth groups.

The famous Trappist Preserves—jams, jellies, marmalades, conserves, and wine jellies—are made, packaged, and sold at this Trappist monastery, which produces more than 20 flavors ranging from apricot to ginger to rhubarb-strawberry, and six choices of wine jellies, including burgundy, port, and sherry. For centuries, monks have preserved food products to offer guests, and being committed to supporting themselves by their labor, the monks of St. Joseph's responded to a market that appreciates products made with quality and care.

In 1954, one of the monks who worked in the herb garden had a surplus of mint and made a small batch of mint jelly. Monastic austerity at that time precluded the monks from using the delicacy, so it was sent down to the porter's lodge, where it quickly sold out to visitors. Varieties of fruit and wine jellies were experimented with, and these too were greeted with enthusiasm, so that by the spring of 1955, plans were under way to turn jelly-making into a monastic enterprise.

For 30 years the same cook refined recipes and techniques to establish gel consistency and texture, and color and distribution of fruit in each jar. The process of vacuum-pan cooking, which they use, allows the fruit to be cooked at lower temperatures and results in better color and flavor retention. Only the best fruits are selected, and no artificial preservatives, colorings, or flavors are used. The monks use two kinds of strawberries in their strawberry preserve, one for flavor and the other because the texture holds up well in the cooking process; in the apricot preserve, special slicing guarantees equal fruit distribution in the jar. To keep the fruit in the blueberry and cherry preserves from floating to the top, the batches are carefully monitored and their temperature adjusted as the fruit is mixed, cooked, and poured. The monks are true masters of this art. The preserves are available in most fine food stores and may also be ordered directly from the monastery in various gift packages.

The monks also make high-quality liturgical vestments under the name Holy Rood Guild. Over the years,

ST. JOSEPH'S ABBEY

◆

Spencer, MA 01562
(508) 885-8730/885-4687
fax: preserves mail order
(508) 885-8750/885-8701
fax: Holy Rood
(508) 885-8710/885-8701
fax: guesthouse

TRAPPIST PRESERVES

VESTMENTS

ALTAR VESSELS AND FURNISHINGS FOR THE SACRED LITURGY

RETREATS

M
A
S
S
A
C
H
U
S
E
T
T
S

◈

Silver altar vessels (HOLY ROOD GUILD)

Guild vestments and other products, including exquisite altar vessels and furnishings for the sacred liturgy, have found their place in worship services of Protestants and Orthodox Christians, as well as Catholic parishes and religious houses. This is a large Trappist community that has retreat rooms for men in a separate wing of the complex. Women and couples can stay at nearby Mary House.

JELLIES AND JAMS

Jellies and jams have historically enjoyed an affiliation with religion. The Crusaders are believed to have brought jelly and jam from the Middle East to the West as part of the "fruits" of their expedition. Soon popular in Europe, the making of jellies and jams naturally found its way to American soil centuries later, where anyone from the individual cook to the corporate giant can produce sweet spreads for pleasure and for profit.

Jellies and jams alike are typically made by adding sugar to boiled fruit or fruit juice. The main difference between the two is that jelly is made only from fruit juice, while jam is made from fruit pulp that has been crushed, mashed, ground, or chopped into pieces. Preserves and marmalades fall under the larger "jam" category, a preserve being a jam containing whole fruits, a marmalade being a jam with both a fruit peel and pulp. Another difference between jelly and jam is that jam usually has a thicker consistency than jelly, and quivers to the touch. Consistency is determined by the proportions and handling of the fruit or juice and the content of acid, sugar, and pectin. Generally, a higher sugar content also produces greater thickness. The monks of St. Joseph's Abbey in Spencer, Massachusetts, will tell you that production rewards the careful, the creative, and the dedicated, making it an ideal spiritual endeavor.

◆

Based on material in the Encyclopedia Americana

Using a secret formula from the thirteenth century shared with them by Pluscarden Abbey in northern Scotland, these Catholic Benedictine monks make and sell Benedictine Balm. This salve is used to soothe and heal cuts, lesions, pimples, sores, and chapped lips. Another product, St. Mary's Duo Cream, is a smooth blend of rich oils that serves a dual purpose: it cleanses and lubricates the skin to make and keep the complexion soft, clear, and youthful. The monks claim it is better than any other skin cream and works wonders on rough, chapped skin and sunburn, too. They provide directions for morning and evening application. Duo Cream has no wax, water, or fillers. The cream contains only petrolatum, mineral oil, zinc oxide, and fragrance. They also make Beeswax Furniture Polish from natural ingredients, which nourishes wood and adds a deep lustre.

The Catholic Benedictine nuns of this priory have developed their own publishing house, St. Bede's Publications, and their recent catalog has over 90 titles available, as well as cassette tapes and CDs, all on spiritual and religious topics. The sisters design, edit, and typeset their own books using laptop computers. When asked how they find their authors, the reply was "They find us."

Among their best-sellers is *The Life of Prayer and the Way to God* by Mother Mary Clare Vincent, O.S.B., who drew on her many years of experience as head of the priory to write a classic guide using the teachings of past and present masters. First printed in 1978, *Finding Grace at the Center,* by Thomas Keating, Basil Pennington, and Thomas Clarke, is still finding an audience after twenty years.

The sisters make rosaries of wooden beads strung on a cord with a metal crucifix. These handcrafted rosaries come in six different colors. There are rooms for retreatants in a separate guesthouse. The monastery property is in a rural area of New England, a perfect place for solitude and quiet.

ST. MARY'S MONASTERY

◆

P.O. Box 345
Petersham, MA 01366
(978) 724-3350/
724-3549 fax

**BALM
SKIN CREAM
FURNITURE POLISH**

ST. SCHOLASTICA PRIORY

◆

P.O. Box 606
Petersham, MA 01366
(800) 247-6553:
book orders
(978) 724-3407/
724-3574 fax
(978) 724-3227:
guesthouse
E-mail: info@stbedes.org
Web site:
www.stbedes.org

**BOOKS
AUDIOS
ROSARIES
RETREATS**

MASSACHUSETTS

THE RECEPTION OF GUESTS

All guests who present themselves are to be welcomed as Christ, who said: "I was a stranger and you welcomed me" (Matt. 25:35). "Proper honor must be shown to all, especially to those who share our faith" (Gal. 6:10), and to pilgrims.

Once guests have been announced, the prioress/abbot and the community are to meet them with all the courtesy of love. First of all, they are to pray together and thus be united in peace, but prayer must always precede the kiss of peace because of the delusions of the devil.

All humility should be shown in addressing a guest on arrival or departure. By a bow of the head or by a complete prostration of the body, Christ is to be adored and welcomed in them. After the guests have been received, they should be invited to pray; then the prioress/abbot or an appointed member will sit with them. The divine law is read to all guests for their instruction, and after that every kindness is shown to them. The prioress/abbot may break her/his fast for the sake of a guest, unless it is a day of special fast which cannot be broken. The members, however, observe the usual fast. The prioress/abbot shall pour water on the hands of the guests, and the prioress/abbot with the entire community shall wash their feet. After the washing they will recite this verse: "God, we have received your mercy in the midst of your temple" (Ps. 48:10).

Great care and concern are to be shown in receiving poor people and pilgrims, because in them more particularly Christ is received; our very awe of the rich guarantees them special respect.

The kitchen for the prioress/abbot and guests ought to be separate, so that guests—and monasteries are never without them—need not disturb the community when they present themselves at unpredictable hours. Each year, two members who can do the work competently are to be assigned to this kitchen. Additional help should be available when needed, so that they can perform this service without grumbling. On the other hand, when the work slackens, they are to go wherever other duties are assigned them. This consideration is not for them alone, but applies to all duties in the monastery; members are to be given help when it is needed, and whenever they are free, they work wherever they are assigned. The guest quarters are to be entrusted to a God-fearing member. Adequate bedding should be available there. The house of God should be in the care of members who will manage it wisely.

No one is to speak or associate with guests unless s/he is bidden; however, if a member meets or sees guests, s/he is to greet them humbly, as we have said. S/he asks for a blessing and continues on her/his way, explaining that s/he is not allowed to speak.

◆

Chapter 53, A Reader's Version of the Rule of Saint Benedict in Inclusive Language

Michigan

This Romanian Orthodox monastery makes pure-wool prayer ropes in black or with smooth, shiny cord in six colors with 33 to 100 knots, and up to 500 knots on special order. Prayer ropes have been used for centuries by Orthodox worshippers as an aid to practicing the "continual prayer of the heart." When a rope is worn on the wrist, it serves as a visual and tactile reminder of the prayer. The monastery has produced two videos: one that shows how to make a prayer rope and another in which Mother Apolinaria demonstrates the preparation of *Prosfora*, the special altar bread used for Holy Communion. One very popular product made here is exquisitely beaded and decorated eggs which come in a variety of patterns and a broad range of colors. The eggs can be decorated to order on special request.

The monastery was founded in 1987 by Mother Benedicta, and its HDM Press has published the story of their spiritual father, and her brother, Archimandrite Roman Braga, who spent five years in a Communist prison and says, "When I went in, I was an intellectual. When I came out, I was a believer." He then became a monk, served five more years in a labor camp, and was eventually ordained. The bilingual *Burning Bush*, the monastery journal, is published three times a year.

The property was purchased mainly with funds raised by the nuns from sewing vestments and altar cloths, which continues to be a significant part of their income today, in addition to painting icons and making beeswax candles. For the last few years a weeklong workshop in Byzantine icon-painting has been offered to participants who are also able to experience monastery life firsthand.

DORMITION OF THE MOTHER OF GOD ORTHODOX MONASTERY

◆

**3389 Rives Eaton Rd.
Rives Junction, MI 49277
(517) 569-2873 phone/fax**

BEADED EGGS

CANDLES

PRAYER ROPES

VESTMENTS

BOOKS

ICONS

CASSETTES OF ROMANIAN CAROLS AND LITURGICAL MUSIC

INSTRUCTIONAL VIDEOS

BYZANTINE PAINTING WORKSHOP

JOURNAL

CELEBRATIONS

RETREATS

The brochure explains: "In iconography, everything is symbolic, not realistic. The iconographer writes icons, they are not painted. Icons are theophanies, not mere decorations. They are snapshots of the divinity, they are the revelations of God's image in humanity. The manner of painting or the art style are not important, but the theocentric character of the icon is. The icon is an archetype of the Divine Mystery and functions as the glass through which we look. The icon becomes transparent, as we look through this window to heaven. Our eyes must not stop at the glass but our entire attention must be directed to what happens beyond. Thus, icons, nature, spiritual persons are only instruments of revelation. Each figure is an expression of the divine in the symphony of the whole. After a few minutes of contemplation, you are filled with joy and inner peace."

Another way the nuns earn money is through speaking engagements at other churches and groups. They have celebrations on Christmas, Easter, and August 15, which is the feast commemorating the Dormition or Assumption of Mary, after which the monastery is named. At this feast 500 to 600 people come for liturgy, lunch, confession, and an unction service for the sick. During the year meals are served after

Saturday and Sunday liturgy featuring Romanian-American food. The large garden provides fresh vegetables in the summer and enough for canning to last the winter. There is also a free two-acre cemetery for Orthodox Christians.

The monastery has retreat accommodations for 14 guests who can enjoy the gardens, an orchard, an outdoor pavilion used for the celebrations, a farmhouse, and the chapel.

HOW TO MAKE ORTHODOX * PROSFORA * (Altar Bread)

Prosfora Seal

ST. MARY OF EGYPT

HOW TO MAKE AN ORTHODOX * PRAYER ROPE *

ICONS

Debate and violent conflict color the history of religious icons. When one looks at beautifully crafted traditional icons, or Brother John Giuliani's Native American icons and prints for the Benedictine Grange, it is hard to imagine the controversy that such objects generated in past centuries. The storm of conflict centers on the Second Commandment, which prohibits the use of graven images (*icon* comes from the Greek *eikon,* meaning "likeness" or "image"). In the Judeo-Christian tradition, concern about idolatry has persisted through the ages. Yet according to Edward N. West, writing on icons in the *Encyclopedia Americana,* the early Christian church saw icons as powerful tools for evangelism. West writes that in this crucial period of mission, icons were "used didactically to inform the picture-minded Greeks and Latins of 'the mighty acts of God.'" But cries of idolatry, voiced most loudly in western Europe, erupted in the eighth and ninth centuries, and the use of icons was outlawed. St. John Damascene responded with three famous Discourses Against the Iconoclasts (726–730), in which he argued for the distinction between *latria,* the expression of worship due to God alone, and *dulia,* the reverence displayed for the saints. The debate, one still strikingly relevant for the modern age, concerns whether material reality is an impediment to awareness of divine reality, or a vehicle for it. St. John Damascene argued fervently that the material can offer a window to (not a substitute for) the divine; for him, this was proven in the radical, creation-affirming Incarnation.

ST. GREGORY'S ABBEY

◆

56500 Abbey Rd.
Three Rivers, MI 49093
(616) 244-5893

SPIRITUAL EXAMINATION
RETREATS

From June through August, men can come for two weeks or longer to live with Episcopal Benedictine monks to examine their lives in a spiritual context, reflect on a religious vocation, or see more clearly the direction of their lives. This is the oldest Episcopal Benedictine monastery in the United States, located on 604 farmland acres in southern Michigan. Men and women retreatants are welcome throughout the year.

UPLAND HILLS ECOLOGICAL AWARENESS CENTER

◆

2575 Indian Lake Rd.
Oxford, MI 48370
(810) 693-1021

PROGRAMS
WORKSHOPS
CELEBRATIONS

Programs and workshops are held here regularly to encourage ecological awareness and develop and promote a responsible role toward the natural world. The berm-designed building on the grounds faces south to use solar energy; it also has a sod roof and a heat-retaining rock wall, and is a good example of energy conservation that works in the Great Lakes bioregion. Solstices and equinoxes are especially celebrated to increase awareness of the natural order of things.

Minnesota

A profound spirituality centered on the cross of Christ and the power of the Holy Spirit has characterized Bethany Fellowship since its founding in 1945. The College of Missions, encompassing 70 acres, provides a three-year training program for missionaries now in 20 foreign countries. The success of Bethany House, which publishes Christian fiction by such writers as Janette Oke, whose current best-seller, *The Tender Years* (84,000 copies sold in the first three months), and Beverly Lewis (*The Shunning* and *The Confession*) enables the college to offer training at minimal fees. The 80 community members and their children live independently on the grounds, but often share the evening meal, along with the students, visiting missionaries, and guests.

BETHANY FELLOWSHIP

◆

6820 Auto Club Rd.
Bloomington, MN 55438
(612) 944-2121/
829-2503 fax

MISSIONARY TRAINING COLLEGE

PUBLISHING

This Russian Orthodox church and monastery celebrates an annual Christmas festival to encourage and maintain the Orthodox traditions. The community of six monks has been in the area for more than ten years. They pray together in the chapel twice a day, and visitors are welcome to attend. Retreats are given on request, and two guest rooms are available. Their gift shop offers icons, crosses, and books. During the year, Russian-language classes are given by two of the monks.

MONASTERY OF THE RESURRECTION OF CHRIST

◆

1201 Hathaway Ln.
Fridley (Minneapolis)
MN 55432
(612) 574-1001

CHRISTMAS FESTIVAL
RUSSIAN CLASSES
RETREATS

PLYMOUTH CHRISTIAN YOUTH CENTER'S WILDERNESS CANOE BASE

◆

**940 Gunflint Trail
Grand Marais, MN 55604
(218) 388-2241 phone/fax
(800) 454-2922**

CANOE TRIPS
YOUTH HOSTEL
WOMEN'S RETREATS
CAMPING

The staff at Wilderness, comprising more than 40 members in the summer and about ten in other seasons, forms an intentional Christian community of thoughtful, supportive, caring people who come from all over the country. The center is affiliated with the Evangelical Lutheran Church in America as a social ministry organization. Experienced guides lead canoe and camping trips for men, women, and children, and youth hostels, some of up to 28 days, and also offer a five-week work/service and trails adventure with an extensive reflection period at the end. The aim is to assist the church in sharing the message of God's love for all humankind and of stewardship for God's creation.

ST. JOHN'S ABBEY

◆

**P.O. Box 7500
Collegeville, MN 56321
(320) 363-2573
(800) 544-1816:
Abbey information
(800) 858-5450:
Liturgical Press**

SEMINARY
PUBLISHING HOUSE
RETREATS

St. John's University shares the 2,400 acres of monastery grounds and was founded by the Benedictine monks who live here. There is a School of Theology that prepares men for the Catholic priesthood. Its Liturgical Press publishes 90 new titles each year and has a backlist of hundreds dealing with major Catholic issues. The university offers courses and workshops for laypeople, and the Spiritual Life Institute has ongoing retreat programs. A notable feature is the Abbey church. Designed by Marcel Breuer and completed in 1961, it is an anomaly or a masterpiece—opinions differ—but it is magnificent, especially in comparison to the "frontier gothic" style of the adjacent structures.

Mississippi

The cloistered nuns at the Carmelite Monastery opened the Carmelite Gift Shop at the request of the local bishop because there is no other Catholic resource within 200 miles. The shop offers Catholic home devotional items such as Christian books for adults and children, Bibles, prayer books, crucifixes, rosary beads, and altar bread. There is also daily mass in the chapel. Since this area is primarily Baptist, it's "mission country" for the Catholics. Alms, "money or goods given to the poor," help the nuns support themselves—when people ask them for prayers they often make a donation in thanks.

CARMELITE MONASTERY

◆

**2155 Terry Rd.
Jackson, MS 39204
(601) 373-1460**

**BOOKS
STATUES
CRUCIFIXES
DEVOTIONAL ITEMS**

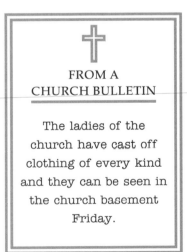

FROM A
CHURCH BULLETIN

The ladies of the church have cast off clothing of every kind and they can be seen in the church basement Friday.

Missouri

ASSUMPTION ABBEY

◆

Rte. 5, Box 1056
Ava, MO 65608
(417) 683-5110/
683-5658 fax

FRUITCAKE

RETREATS

When the Abbey's Trappist monks were planning their bakery in the 1980s, they sought the help of a world-class chef who had once worked for the Duke of Windsor. The monks are grateful for the recipe and production suggestions given by chef Jean-Pierre Auge, who helped them to organize and produce their well-known dark, rich, and traditional Assumption Abbey Fruitcakes. More than 23,000 were made in 1997, and they are sold through Williams-Sonoma, in midwestern specialty stores, by the monastery's mailing list, and at their gift shop. The monks bake from February through Thanksgiving to meet the demand.

The guesthouse has nine single rooms for men and women who share meals in the guest dining room. Many people come who are not Catholic, seeking a private retreat in the Ozark Mountains of southern Missouri where the nights are always cool, surrounded by 3,400 acres of privacy. The monastery was founded in 1950 by monks from New Melleray Abbey near Dubuque, Iowa, on property donated by Mr. and Mrs. Joseph Pierson, who acquired the land from a cooperage firm in St. Louis that had cut down all the white oak to make whiskey barrels. Over the years, the monks have replanted the trees and continue a program of reforestation. There are miles of old logging roads for hiking.

The monastery is 75 miles southeast of Springfield, about 30 miles from the Arkansas border.

In 1874, five Catholic Benedictine sisters left a remote convent in Switzerland by horse-drawn carriage, took a train across France, and embarked on a ship bound for America. One of the sisters kept a journal and reported the ship had no sooner left the harbor than they all fell seasick, admitting: "If the ship were to founder while in the clutches of this illness, one would not move a finger to save herself. Indifference depresses both soul and disposition." By the fourth day, most had recovered, but dreary weather and circumstances continued. One of the crew members, whose job was to shovel coal into the furnace, dropped dead. The body was unceremoniously tossed overboard to the distress of the sisters, "without coffin, song, or sound."

The sisters landed at Hoboken, New Jersey, and stepped onto American soil at high noon. Having loaded their baggage onto a wagon with a team, they were taken at breakneck speed to New York City, which they found grandiose and striking. It reminded one sister of Paris, though she thought Paris might be built to last longer. "Gala vehicles, chaises, omnibuses, horse-drawn street cars, carts drawn by dogs, all ran about in wild confusion, zig-zagging about among each other, and above the heads of all, steam locomotives storm along with great puffs, pants, and snorts. Wagons rattle, whips bang, firemen yell throughout the day." Those of us who currently live in New York City can report that it hasn't changed a bit.

Within a few days they boarded a train to St. Louis for their final destination in northwest Missouri, where they planned to work with German immigrants. The prior of Conception Abbey, who had invited them, had written: "They must not expect too much, and I hope their zeal is greater than their expectations." Zeal could be the only explanation for their success. They were to teach in English, a language none of them knew, using English texts none could read. As they learned English, one sister prayed: "Please God loose my tongue and make me hear right."

By the turn of the century the number of sisters had

BENEDICTINE MONASTERY

◆

**RR 1, Box 101
Clyde, MO 64432
(816) 944-2221/
944-2132 fax
(800) 223-2772**

**ALTAR BREAD
RETREATS**

M
I
S
S
O
U
R
I

◈

grown substantially and they were thriving. The cornerstone of their church was laid in 1901, and the outstanding building was completed in 1911. The Romanesque design was built of Bedford stone, and the interior embellished with a white Carrara marble altar with pillars of onyx and Siena marble. Mosaic murals, elegant statues, and tabernacle doors styled in cloisonné add splendor to the holy space. The monastery is about an hour from St. Joseph, Missouri, and is surrounded by 400 acres of rolling hills and fields. The guesthouse has eight rooms for retreatants.

Since 1910 the sisters have been producing altar breads for parishes and religious communities throughout the United States, and they also ship to Canada, Mexico, Puerto Rico, and Haiti. Their sparkling bright and clean plant is a state-of-the-art operation and has a weekly production of two million hosts, made from 4,000 pounds of flour and 740 gallons of water. This is their primary business, and they are very good at it. Sister Juliana, a very young 92, entered the order in 1920, and explains: "Making altar bread is a very desirable task for our community. We must provide for ourselves, and this work allows us to live in the confines of the monastery. We know that the bread we make will help others in their prayer life. Each of the sisters here spends an hour a day praying in front of the Blessed Sacrament."

CLIFF SPRINGS CAMP

◆

**30330 Jefferies Rd.
Richland, MO 65556
(800) 471-6160, ext. 7**

CAMP

RETREATS

The Episcopal Diocese of West Missouri offers a summer camp for children (grades 1 through 12) from June through August. The rest of the year, adults can camp, use rustic cabins, or live in indoor comfort for retreats in the Ozark wilderness of vistas, woods, and nature.

Catholic Benedictine monks arrived here in the late 1800s and founded a school to train young men for the priesthood, a mission they continue today at Conception Seminary College. The college occupies 30 acres of the 640-acre monastery property in rural northwest Missouri.

The Printery House's 56-page color catalog illustrates a huge selection of high-quality greeting and prayer cards, notes, and outstanding religious art. One of the artists is a Benedictine nun living in Jerusalem who follows the classic Byzantine style of iconography using ancient patterns, applying the colors from dark to light in layers, and abundant gold leaf. The icons are sold unmounted or with a walnut base. The work of other very talented iconographers is shown, dedicated artists who live in monasteries in Minnesota and Oregon. Fine sculpture and crosses are available, made by a Benedictine brother who lived at Conception Abbey until he died at 85. Retreats are at the Abbey Center for Prayer and Ministry.

CONCEPTION ABBEY

◆

**P.O. Box 501
Conception, MO 64433
(816) 944-2211
(800) 322-2737:
The Printery House**

SEMINARY

GREETING AND PRAYER CARDS

RELIGIOUS ART AND JEWELRY

RETREATS

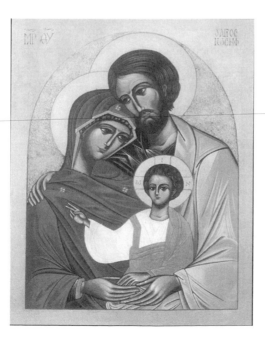

EAST WIND COMMUNITY

◆

HC-3 Box 3370
Tecumseh, MO 65760
(417) 679-4682/
679-4684 fax
(800) 472-0384: crafts
E-mail:
visit@eastwind.org
Web site:
www.crl.com/~eastwind
Web site:
www.well.com/user/
eastwind/bookshelf.html

NUT BUTTERS
HAMMOCKS
SANDALS
MAIL-ORDER BOOKS,
AUDIOS, AND VIDEOS

East Wind Nut Butters are made of natural ingredients without sugar, preservatives, hydrogenated oils, or other stabilizers. The products are certified kosher, and the packaging is recyclable. This worker-owned cooperative makes peanut butter, organic peanut butter, almond butter, cashew butter, and tahini. It also sells roasted peanuts and roasted organic peanuts. The community has published a small cookbook of 30 recipes that use nut butters. Call to find out where their products are sold.

The community is supported entirely from the nut butter business and the sale of Twin Oaks Hammocks and Utopian Sandals. They gross more than $2 million a year. One year they made 17,000 hammocks and 3,000 pairs of rope sandals, and packed 750,000 pounds of nut butters and nuts. An article in the spring 1997 issue of *Communities, Journal of Cooperative Living* gives details of exactly how they make each product.

They are part of the Federation of Egalitarian Communities, a network of groups devoted to building communities rooted in the values of equality, cooperation, and nonviolence. Residents can choose which business they want to participate in depending on their personalities, with hammock-weaving allowing a laid-back work style, while the nut butters demand a very tight schedule. This was one of the first companies to get a loan from the National Co-op Bank in Washington, D.C. They also operate "Community Bookshelf, A Mail Order Resource for Communal and Cooperative Lifestyles" offering selections in print, audio, and video.

NUT BUTTER

East Wind Nut Butters has its own production building, "The Nuthouse," and its own 3,600-square-foot cold-storage warehouse, "Siberia" (it's huge and it's cold). In the mornings, two "roaster" members load and roast from 2,000 to 5,000 pounds of nuts, and mill and pack bulk items: cashew butter into 15-pound containers, peanut butter into 35-pound containers, and boxed, vacuum-packed nuts into 25-pound containers. After lunch, five or six people package jars and/or 5-pound tubs destined for retail shelves. Unlike hammock and sandal production, the work shifts in the nut butters business occur at designated times during the day, and the work is less self-paced and more like an assembly line. The morning roasting shifts require workers with the ability to lift 50-pounds bags of nuts, as well as the ability to operate a serious amount of loud and sometimes ornery equipment. Since a morning's roast can consist of up to $12,000 of raw materials (for example, in making almond butter), it is important that the morning roasters have a high degree of training and attention to detail! In the afternoon a coordinator supervises the packagers, operates the mill, and makes sure the workers are using the right labels and filling the correct containers with accurate amounts of butter. The afternoon coordinator also helps lid, label, box, and/or stack the finished goods.

◆

Anna Young, East Wind Community, reprinted with the permission of
Communities, Journal of Cooperative Living, *"Making a Living" (Spring 1997)*

MARIA FONTE SOLITUDE

◆

**P.O. Box 322
High Ridge, MO 63049
(314) 677-3235**

DESERT EXPERIENCE RETREAT

T hough this retreat is on a ridgetop an hour south of St. Louis, it exemplifies "the starkness of the desert; not its harshness, but an uncompromising refusal to provide distractions." A community of Catholic hermits make it possible for men and women to retreat to single cabins, and provide food and space in a prayerful atmosphere where there is appreciation for solitude and reflection.

SANDHILL FARM

◆

**Rte. 1, Box 155
Rutledge, MO 63563
(660) 883-5543
E-mail: fic@ic.org
cecil@ic.org**

**SORGHUM MOLASSES
HONEY
TEMPEH
HORSERADISH
GARLIC
*COMMUNITIES DIRECTORY***

T his small communal farm in northeast Missouri grows most of its food in large organic gardens and orchards. The foods produced for sale are honey, tempeh, garlic, horseradish, and sorghum molasses. The sorghum brings in about $12,000 a year; the 50 to 70 beehives produce 4,000 pounds of raw honey a year to net about $8,000; the tempeh brings in $1,500, and mustard produces about $1,200, garlic $800, and prepared horseradish $1,000 a year in what they call "community scale business." Visitors who will help (write ahead) during the growing season, and for the sorghum harvest in the fall, are especially welcome.

As members of the Federation of Egalitarian Communities, the farm values equality, nonviolence, and honesty and makes decisions by consensus. Meals, income, vehicles, and recreation are shared by the 8 adults and 3 children who are currently members. They help fund and distribute the *Communities Directory*, the detailed, 440-page guide to cooperative living that we describe in the acknowledgments to this book.

The 100 community members are involved in working in Shepherdsfield's variety of businesses. In the mornings the men drive off in white vans to do window-washing, painting, and wallpapering in nearby Columbia and Jefferson City. The women have an organic bakery with a 200-loaf oven, and sell the products in local farmer's markets and throughout the United States via mail order and health food outlets. Their stone-ground, frozen, whole-wheat waffles are very popular, and they recently began a dog-grooming and boarding kennel.

They operate a school for residents and church members, and pride themselves on their musical programs for the children. Community mealtime is used as a time of nurturing, with songs, prayer, reflective music, and a spiritual or scriptural teaching. They try to live as the early Christians did, "sharing all things in common," and accepting Jesus Christ as the Way, the Truth, and the Life. They have what they call a "literature mission," which publishes various pamphlets and brochures from Christian writings in an effort to reach "those enmeshed in mysticism and New Age thought."

SHEPHERDSFIELD

◆

**777 Shepherdsfield Rd.
Fulton, MO 65251
(573) 642-1439**

ORGANIC BAKERY

WALLPAPERING AND
PAINTING

WINDOW-WASHING

PRINTING

PUBLISHING

DOG GROOMING AND
BOARDING

OUR BREAD

These products are made from the finest organic, fresh grains and flour. Sweetened with Missouri honey and/or molasses or dates (plus deliciously sweet raisins in our Cinnamon/Raisin Bread). You will find no added colorings, preservatives, synthetic vitamins, or fiber. Our rye and whole wheat flours are stone ground on our premises (except for our potato roll wheat flour) and little time is lost before they are mixed and baked into our tasty, award-winning breads in our state-inspected and approved modern, clean kitchen facilities. Clear, cold, sparkling, absolutely delicious water from our 490-foot tested deep well has been one of God's blessings to us and a vital ingredient in our baked goods. Come visit us at our country store. You may call about our hours. It is our sincere pleasure to serve you.

◆

Shepherdsfield Country Store & Bakery, Fulton, Missouri; (573) 642-1439

Montana

◆——————◆——————◆

URSULINE RETREAT CENTER

◆

2300 Central Ave.
Great Falls, MT 59401
(406) 452-8585

DAY CARE

CARE FOR THE ELDERLY

HUNGER AND HOMELESSNESS
PROJECT

MUSEUM

ECUMENICAL RETREATS

The mission of the Ursuline Center is to meet the ever-changing needs of the people of Montana by providing a setting and an atmosphere for spiritual and intellectual growth. In their early days in Montana, the Ursuline sisters educated and cared for the children of many local Native American tribes.

This center was opened in 1912 as a boarding school for girls and a day school for boys. Since its current aim is to meet the needs of the community, it provides day care for local children, care for the elderly, runs a hunger and homelessness project, and offers the center to ecumenical groups for retreats. Catholics, Lutherans, Ba'his and many others feel welcome to hold their events here. The gymnasium provides space for such organizations as the Great Falls dog-training club and the Dudes and Dolls Square Dance group. "We're self-sufficient," says the director, "although some months it's nip and tuck."

Designed in the Gothic Revival style by the architect George Shanley, the four-story, richly patterned brick and terra-cotta structure, complete with a five-story tower, crenellated parapets, and eight winged gargoyles, is listed in the National Register of Historic Places. The chapel is filled with the work of their own Sister Raphael, who taught here for fifty years, and includes St. Ursula and her band of virgins and founder St. Angela Merici's vision of young women ascending the ladder to heaven.

The sisters urge guests to visit their museum to see a treasury of murals, Indian relics, antiques, musical instruments, and other artifacts from over 100 years of their history in Montana.

Nebraska

These Benedictine monks have been in Nebraska since 1935 and offer the Schuyler Book Series through their publishing house, BMH Publications. One of their most popular titles, *The Challenge of Midlife* by Anselm Gruen, examines the critical period of midlife as an opportunity to grow spiritually, addressing midlife crisis from a Jungian viewpoint and that of the mystic Tauler. The giftshop offers card assortments, one featuring words of Mother Teresa, and statues, medals, and rosaries. The monks are part of the Ottilien Congregation of Benedictines, which is active in missionary work worldwide. The retreat and guesthouse, St. Benedict Center, was completed in 1997 and welcomes people of all Christian faiths.

BENEDICTINE MISSION HOUSE

◆

**P.O. Box 528
RR 1
Schuyler, NE 68661
(402) 352-2177/
352-2176 fax
(402) 352-8819/8884 fax:
guest and retreat house**

BOOK PUBLISHING
RETREATS

✝

FROM A
CHURCH BULLETIN

Tuesday at 4 P.M.
there will be an ice
cream social. All ladies
giving milk will please
come early.

Nevada

◆ ◆ ◆

WELLSPRING RETREAT HOUSE

◆

P.O. Box 60818
Boulder City, NV 89006
(702) 293-4988

GREETING CARDS
CROCHETED AND KNITTED
GOODS
PAINTINGS
PLAQUES
RETREATS

The Sisters of Charity run the Wellspring Retreat House in Boulder City, Nevada, located on a hill overlooking Lake Mead. They are highly motivated to make a large variety of crafts, because the earnings from the sales of these items go into a special "airplane ticket fund." Whenever they have enough money saved to buy their tickets, they fly to England to visit their motherhouse in Plimpton's Morris, near Plymouth.

Each of these crafts is a specialty or hobby of a different sister. One loves wildflowers and gathers, presses, and dries them to make charming note cards and cards for special occasions. Some have hand-inscribed verses, such as "A man who pulls on the oars doesn't have time to rock the boat," or the parents' creed: "We want you to feel free to grow and change and to follow your life's path, knowing that we love you for who you are and what you are," or "Good character is like good soup, it is made at home." Some of the sisters crochet or knit; others are artists who do paintings or frame plaques with verses on them. But the crafts are just a sideline, as the sisters are fully engaged in running their retreat house, which houses up to 40 people.

New Hampshire

◆――◆――◆

Numerous books and booklets dealing with Buddhist meditation at all levels, as well as art and poetry, are for sale here. The story of Sangarakshita, an Englishman born in the 1930s, is a fascinating tale of a man who founded a successful movement dedicated to communicating Buddhist spiritual traditions to Western culture. In his book *A Guide to the Buddhist Path,* he sorts fact from myth, essence from cultural accident, and draws a reliable map of the Buddhist path anyone can follow. There are more than 150 lectures available of Sangarakshita on tape. Meditation benches, cushions, and mats are made by a member

of the sangha, and incense, pictures, and postcards are for sale. Meditation instruction and retreats are ongoing.

ARYALOKA BUDDHIST CENTER

◆

14 Heartwood Circle
Newmarket, NH 03857
(603) 659-5456
(800) 303-5728 orders
E-mail:
aryaloka@aol.com

BOOKS
TAPES
BUDDHIST SUPPLIES
INSTRUCTION
RETREATS

An annual festival, "The Faire," is held the Sunday after Labor Day to celebrate the history of this New England area, which dates back to 1738, when ten acres of this hilltop were designated as the town center or common. The property is now a retreat center managed by Catholic Carmelites who give programs and retreats throughout the year.

THE COMMON

◆

182 Old Street Rd.
Peterborough, NH 03458
(603) 924-6060

FESTIVAL
PROGRAMS
RETREATS

New Jersey

ST. MARY'S ABBEY–DELBARTON

◆

**230 Mendham Rd.
Morristown, NJ 07960
(973) 538-3231**

BOYS' PREP SCHOOL

BOOKS AND CARDS

RETREATS

Catholic Benedictine monks acquired this 400-acre estate in the 1920s and farmed it until the local bishop asked them to start a boys' prep school, which they did in 1939. From the original 12 students, it has become a distinguished Catholic prep school (grades 7–12) with an enrollment close to 500. The farmland has been turned into playing fields for soccer, football, and baseball as the monks adjusted to the needs of a growing society. Their gift shop has books, cards, and religious articles, and retreats are held periodically.

ST. PAUL'S ABBEY

◆

**Newton, NJ 07860
(973) 383-2470/383-5782
fax: monastery
(973) 383-0660:
retreat house**

CHRISTMAS TREES

TREE TRANSPLANTS AND SEEDLINGS

RETREATS

These Catholic Benedictine monks raise Christmas trees on their 500 acres and plant thousands of seedlings to replace the ones sold at the end of each year. From December 1 through December 23, customers can choose and cut their own Christmas trees. During the spring and fall, a limited number of transplants, from 18 inches to 6 feet, are available for purchase. The gift shop sells religious articles and books.

The monks came here in 1924 from Bavaria. They are part of the St. Ottilien branch of Benedictines, and are active in mission work throughout the world. They have established missions in Africa, South America, and the Far East. There are ongoing retreat programs at the Queen of Peace Retreat House.

New Mexico

◆———◆———◆

Father Richard Rohr, a Franciscan priest, founded the center in the 1980s to establish a place where laypeople could integrate their spirituality with active, compassionate service. There is a two-to-six-week program for individuals to live communally in Tepeyac, a former motherhouse of the Franciscan province, and learn to develop contemplation with action. The program offers a renewed dimension of life, and challenges participants to live their faith. Rohr, a well-known writer and speaker, has many tapes that are wise and provocative. His *Images of Jesus* talks about how "exclusive religion" looks at Jesus as a totem or mascot while "inclusive Christianity" sees Jesus more as a way, a door, a vine. These images, he explains, make Christianity a way of living rather than a set of rules: Watch how they walk, not how they talk. CAC puts out a newsletter, *Radical Grace*, and sponsors programs and retreats regularly.

CENTER FOR ACTION AND CONTEMPLATION

◆

P.O. Box 12464
Albuquerque, NM 87195
(505) 242-9588/242-9518
fax: information

(505) 242-1846:
Tepeyac guesthouse

(800) 333-7373:
cassette catalog

INSTRUCTION

TAPES

NEWSLETTER

RETREATS

GHOST RANCH

◆

HC 77, Box 11
Abiquiu, NM 87510
(505) 685-4333

SEMINARS
WORKSHOPS
COURSES
BOOKS
CARDS
RETREATS

Ghost Ranch is 21,000 acres of magnificent high desert owned by the Presbyterian Church, which operates it as an education center and makes it available for retreats and conferences. Throughout the year, seminars and workshops are held on paleontology, sociology, theology, history, literature, music, psychology, environmental concerns, solar housing, and land-use programs. Instruction and classes are given in pottery, photography, geology, and archeology. This area was a swamp 250 million years ago, and the ranch is designated a Registered National Landmark. Attracted by the stark beauty of the desert and the quality of the light, the artist Georgia O'Keeffe lived nearby for many years painting the cliffs and sky, bones, trees, and mountains. Books and cards are available from the gift shop. Retreatants are welcome.

GLORIETA BAPTIST CONFERENCE CENTER

◆

P.O. Box 8
Glorieta, NM 87535
(505) 757-6161/
757-6149 fax

INSTRUCTION
PROGRAMS
RETREATS

A full range of programs and instruction is available year-round in Bible study, church music, Sunday-school teaching, and missionary work. This is a church leadership training center for every phase of Baptist life and work, and a first-rate facility of more than 150 buildings that can accommodate 2,700 visitors, some for retreats. Located at 7,500 feet in the Sangre de Cristo Mountains, the 2,500 acres of the center are surrounded by the 380,000-acre Santa Fe National Forest.

Lama was founded in the 1960s as an ecumenical spiritual community by a group of hippie activists who followed the teachings of the Indian guru Meher Baba. They were aided and encouraged by several other teachers such as Pir Vilayat Khan, Ram Dass, and Sam Lewis (Sufi Sam), who commingled their visions to establish a place that would serve to draw all religions together to celebrate one truth . . . many paths but one mountain. Cottage industries were created by the resourceful people who live here year-round. They design and print colorful prayer flags, banners, and T-shirts that reflect and embody new waves of spirituality. Lama is located at 8,600 feet on the side of Lama Mountain, a wilderness site facing the broad expanse of the Rio Grande gorge and the mountains beyond. Workshops and retreats are given during the summer. Demonstrating the ecumenical nature of the place, Sufis, Hindus, Roman Catholics, and people of many other spiritual paths have benefited from being here. A devastating forest fire in May 1996 consumed 17 of the 23 buildings, and Lama is now in the challenging process of rebuilding, restoring, and reemerging. They welcome all help, in the form of donations, materials, resources, and inspired spirits who would like to help in this major rebirth.

LAMA FOUNDATION

◆

P.O. Box 240
San Cristobal, NM 87564
(505) 586-1269
E-mail: 76375.2726
@compuserve.com

PRAYER FLAGS
BANNERS
T-SHIRTS
PROGRAMS
RETREATS

(JACK KELLY)

(JACK KELLY)

PRAYER FLAGS

As one of its cottage industries, the Lama Foundation in San Cristobal, New Mexico, makes silk-screened prayer flags. Tibetan in origin, the flags are produced now for use by members of all faith traditions. According to a Lama Foundation brochure, "In Tibetan tradition, flags containing sacred images and phrases are flown in the thousands, offering with each gust of wind, prayers for the peace and happiness of all beings. We've taken this tradition and expanded it to embrace all traditions and walks of life." With just a hasty glance through their catalog, one can find prayer flags that depict Allah, the Virgin Mary, or the Buddha, as well as Hindu, Taoist, Jewish, and Native American symbols. One flag, entitled "Meeting of the Ways," incorporates Taoist, Hindu, Buddhist, Zoroastrian, Jewish, Christian, Sufi, and Sikh symbols. A devastating fire ripped through the Lama Foundation community in 1996, destroying Lama's printing screens, but, incredibly, production capability has been almost entirely restored.

◆

For a Lama Foundation catalog, call (505) 586-1269 between 10:00 a.m. and noon, Mountain Time.

MONASTERY OF CHRIST IN THE DESERT

◆

**P.O. Box 270
Abiquiu, NM 87510
(505) 470-4515
(201) 784-8488:
video orders**

**VIDEO
AUDIO
DESERT EXPERIENCE
RETREATS**

The video *Seeking God: The Way of the Monk* is the story of the monk's life at this remote desert community, 12 miles down an unpaved road difficult to traverse, perhaps a metaphor for life's journey to discover peace and tranquillity. Also available is a CD or cassette of Gregorian chant, *Monastic Chants in the High Desert,* sung by the monks here. Private retreats are available for those seeking a desert experience in a remote setting with a prayerful atmosphere where life is simple, organized around the canonical hours, and surrounded by the spectacular beauty of the New Mexican desert.

The distinguishing mark of this Catholic Benedictine monastery is that monastic men and women live here together as one community, observing poverty, stability, and chastity. It has a wide reputation for Charismatic renewal. Twice a year they give month-long training sessions for the School for Charismatic Spiritual Directors, where people are trained to serve their home communities in this dynamic spirituality. Spiritual books and cards are available, as well as rooms for retreatants.

**PECOS
BENEDICTINE
MONASTERY**

◆

**Pecos, NM 87522
(505) 757-6415**

**INSTRUCTION
SPIRITUAL BOOKS
CARDS
RETREATS**

BAKERIES

Visiting a community on baking day can provide a series of sensual delights: smelling and seeing the finished products, and then sampling each variety. Many communities specialize in baked goods ranging from basic breads to cheesecake, pies, and cookies; the fruitcake, thanks to some monasteries, is enjoying a rebirth of appreciation. It's fascinating to discover so many different places in various parts of the country that consistently satisfy their customers with an assortment of choices.

The Abbey of the Genesee, a Trappist monastery in Piffard, New York, is the home of Monk's Bread, made in white, whole wheat, sunflower, and more, and can be found on store shelves in the Northeast. The Greyston Bakery, part of a Buddhist community in Yonkers, New York, creates high-quality cakes, pies, tarts, cookies, and brownies. The New Skete Communities of Cambridge, New York, Orthodox Catholic monks and sisters, sell first-rate cheesecakes. Fruitcake is the specialty of the Holy Cross Abbey in Berryville, Virginia, the Abbey of Gethsemani in Kentucky, Corpus Christi Abbey in Sandia, Texas, and Assumption Abbey of Ava, Missouri. St. Benedict's Monastery of Snowmass, Colorado, creates cookies, and on the West Coast, Our Lady of Guadalupe Trappist Abbey in Lafayette, Oregon, makes and sells fruitcake, nut cake, and biscotti.

◆

Abbey of the Genesee (716) 243-2220, Greyston Bakery (914) 375-1514, New Skete Communities (518) 677-3928, Holy Cross Abbey (540) 955-3124, Abbey of Gethsemani (502) 549-3117, Corpus Christi (512) 547-3257, Assumption Abbey (417) 683-5110, Our Lady of Guadalupe Trappist Abbey (800) 294-0105.

New York

ABBEY OF THE GENESEE

◆

3258 River Rd.
Piffard, NY 14533
(716) 243-2220
E-mail: abbeygen
@frontier.net

BREAD
FRUITCAKES
RETREATS

This is the home of the famous Monk's Bread, which is widely distributed in the Northeast. When Trappist monks came here from Gethsemani, Kentucky, in the 1950s to farm land that had been given them, the cook, an ex–navy chef, made such good bread that visitors wanted to take some home. So a business was started and evolved into a highly mechanized bakery, which now produces thousands of loaves weekly, yet enables the monks to maintain their spiritual lives. They also make fruitcakes in a variety of flavors, including an outstanding butterscotch. There are guest rooms for retreatants.

ADIRONDACK HERBS

◆

Fish House Rd.
Galway, NY 12074
(518) 883-3453

MEDICINAL HERBS
HERBAL TEA BAGS
WOOD-FIRED WATER
HEATERS

Made up of two farms 30 miles apart, this community seems to be attempting to create its own vision of Utopia. People can start their own business, or work in one of the cooperative ventures, such as growing medicinal herbs for sale to health-food stores, or producing herbal tea bags. They hope to open their own health-food store and an electronics repair shop. The wood-fired water heaters they make for themselves are not yet for sale. In the *Communities Directory* they write: "We have a good library, piano, sailboats, windsurfer . . . are very interested in bees, flywheels, alternative energy vehicles, small airships, aquaculture . . . and prefer using dumped or surplus material, such as paper, envelopes, lumber, steel, bananas with brown spots. We'd rather pick firewood at the town dump than cut down trees. We respect all religions/spiritual paths, and propose herbal medicine as an adjunct rather than an alternative to regular medicine."

One of seven North American communities that seek to create a renewed village life and to establish social forms of human interdependence between disabled and nondisabled people. Their approach is a nondenominational Christian way of life based on Rudolf Steiner's anthroposophy and the innovative therapeutic work of Karl Koenig, M.D. The 600-acre village in Copake is made up of over two hundred people, half of whom are mentally disabled adults. The only requirement is a dedication to maintain active interest, care, and concern for one's fellows.

Support comes mainly from the fees residents pay, donations, income from the gift shop, crafts made by community members, baked goods, and the famous "Anne Ratner Concert Series" where musicians such as Richard Goode, André Watts, and Ani and Ida Kavafian donate their music for private evening recitals and buffets in the New York apartment of a Camphill supporter. A member of Triform, another one of their communities in Hudson, New York, said, "Our farm, garden, bake shop, and weavery provide dignified and meaningful work for our handicapped friends who live here. The gardens they tend supply food that we eat, the bakery our own bread and granola. We do sell a little surplus organic meat from our beef cattle, and a few of our weavery products, but it is not a significant source of our income like it is at Camphill."

CAMPHILL VILLAGE USA

◆

**Camphill Rd.
Copake, NY 12516
(518) 329-7924/329-4511
(gift shop, after 2:30 P.M.)**

**CONCERTS
CRAFTS
BAKERY
BOOKBINDING
POTTERY
WEAVING
SUMMER FESTIVAL**

CHAUTAUQUA INSTITUTION

◆

P.O. Box 28
Chautauqua, NY 14722
(800) 836-ARTS

SUMMER CULTURAL FESTIVAL
LECTURES
PROGRAMS
WORKSHOPS
BOOK CLUB

The Chautauqua program started in the 1870s as a summer camp held on the shores of Lake Chautauqua to instruct Sunday-school teachers in organization, management, and teaching methods. Today there is a nine-week summer schedule from mid-June until the end of August.

The Chautauqua Institution holds daily prayer services and lectures, provides world-class instructors in art, music, dance, and writing, and holds nightly classical and popular concerts given by well known artists. A typical nine-week season might include weekly topics such as "The Politics of the Environment" with talks by John Sawhill, president of the Nature Conservancy; or "Voices of the African-American Community" with Calvin O. Butts III as one of the featured speakers; or a week on "The Mystery of Good and Evil" with Huston Smith, author of *The World's Religions.* Evening programs include the Chautauqua Symphony Orchestra, featuring performers from major orchestras around the world, or the Chautauqua Ballet Company led by Jean-Pierre Bonnefoux. Willie Nelson and Kenny Rogers have also performed here.

Many Christian denominations maintain houses here and offer rooms at reasonable rates for those who would like to take advantage of the many spiritual opportunities available. The Chautauqua Book Club and bookstore select and sell titles that are in keeping with espoused values, and the gift shop has high-quality memorabilia, including cards and art by local artists.

Twenty-three adults and 14 children live in this land-trust cooperative community. There are 12 owner-built solar homes on the land, and over 20 years the Cooperative's members have come to agreement on 11 core ideals that define and guide the community, including land stewardship and trust, consensus decision making, voluntary simplicity, welcoming diversity, and community participation. Members support themselves with jobs outside the community, and each contributes $60 a month. The late-June Strawberry Festival and the August Summer Gathering are fund-raisers and happy social events for community members and those interested in learning more.

Sixty adults and children have joined together in a "covenant of love with others" to form this community. They build and remodel homes and small businesses through Winterset Builders, although they prefer to use these skills within their own community. All the members also enjoy working together in the big garden that helps feed the community.

They have opened the Common Sense Store, which sells products made by sister communities. A bakery and cafe features great chocolate-chip cookies, muffins, and pies. They also make soaps, shampoos, vinegars, and dressings.

The Common Blacksmith forge creates beautiful lamps, candleholders, chandeliers, coatracks, coffee tables, and fireplace implements. Each of these items is shown in the lovely catalog. (Common Blacksmith, P.O. Box 42, Lakeview, NY 14085, [716] 627-1120). As in many communities, this craft grew out of the skills of one member, now no longer with the community, who taught others what he knew.

COMMON PLACE LAND COOPERATIVE

◆

**4211 Rte. 13
Truxton, NY 13158
(607) 842-6849 or
842-6858**

FESTIVALS

COMMUNITY IN BUFFALO NEW SOCIAL ORDER IN MESSIAH

◆

**2051 North Creek Rd.
Lakeview, NY 14085
(716) 627-2098 or
649-4967/627-1120 fax**

**IRONWORK
SOAPS
SHAMPOOS
VINEGARS
DRESSINGS
BAKERY/CAFÉ
BUILDING AND REMODELING
HOMES**

N
E
W

Y
O
R
K

◈

 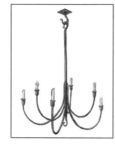 

Common Blacksmith

BEEKEEPING

Honeybees form only one genus of the bee species, but they are the most economically productive type of bee. According to Miller's Honey Company, a colony of honeybees makes between 60 and 100 pounds of honey per year. In a typical hive, one finds one queen bee, perhaps thousands of worker bees, and hundreds of drones. Laying up to 2,000 eggs in a day, the queen bee never leaves the hive. The worker bees, sterile females, live up to their name—it takes 154 trips between nectar source and hive to yield one teaspoon of honey. The drones, which are males, utterly incapable of stinging or even of feeding themselves, exist only to mate with the queen. (If Saint Augustine ever looked for a natural model to support his theories about the position of women within a society, he surely did not look to bees.) Humans are not the only ones who enjoy the product of these bees' tireless labor; for bears and badgers, honey is one of the major food groups.

The Seva Foundation (Berkeley, California), through its Gifts of Service program, supports beekeeping projects in Chiapas, Mexico. According to Seva, "Beekeeping supports a community . . . in several ways: honey, a by-product, is exported to Europe; coffee and corn plants are pollinated by the bees; and the beeswax is used in making candles."

Of the many enterprises undertaken by spiritual communities, beekeeping can perhaps best uphold a claim to be truly sanctified. In Saint Ambrosius, a fourth-century bishop of Milano, beekeeping finds its very own patron saint.

◆

Visit Miller's Honey Company at www.millershoney.com *and find out more about all the different types of bees at* www.ifi.unit.no/~janne/bees.html.

This magnificent Zen temple was completed in 1976 to aid the Zen Studies Society in bringing Zen Buddhism to the West, and gives students an opportunity for intensive training in a traditional environment. Training programs, classes, and sittings are scheduled throughout the year. A very good selection of Zen Buddhist books is available and described in a catalog. In a 1996 release on *Endless Vow: The Zen Path of Soen Nakagawa*, Eido Roshi, the founder of Dai Bosatsu, described Soen as "hard to grab . . . he was the greatest koan of my life. He had many faces; he was a simple monk, a crazy-wisdom Zen master, a genius in the arts, a spiritually realized being of the highest attainment, a dedicated student of the Dharma, a master manipulator, a troubled human being, a skillful politician, a tactful diplomat, a stupendous host, an inspired guest."

Dai Bosatsu Zendo has Buddhist supplies for sitting: cushions, benches, encouragement sticks, robes, incense. There are audiotapes of Diamond Sutra chanting and other services here, and a video of DBZ: *Portrait of an American Rinzai Zen Monastery.*

DAI BOSATSU ZENDO

◆

**HCR 1, Box 171
Livingston Manor
NY 12758
(914) 439-4566
(10:00 A.M.–noon,
2:00–4:00 P.M.)/
439-3119 fax**

**INSTRUCTION
BOOKS
BUDDHIST SUPPLIES
AUDIOS
VIDEO**

EMMAUS COMMUNITY OF THE HOMELESS

◆

**2027 Lexington Ave.
P.O. Box 1177
New York, NY 10035
(212) 410-6006**

**W. E. B. DU BOIS ROOM
BED-AND-BREAKFAST**

More than 30 years ago, Father David Kirk founded Emmaus House to serve the "poorest of the poor" in Harlem. It continues to this day, a community of homeless and poor people who build new lives while helping each other. Father David recently wrote a letter to the editor of *The New York Times:* "We want to invite all those funders who slept in the Lincoln Bedroom in the White House to come sleep in our W. E. B. Du Bois Room, which was once a place for slavery to drugs and prostitution and is now a place of hope. Visit our community of those recovering from homelessness and addiction; enjoy a delicious home-cooked meal in our dining room; listen to our talented musicians and poets. There is no charge, but if you are moved to put a check in our hands as you say good-bye, it will be gratefully accepted and put to good use."

GANAS

◆

**135 Corson Ave.
Staten Island, NY 10301
(718) 720-5378 or
981-7365/448-6842 fax
E-mail: ganas@well.com
Web site:
www.well.com
/~ganas**

**FOUR RETAIL STORES THAT
RESTORE, REPACKAGE,
AND RECYCLE**

RETREAT CENTER

This nonreligious community of 70 adults has remodeled seven houses in Staten Island to create a comfortable, spacious setting for its autonomous cooperative community. Its projects include the innovative use of video and other feedback learning devices for learning how to learn. Community members work at jobs in New York and contribute financially to the community, or pay their way by working in the four large retail stores called Every Thing Goes that restore, repackage, and recycle furniture, clothing, household goods, books, records, artwork, and crafts. Their idea is to do it happily, beautifully, efficiently, inexpensively, and profitably for everyone.

A new retreat and conference center in the Catskills, G.R.O.W. II in Parksville, New York, which was purchased with the profits from their stores, will offer a variety of programs for retreatants and is available for rent by groups of up to 150. The purpose of the community is to reduce the waste of human resources by learning how to restore minds to creative thinking, hearts to joyful loving, and hands to productive work.

EVERY THING GOES STORES

The Ganas Community in Staten Island, New York, has four stores that carry literally everything, as the stores' name indicates. Here are some unusual examples:

Mardi Gras headdresses

Camel saddles

African spears/masks

Player pianos

Elephant stands

Antique wine presses

Fondue sets

Vintage hats

Exotic Caribbean Carnival headdresses

Clown costumes

Vintage stockings

Handmade shawls and ponchos

Fur collars and muffs

Parachutes

Bowling balls

American flags, all sizes

Ganas, in Spanish, means to want something in a compelling manner, to be motivated to act. This was clearly illustrated during our visit. We were picked up at the Staten Island ferry, after a quick trip across the harbor, and whisked to all four Every Thing Goes stores. Each store was a model of organization, filled with fabulous things, all displayed with flair: thousands of pieces of great costume jewelry, neatly arranged for easy selection; housewares galore, from toasters to fine china, from blenders to crystal, and at such low prices we were tempted to buy everything. The clothing store belonged in a fashion magazine! Straw hats wound with beautiful scarves topped colorful outfits; exotic headpieces from stage productions were on walls and shelves; and lots of great clothing for women, men, and children was arranged for easy access.

The furniture store was a beehive of activity, with community members sanding, refinishing, and polishing items as diverse as elegant birdcages hanging from the ceiling, and dining room tables and chairs. Seeing all these discarded items turned into treasures was exhilarating. This community's gift of renewing and recycling is an extraordinary model for us all.

GREYSTON FOUNDATION

◆

**21 Park Ave.
Yonkers, NY 10703
(914) 376-3900/
376-1333 fax
(800) BUY-CAKE
(914) 375-2515/375-1514
fax: bakery**

BAKED GOODS

HOUSING AND HEALTH CARE FOR THOSE WITH HIV/AIDS

APARTMENTS FOR HOMELESS FAMILIES

The Greyston Bakery is a premier baker of high-quality cakes, pies, tarts, cookies, and brownies. The pecan tart made with a shortbread crust is just one of their outstanding creations, as is the prize-winning cheesecake. Founded by American-born Zen abbot Bernie Glassman in 1982, the bakery has given work opportunity to the poor, and is a major example of Buddhist spirituality responding to the needs of society. Roshi Glassman, in his recent book Instructions to the Cook, uses the metaphor of cooking to write about faith, doubt, right livelihood, social service, and all the things that make up a good life. It challenges those who see practicing Zen as merely a refuge from the messiness of society.

The foundation also runs Issan House, the Maitri Day Program, an extraordinary housing and health-care program for those living with HIV/AIDS, and the Greyston Family Inn for formerly homeless families. Glassman is now living in Santa Fe, New Mexico, devoting himself full-time to his latest project, the Zen Peacemaker Order, which he founded with his late wife, Sensei Jishu Holmes.

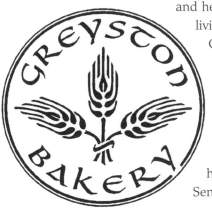

HOLY CROSS MONASTERY

◆

**P.O. Box 99, Rte. 9W
West Park, NY 12493
(914) 384-6660/
384-6031 fax
E-mail:
holycross@idsi.net**

**BOOKS
AUDIOS
VIDEOS
INCENSE
INSTRUCTION
WORKSHOPS
RETREATS**

These Episcopal Benedictine monks of the Order of the Holy Cross have their own publishing list that includes titles by Bonnell Spencer, OHC, whose latest work, *Paul According to Paul,* recognizes discrepancies between the Apostle Paul's life in the book of Acts and what Paul described in his letters. They also produce video- and audiotapes of Gregorian chanting done here at daily prayer services, and a CD of one of the monks playing the Celtic harp. The Monk's Cell Gift Shop has a wide selection of spiritual books and gifts, including Holy Cross Incense, a high-quality liturgical incense made from a blend of frankincense and myrrh with balsam and perfumed oils.

Each spring the monks offer a weeklong Benedictine Experience when individuals share the life of the monastic community in prayer, work, guided meditation, and daily discussions and reflection. Workshops and retreats are scheduled regularly. The monastery is on 26 secluded acres along the Hudson River, about an hour north of New York City.

HOLY CROSS
INCENSE

N
E
W

Y
O
R
K

◈

EXCERPTS FROM A JOURNAL

One guest at Holy Cross Monastery shared the following journal entries made during recent visits:

Left home at 5:00 A.M. Coming down the monastery driveway, the Hudson shimmered a breathtaking sunrise orange on massive crinkled ice floes. Great breakfast of hot oatmeal, raisins, bananas, toast, and tea. It seems odd, at first, to see your friends, the monks, after several months' absence, and have to remain silent. But in the silence there are many profound greetings, real heart-to-heart greetings.

It is completely silent in this large, comfortable living room/library . . . so many of the great religious classics. Just read this from Carlo Carretto, "If you asked me how God has revealed himself to me, I should reply, He reveals himself as Newness." God is eternally new. He never repeats Himself. Oh, to spend a month in this library.

The Eucharist is over. I'm sitting here in the cloister just looking at the magnificent oak tree that was here when Henry Hudson sailed up the river. The tree seems to have great strength, great peace. It has humbly accepted all that has come to it in the hundreds of years since it appeared from the earth. I think I have just been given a message.

A priest, his wife, and daughter dropped in today before lunch. Great conversations at lunch. There's a light but steady trickle of fascinating people coming here from literally all parts of the world. (God's voice in various disguises!)

Been thinking about what Br. Timothy said at the beginning of this retreat. "You can go to all five services if you like, or to none. In the next two days, I invite you to simply rest in God's arms."

◆

Mundi Medicina, *The Newsletter of Holy Cross Monastery, October 1996*

Located not far from historic Cooperstown, this monastery/farm on 150 acres is just beginning its wool and meat business with 12 ewes and a ram, 10 goat does and a buck. The annual catalog, mailed just before Lent, lists an extensive selection of Orthodox Christian cards for Christmas, Easter, birthdays, and baptisms, including cards of the saints and illuminated prayers with beautiful calligraphy by Mother Raphaela. The monastery has been fortunate enough to acquire a custom design for gorgeous baptismal gowns, bonnets, and towels and will begin to sell these in 1999.

On the second weekend in October the archbishop comes for the annual pilgrimage and conducts liturgy and healing followed by supper for all. Myrrhbearers Sunday, the monastery feast day, is always the second Sunday after Easter. Guest rooms are available for five.

HOLY MYRRHBEARERS MONASTERY

◆

**144 Bert Washburn Rd.
Otego, NY 13825
(607) 432-3179/
432-0794 fax
E-mail:
otegonuns@aol.com
Web site:
www.oca.org/OCA/pim/
oca-st-otechm.html**

**BAPTISMAL GOWNS,
BONNETS, AND TOWELS**

ORTHODOX CARDS

PRAYER BOOKS

CHURCH SUPPLIES

LAMBS

GOATS

CELEBRATIONS

GUEST ROOMS

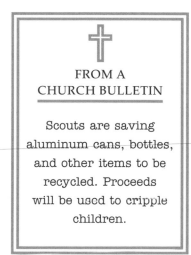

FROM A CHURCH BULLETIN

Scouts are saving aluminum cans, bottles, and other items to be recycled. Proceeds will be used to cripple children.

MONASTERY OF BETHLEHEM

◆

**Grooville Rd., Box 258
Livingston Manor
NY 12758
(914) 439-4300/
439-3069 fax**

CHINAWARE
ICONS
FINE ART MEDALS
DOLOMITE ART
RETREATS

The Monastic Family of Bethlehem and of the Assumption of the Virgin Mary creates exquisite tea and coffee sets, plates, vases, and serving pieces from a pure, fine-textured clay with high kaolin content. The chinaware is fired at a high temperature to produce dinnerware of great strength, hardness, clarity, and beauty. The decorations are from ancient motifs, painted by hand, and every piece is color-fast and dish-washer safe. The catalog resembles a Sotheby's auction presentation or that of a museum gift shop. The sisters, who live contemplative lives in this quiet section of the Catskill Mountains, believe that through their artwork they convey something of God's beauty and truth. They also sell framed icons reproduced on wood; gold, silver, and enamel medals of the faces of Christ and mother Mary; and religious figures, statues, and reliefs in dolomite. There are a few rooms for retreatants who seek silence and solitude.

(JACK KELLY)

High in the Allegheny hills of western New York, Mount Irenaeus, a Franciscan mountain retreat associated with St. Bonaventure University, celebrates the joy and contemplation of Saint Francis of Assisi. When this "spirited friend of all creation" found himself in a woodland setting, he was caught up with overflowing happiness and took up two sticks and played them as if they were a violin, inviting others to enjoy the music.

In this same spirit, Mount Irenaeus often celebrates Music on the Mountain in spring or autumn. This afternoon concert follows Sunday Eucharist and a picnic brunch for all who attend, on the porch and lawn of their new common home, "House of Peace." Music of various cultures is presented, including steel-drum bands, guitars, and singing. Guests hike the trails to see the fall leaves at their colorful height.

During the summer, Wednesdays are observed as "mid-week Sabbaths for prayer and peaceful recreation." At noon the friars complete their work in the woods, gardens, and house, and begin an afternoon of contemplative leisure, welcoming guests to walk in the woods or take time in Holy Peace Chapel. At 4:00 P.M., those who wish to do so gather with the community in the chapel for sitting meditation or centering prayer, and at 4:45, Eucharist is celebrated. Everyone gathers for a potluck supper before heading back up the hill to the chapel for a 7:30 presentation, conversation, and meditation, sometimes on themes written by Thomas Merton, or inspired by the thoughts and actions of Saint Francis.

Outdoor work is available in abundance on this 228-acre property, and guests are welcome to take on various projects, from helping care for the beautiful flowers or tending the vegetable and fruit gardens to gathering firewood or clearing new paths through the woods. "Prayer and weeding" is a favorite among volunteers! Sunday Eucharist at 11:00 A.M. always includes time for guests to share their thoughts, followed by a potluck brunch with a glorious abundance of delicious food and high spirits. Since they feel their main calling is to "feed each other," they have designed a lovely dinner plate as

MOUNT IRENAEUS FRANCISCAN MOUNTAIN RETREAT

◆

P.O. Box 100
West Clarksville, NY
14786
(716) 973-2470

MUSIC FESTIVAL

SUMMER EVENINGS OF
RECREATION

SUNDAY "DISH TO SHARE"
FOLLOWING MASS

PRAYER AND WEEDING

ARTIST-IN-RESIDENCE
PROGRAM

CDS

FELLOWSHIP PLATES

T-SHIRTS

NEWSLETTER

RETREATS

N
E
W

Y
O
R
K

◈

Chapel raising

a reminder of the importance of this time together. It is inscribed with the words *God is like a circle whose center is everywhere and whose circumference is infinite.*

The new artist-in-residence program has a musician who is a gifted vocalist and a leader in prayerful song. He helps people find their "musical voices" based on everyday experience, using chant and simple responses. His dulcimer CDs are available.

Mount Irenaeus, named after a beloved friar who ran the St. Bonaventure library, was started by Father Dan Riley, O.F.M., an artist who uses his art in a variety of ways, including designing beautiful T-shirts for special occasions. Retreats can be taken in one of the cabins in the woods, or in a room in the main house.

BOTTLING SANCTITY

Mount Irenaeus, the Franciscan Mountain Retreat, is located in the lush green hills of western New York. There is a core community that currently consists of five Franciscan friars, who attempt to live a contemplative life. We have 228 acres, with hermitages, a chapel, and a new main house. On the grounds we have a vegetable garden that has 13 raised beds, and many flower gardens in different places. Our vegetable garden is very productive. We are blessed with a delicious source of summer greens and an abundant crop of root vegetables for the winter. Also, we can pickles, beans, and tomatoes. However, our number-one crop comes in clear jars, and you would say that there is nothing in them. Can you guess what it is? The answer is sanctity!

No, we don't claim to bottle or can or sell sanctity as a product. The definition of *sanctity* is "holiness of life; the quality or condition of being considered sacred." We believe that we are children of God and therefore we are sacred. As a community we attempt to encourage people to see that sanctity is their gift from God.

We feel confident that one way we can help people to experience sanctity is through gardening. Thus, we invite people to get in touch with Mother Earth and to experience the holiness of life. We stand in awe of how many people leave the Mountain renewed in their sense of holiness, and we are all blessed with another jar of sanctity.

◆

Br. Joseph A. Kotula, O.F.M.

Catholic Benedictine monks came to this hilltop in the early 1950s and found the rolling fields and climate suitable for raising Scottish Blackface sheep, prized for their wool. Spring shearing is an exciting and busy time as the monks round up the balky flock to relieve them of their winter coats. The wool is processed and made into many fine products: bed pads, comforters, pillows, slippers, and mittens. Yarn is available for knitters. The bed pads and comforters are available in crib- to king-size with beautiful floral patterns.

The gift shop has an extensive book selection as well as religious articles from rosaries to icons. The shop stocks a good supply of products from other monasteries, such as preserves, candy, and cards. One of the monks, Brother Luke Pape, is an accomplished watercolor artist, and his original art and prints of his monastery scenes

can be purchased. Male retreatants can stay in the old monastery building, while couples and women stay in St. Gertrude's guesthouse.

MOUNT SAVIOUR MONASTERY

◆

**213 Monastery Rd.
Pine City, NY 14871
(607) 734-1688/
734-1689 fax
E-mail:
msaviour@servtech.com
Website:
www.servtech.com/
public/msaviour**

**SHEEP
BEEF CATTLE
WOOL PRODUCTS
RELIGIOUS ARTICLES
FINE ART
RETREATS**

(JACK KELLY)

(JACK KELLY)

N E W   Y O R K

◈

(BROTHER LUKE PAPE)

SUMMER PROGRAM

The monks of Mount Saviour conduct an annual summer program for men between the ages of 20 and 35. There is no fee for the five weeks, but the participants are responsible for their own transportation to and from the monastery. The number of participants is limited to ten.

The summer program consists of spending a five-week period inside the monastery, sharing the communal and prayer life of the monks. Because Mount Saviour is a small Christian community, one can sense there the specifically Christian dimension of life together. This experience and the faith that comes with it are helpful to people throughout their lives as laypersons.

The mornings are divided between communal and private prayer, with several hours to study. Brief courses are taught by monks and oblates (lay affiliates) of the monastery on such topics as prayer, scripture, history, and theology. The afternoons are spent joining the brothers in the work of the monastery. Members of the group also spend time with each other and the directors to process the experience and place it in perspective.

◆

Mount Saviour Monastery, Pine City, New York

A POLITICAL ALPHABET BOOK

Born in Canada on February 1, 1910, the first of 10 children, Brother Luke Pape showed an early interest in art. His family took him to Saturday-morning art classes in Toronto, and though he failed the first entrance exam, on his second try he was accepted and eventually went on to win their four-year scholarship to the Ontario College of Art. Following his graduation in 1929, he studied ballet with Boris Volkoff and performed with his company until 1942 when he joined the Canadian Army Medical Corps for service in Canada and Europe. One of the European hospitals he worked in was next door to the Monte Vergine Benedictine Monastery in Italy. Here for the first time Brother Luke encountered monasticism. After the war he went on retreat at a Canadian Benedictine monastery, St. Benoit du Lac, where he heard about Mt. Saviour. In 1949, he and a group of friends interested in dance decided to hold a dance festival in Toronto. It was such a success, drawing companies from all over Canada, that one of the committee members brought Celia Franca from England, and in 1951 she picked 29 dancers and began the National Ballet of Canada. Brother Luke helped with the early productions, then joined the monastery in 1952.

"After more than 25 years as a monk helping to build this monastery farm at Mount Saviour, with scant time for art, the Prior, Father Martin Boler, took pity on my artistic struggles and arranged for me to be a guest student at Syracuse University in Professor John Vargo's illustration class. Once a week I traveled from the monastery near Elmira to the bustling campus of Syracuse for evening classes from 6:00 to 10:00 P.M. Renaissance art professor Tim Verdon fed and housed me overnight for the semester. He bravely gave up his one bed to me and slept on the floor! In 1978 I attended full-day classes for two semesters, and was hosted by Professor Joseph and Sally Weber and family. So 1978 was the time when I got the assignment for a political alphabet, picking subjects of current interest politically and illustrating them (I could take all semester to finish)—wow, 26 letters! The real students took a medium-size piece of paper, drew 26 little squares, and finished in two weeks. Here is what a Canadian rookie came up with: I chose to use a large classic letter type in a five-and-a-half-by-five-and-a-half-inch square, painted on Arches 140-pound cold-press paper with bright opaque gouache paints. Six panels of four letters and one of letters V and Z.

"This two-year work/study time was a wonderful inspiration. I joined the Elmira Art Club, began their meeting and exhibition schedules; at the monastery I found studio space and was given more time for artwork and a new addition to my monastic life and vocation."

NEW SKETE COMMUNITIES

◆

**P.O. Box 128,
New Skete Rd.
Cambridge, NY 12816
(518) 677-3928/
677-2373 fax: monks
(518) 677-3810: nuns
(888) 777-5383:
books and videos**

DOG TRAINING

**BOOKS AND VIDEOS ON DOG
CARE**

LEATHER LEASHES

DOG BEDS

DOG BISCUITS

GOURMET FOODS

CHEESECAKE

**LITURGICAL BOOKS, MUSIC,
AND RECORDINGS**

ART

RETREATS

The monks, nuns, and lay companions of New Skete belong to the Orthodox Catholic Church and have developed products and services that support their monastic lifestyle in a complex of buildings on 500 acres in a rural area north of Albany. They breed and train German shepherds, which are in great demand, and have written two definitive books on dog care: *How to Be Your Dog's Best Friend* and *The Art of Raising a Puppy.* Coming from more than 20 years' experience, these books are a wealth of wisdom, information, and inspiration for dog lovers. The monks have a three-tape video series, *Raising Your Dog with the Monks of New Skete,* which provides an enlightened understanding of dog behavior and the techniques to develop a healthy relationship with your dog.

Their four-color catalog illustrates smoked meats, cheeses, and cheesecakes available by mail order. The pumpkin cheesecake and the white chocolate cheesecake have taken cheesecake to a higher level of temptation. Liturgical music and recordings of their offices and some religious art are also for sale. Retreats are available for those willing to share their work, meals, and prayer.

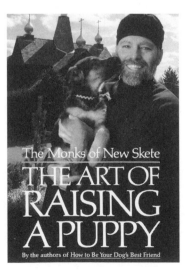

THE COMPANIONS OF NEW SKETE: A REFLECTION BY PATRICIA REID

This fall the Companions of New Skete begin their ninth year as one of the communities of New Skete. The time seems ripe for a review of who and what we are and are not. At present we are six people (three couples, married anywhere from 11 to 39 years), who are striving to live a radical and authentic Christian life. We follow the monastic tradition of common life, prayer, discipline, and repentance, under the leadership of a spiritual father. We live the same life as the monks and nuns of New Skete, except that we live it with our spouses and without the obligation of celibacy. Being married colors our experience of monastic life, but doesn't change its essence. Like the monks and nuns, we too have but one rule, the gospel of Jesus Christ.

Since this kind of monastic experience is unusual in the Orthodox Church, it seems usually to be misunderstood. We would like to dispel a few of the most common misreadings. First of all, we are not a religious boardinghouse, conveniently located near the church to provide a pious atmosphere for our golden years. It's true we share a common table, but we don't board here. Our lives are integrally connected, not parallel. So we try to think of ourselves as a community of six, not of three two's. Besides sharing a common goal and vision of life, we share all aspects of daily living: one common fund, one kitchen, living room, and dining room, one car for the five who work at home. It's also true that we live geographically close to the church, but we don't choose when to attend services. Singing in choir is part of our monastic work, and so, like the monks and nuns, we are there, rain or shine, rested or tired, in spiritual consolation or dryness.

Another misconception is that we are condominium owners. Not so. In the spirit of monastic poverty, we own nothing, whether as individuals or as couples. To build Emmaus House (our residence), we sold or gave away everything we couldn't use in our new life. With the proceeds we built our simple and practical six-unit bedroom wing and an ample common area. From the moment we moved in, all income and savings became common property, administered by the superior we elect for our house.

Some have thought that we live on contributions. On the contrary, we are not dependent on the Orthodox Church in America or on the parish here for financial support. We are self-sustaining, with a number of small but growing enterprises. Foremost among these is the production of a high-quality dog bed and of handcrafted leather leashes [and, in 1997, dog biscuits]. [These] items are excellent complements to our work with the German Shepherds.

Other income-producing projects include carpentry, a drapery and slipcover business, iconography, calligraphy, and floral dried arrangements made from our own gardens.

Pensions and Social Security? Yes, but we are not a retirement community, either. Though our ages range from 52 to 69, we don't consider ourselves retired. In addition to a full five-hour day at our special assignment, we take time for the care and training of our dogs, for our outdoor lawn, road, garden work, for cooking (which we rotate), and for household tasks. Of course, we reserve time for daily prayer, spiritual reading, and quiet reflection. By the time the evening meal and community recreation is over (and sometimes well before), we're ready to retire in another sense.

We are quite ordinary people, special only in our good fortune in finding this way of life . . . and in having a spiritual guide willing to take a chance on us and put up with the fumbling attempts of middle-aged, set-in-their-ways novices from different backgrounds. What matters is for us to achieve what we were created for: full human and Christian maturity and its consequent happiness, even in this life.

◆

Thoughts from New Skete, *Fall 1991, Monks of New Skete, Cambridge, New York*

PROFILE: BROTHER ELIAS

Brother Elias sings baritone in our choir, raised our German shepherds Joy, Masha, and Elfie . . . raised calves, worked on building construction for the monks' and the nuns' monasteries, took charge of the Farms in 1972, developed the mail-order department and recipes and marinades for production of the cheese spreads, country sausage, chutneys, etc.; conversant on the ins and outs of marketing and catalogue sales, the FDA, and even the pecularities of various hardwoods for the smokehouse . . . one of the permanent cooks for the monks . . . enjoys working with hands, at first on pottery, then silver and gold jewelry, cloisonné enameling (on pectoral and processional crosses), rings, precious stones, metal castings . . . gardening, trout fishing, and especially birdwatching, about which he has written. Continues to keep up with scripture and canon law studies.

◆

Thoughts from New Skete, *Summer 1992, Monks of New Skete, Cambridge, New York*

MONASTERY SOUPS

Eat soup first and eat it last
and live till a hundred years be past.

French Proverb

◆

In an age of fast food and TV dinners, a bowl of homemade soup can do wonders for the body and the spirit. From a steaming bowl of chicken broth to nurse a cold to a refreshing dish of cold zucchini soup on a sweltering summer night, nothing nourishes or comforts as much as soup does. That is why soups are often referred to as comfort food. Besides being nutritious and economical, soups in general are easy to make, and they can be served as first course, main meal, or even as late-night snack.

From the beginning, soups have held a unique place in the daily fare of monasteries. That is still true today in France, Spain, Greece, Italy, and other countries, and is the origin of the book *Twelve Months of Monastery Soups.* When you have to eat soup often, as we do in monasteries, then you might as well be creative and design a large variety of soups so that the monks and nuns don't get bored. The book took six years to complete, and it finally came to light in September 1996, with 175 soup recipes. Like monastic life itself, the recipes follow the rhythm of the seasons and rely on the fresh produce available at that particular season of the year. Because soups have a universal appeal, the book became a great success. Here is a soup recipe not included in the book, but very much loved by monks and nuns of all places.

SAINT SERAPHIM SOUP

4 tablespoons vegetable oil	1 celery stalk, sliced
1 onion, finely chopped	2 bouillon cubes
3 garlic cloves, minced	1½ cups vermicelli pasta
2 quarts water	½ cup fresh chopped parsley
2 carrots, peeled and cubed	Salt and pepper to taste
1 turnip, cubed	

1. Pour oil in a soup pot and sauté the onion for about 1 minute over medium heat. Add the garlic, stir, and continue sautéing for another ½ minute. Add the water and the remaining ingredients, except the pasta, parsley, and seasonings. Bring the water to a boil, cover the pot, and cook for about 25 to 30 minutes.

2. Add the pasta, parsley, and salt and pepper. Stir well and simmer the soup over low-to-medium heat for 12 to 15 minutes, with the pot covered. Stir one more time, check the seasonings, and then serve the soup.

◆

Brother Victor-Antoine d'Avila-Latourette, Our Lady of the Resurrection Monastery, La Grangeville, New York

OUR LADY OF THE RESURRECTION MONASTERY

◆

**Barmore Rd.
La Grangeville, NY 12540**

COOKBOOKS

FARMER'S MARKET
PRODUCTS

ICONS

POSTCARDS

RETREATS

T hree wonderful cookbooks, as well as other books, have come from this monastery, all by Benedictine monk Brother Victor-Antoine d'Avila-Latourette. More than 20 years ago, Brother Victor found this 22 acres of hilltop land and developed the monastery. In the 1980s he wrote his famous *From a Monastery Kitchen* and *This Good Food.* These books established his reputation as a skilled chef, and his more recent *Twelve Months of Monastery Soups* was a brilliant idea for nutritious and hearty eating throughout the year. This book is thoughtfully developed and beautifully presented. All of the titles may be purchased as well in bookstores. The monastery also makes preserves, dips, and other edibles that are sold at the local Millbrook Farmer's Market during the summer and fall. Icons and postcards are available at the monastery, and there are a few rooms for private retreatants.

Brother Victor, who leads the simple life of a monk and farmer, prefers to be contacted by letter than by fax or phone.

Pumpkin Hollow Farm was founded in 1937 by the Theosophical Society to provide a peaceful, harmonious, natural setting in which the essential spirituality of the individual could thrive and be integrated into day-by-day relationships with others. The Theosophical Society encourages the comparative study of religion, philosophy, and science so that people may better understand themselves and their place in the universe. It encourages investigation of the unexplained laws of nature and the powers latent in humanity. Courses here include therapeutic touch, taught by Dr. Dolores Krieger and by Dora Kunz, whose extensive tapes are for sale: "The Wisdom in the Gospel of St. Thomas," "The Mystery of the Sphinx: Studies in Symbolist Egypt," and "Working with the Devas" (nature's subtle energies). Long- and short-term residents contribute with vegetarian cooking, office work, housekeeping, gardening, landscaping, and general maintenance. There is a general program of work, study, meditation, discussion, and relaxation.

PUMPKIN HOLLOW FARM

◆

1184 Rte. 11
Craryville, NY 12521
(518) 325-3583 or
325-7105
E-mail:
pumpkin@taconic.net
Web site: www
.theosophical.org
/pumpkin.html

RETREATS
WORKSHOPS
SEMINARS
TAPES

CRAFTS APPRENTICESHIP PROGRAM

The Rochester Folk Art Guild is a place where one's inner possibilities are explored and expressed through quality of work and community living. Beginning with the conviction that the education of one's hands, heart, and mind is a lifelong process, the Guild strives to cultivate what is needed to practice in this daily life. The discipline of the crafts and close living and working relationships with others help greatly in this process of educating the whole human being.

The Rochester Folk Art Guild Apprenticeship Program is designed for young people who are searching for a practical, hands-on approach to learning and living. Working alongside experienced master craftspeople, participants are offered a focus in pottery, woodworking, weaving, or glass-blowing. Apprentices take part in the daily life of the community, sharing the work as well as the seasonal celebrations and numerous special events. In addition to working in one or more of the craft shops, apprentices share in resident activities, which include meal preparation, cleaning, maintenance, farming, and gardening, depending on the season. Study of the Gurdjieff teaching is available to apprentices, but participation in this side of the Guild life is voluntary.

The Guild is located at East Hill Farm in the Finger Lakes region of upstate New York, an area of rolling hills and vineyards. Plenty of time is available for apprentices to explore the surrounding ponds, fields, woods, and lakes. The physical beauty of the surroundings evokes themes in the crafts and provides natural materials such as wood, wool, vine, and clay.

To apply to the apprenticeship program, write a letter that gives a brief personal background and your reasons for applying. The next step is a preliminary visit to the Guild of two to three days. If you are accepted, there is a fee of $100 per week for the first two weeks. After that, financial arrangements and duration of apprenticeship are decided on an individual basis. Stipends and scholarships are sometimes available to those accepted for six months or longer. Acceptance is based on a variety of factors, including maturity, motivation, and a willingness to learn new ways of living and working with others. Previous experience or skill in craft work is useful but not required. The nonresident program makes it possible to study with Guild craftspeople while living elsewhere.

"Each of us has had to ask, in one way or another, what is worth pursuing in this hurried, ambitious life. Together we have come to share a yearning to discover a worthwhile purpose for ourselves. The crafts and our common life are a road to this discovery, along which we see how we can stretch ourselves, whether it's making a porcelain vase or washing the kitchen floor and per-haps, with repeated efforts, actually experiencing how we go about doing it!"

◆

For information, write to Apprenticeship Program, Rochester Folk Art Guild, 1445 Upper Hill Rd.,
Middlesex, NY 14507.

Based on the ideas of the Russian philosopher G. I. Gurdjieff, this community began in the late 1950s and is now located on a 350-acre working farm in the Finger Lakes region. The late Louise March, a student of Gurdjieff, was instrumental in guiding the farm's development. "Each of us had to ask, in one way or another, what is worth pursuing in this hurried, ambitious life. Together we have come to share a yearning to discover a worthwhile purpose for ourselves. The crafts and our common life are a road to this discovery." Believing that each person has untapped wells of creativity, Mrs. March encouraged each member to pick a craft and to use that craft as a means for self-study and growth. The guild has received national recognition for its fine arts and crafts, which include exquisite blown glass, prizewinning handcrafted furniture, pottery, and weaving. The public is invited two weekends a year, in June and September, to visit the workshops and sample delicious food and local wine. The crafts shop is open four days a week the rest of the year. In addition, the guild mounts several major shows a year in nearby cities.

ROCHESTER FOLK ART GUILD

◆

**1445 Upper Hill Rd.
Middlesex, NY 14507
(716) 554-3539/6401:
glass shop**

POTTERY
WOODWORKING
GLASSBLOWING
GRAPHIC ARTS
CLOTHING DESIGN
BASKETMAKING

GLASSMAKING

Glass is one of the most common materials of our time. It is made from abundant and available elements: sand, soda ash, and lime. Melted together at a high temperature (2,400°F), these form a liquid that, when cooled to room temperature, is solid yet never crystallizes. This is one of the properties of glass that make it workable: it becomes soft and fluid again whenever it is reheated.

The colors in the glass generally come from metal oxide: cobalt for blue, chrome for green; gold gives cranberry red with a rubylike glow. Mixing these and other metal oxides in varying proportions gives an entire spectrum of colors.

This spectacular substance, which we see today in everything from lightbulbs to windows to TV tubes to tableware, was once rare and precious. When I work it by hand with the simple tools of the glassblower, I can begin to see its mystery and magic. The material glows with incandescent heat when it is taken from the furnace at the end of the blowpipe. As the piece takes form, responding to gravity and breath, it is engaged in a dance with the forces of nature. I participate in the movement of both the material and the forces that shape it. When I give the process my full attention, it enables me to connect with the silent, calm center in myself.

◆

Ben Bennett (GafferBen@AOL.com), *Rochester Folk Art Guild, Middlesex, New York*

This community of 200 is based on the teachings of Rudolf Steiner, the Austrian scientist, philosopher, and educator whose image of the human being was based on the physical, psychological, and spiritual dimensions of human life. According to their brochure, "This threefold imagination lies at the heart of Waldorf education, giving rise to over 500 schools worldwide. It has inspired extensive work in curative education, social and economic development, agriculture, medicine, and the arts with the potential to transform the social ills that have attended our rush to progress." The Fellowship Community has several businesses that provide a meaningful way for community members of all ages to interact with each other and the public; besides selling weaving, candles, and pottery, they run the Mercury Press print shop, a store called Hand and Hoe, Sunbridge (an adult college for Waldorf teacher training), and Green Meadow, a Waldorf school for children, plus a variety of health and medical enterprises such as the Weleda Pharmacy, based on natural practices, Hilltop House for the elderly, and the School of Eurythmy.

RUDOLF STEINER FELLOWSHIP COMMUNITY

◆

**241 Hungry Hollow Rd.
Spring Valley, NY 10977
(914) 356-8494/
356-8468 fax**

**WALDORF SCHOOL
TEACHER TRAINING COLLEGE
EURYTHMY SCHOOL
PHARMACY
MEDICAL PRACTICE
PRINT SHOP
RESIDENCE FOR SENIORS
WEAVERY
CANDLE SHOP
POTTERY**

To supplement the income earned in the outside world by many of these Episcopal sisters, the community sells a mail-order tape ministry of talks given at its retreats, such as "Feminine Voices of the Holy" and "Experiences of the Mystics." Each winter they hold a benefit dinner at St. Michael's Church, which in the past has featured performances such as "Miracles of Santiago" by the famed singers of medieval chant, the Anonymous Four.

Both St. Hilda's House in New York and its community in the country (St. Cuthbert's Retreat House, Federal Hill Rd., Brewster, NY 10509; [914] 278-2610), with 127 acres of fields and woods, have gift shops with crafts made by the sisters and guest rooms available. Each fall

ST. HILDA'S HOUSE

◆

**621 W. 113th St.
New York, NY 10025
(212) 932-8098**

**BOOKS
TAPES AND CDS
CRAFTS
ANNUAL BENEFIT
NATIVE AMERICAN CORN
FEST IN BREWSTER
GUEST ROOMS IN THE CITY
AND THE COUNTRY**

N
E
W

Y
O
R
K

◆

St. Hilda's holds a Native American Corn Fest at St. Cuthbert's with crafts, music, and dancing by Native American members.

MEDICAL AND PSYCHOLOGICAL CARE

Some spiritual communities provide medical and psychological treatment that is both nurturing and experimental. Aquarian Concepts in West Sedona, Arizona, "incorporates both spiritual and scientific techniques such as psycho-spiritual counseling, personal transmissions, light body visualization, and Tron therapy." In general, care emphasizes "how the thought processes affect the reality of your life."

The Rudolf Steiner Fellowship Community in Spring Valley, New York, blends traditional clinical medicine with anthroposophy, "a way of life and thought that synthesizes spirituality and science" and enhances consciousness (from "Blueprint for a New Culture," a brochure published by Steiner Fellowship Communities). The doctors in the community are not paid directly by their patients, but are allotted monies taken from a larger, more general pool of resources. By offering such care within the community, the Steiner community hopes to foster a sense of charity and donation. According to the members' brochure, the community "consider[s] the qualities of charity and donation as constituting a better basis for care than being paid for services rendered."

The Steiner pharmacy offers herbal and homeopathic prescription medicines, and it receives orders from all over the world. Balancing service to those within and outside the community, it serves a core of thirty doctors around the country.

◆

For information on the Steiner Community, call (914) 356-8494. The pharmacy's mail-order phone number is (914) 268-8572. To reach Aquarian Concepts, call (502) 204-1206 or visit www.sedona.net/sd/aquarian.

This former estate of the Alexander Hamilton family, about an hour north of New York City, is now occupied by Sisters of the Eastern Catholic Rite. These Ukrainian Sisters serve as a focal point for the Ukrainian Church, which holds an annual pilgrimage on the Sunday on or before August 15, when thousands of people come to celebrate the Feast of the Assumption. During the year, seminars and retreats are held on the beautiful grounds.

ST. MARY'S VILLA

◆

**50 Table Rock Rd.
Sloatsburg, NY 10974
(914) 753-5100**

FESTIVAL
SEMINARS
RETREATS

In the early 1980s, Toni Packer founded this center in rural western New York, an hour from Rochester, as a place for meditative inquiry and retreats. Her books, tapes, and videos and the center's newsletter reflect the philosophy that "emergence and blossoming of understanding, love and intelligence has nothing to do with any tradition, no matter how ancient or impressive—it has nothing to do with time. It happens completely on its own when a human being questions, wonders, listens and looks without getting stuck in fear, pleasure, and pain. When self-concerns are quiet, in abeyance, heaven and earth are open." There are approximately eight seven-day silent retreats with Toni each year, but it is possible to stay here at other times, too. The center has 200 acres of rolling hills, open fields, abundant deer, woods, ponds, and streams.

SPRINGWATER CENTER

◆

**7179 Mill St.
Springwater, NY 14560
(716) 669-2141/
669-9573 fax
E-mail:
spwtrctr@servtech.com
Web site:
www.servtech.com
/public/spwtrctr**

BOOKS, TAPES, AND
VIDEOS
NEWSLETTER
RETREATS

NEW YORK

◈

TIBET HOUSE
CULTURAL CENTER

◆

**22 West 15th St.
New York, NY 10011
(212) 807-0563
E-mail:
mail@tibethouse.org
Web site: www
.tibethouse.org**

NEWSLETTER

CRAFTS

CLASSES

GALLERY

INTERNSHIPS

TIBETAN NEW YEAR BENEFIT

Tibet House was co-founded by the actor Richard Gere and Robert A. F. Thurman, who left Harvard as a student to learn Tibetan and became a Tibetan Buddhist monk and the first American translator for the Dalai Lama. Now professor of Indo-Tibetan Studies at Columbia University (and the father of actress Uma Thurman), Thurman and his wife, Nena, along with many others, are putting great effort into building a center in New York dedicated to preserving the living culture of Tibet. "We feel that the wisdom and art of all nonindustrial civilizations add meaning to life and enrich the emerging global culture. We share a special love for Tibet, its people, and its civilization of extraordinary beauty. Because this thousand-year-old Buddhist civilization is under threat of extinction from the Chinese, by presenting Tibetan culture and its special art of freedom we hope to inspire people to join in our effort to save it. Tibet House is part of a worldwide network of similar institutions committed to ensuring that the light of the Tibetan spirit never disappears from the face of the earth."

Tibet House publishes a newsletter, *Tibet House Drum,* and offers a wide range of courses taught by Professor Thurman and such guests as Roshi Bernard Glassman, Philip Glass, Melissa Mathison, and Milton Glaser, with titles like "Tibetan Buddhism, History, and Culture," "Evolutionary Sport in the 21st Century," "The Wisdom of Compassion," "The Politics of Enlightenment and Social Action," "Mandala: Spaces and Symbols of Enlightenment," "Buddhism and Popular Culture," and "Buddhism and Creativity." Its Museum Without Walls promotes the future repatriation of outstanding examples of Tibetan art. There is also a photographic archive and resource library. In cooperation with other educational, historical, and cultural institutions, Tibet House is engaged in ongoing efforts to share with the world Tibet's practical systems of spiritual philosophy and science of the mind, as well as its nonviolent approach to conflict and human development.

The gift shop sells handicrafts and merchandise made by Tibetan artisans, as well as books. Tibet House offers internships in archiving, exhibition planning, and research to people who would like to be part of the worldwide network of those working to save the culture of Tibet. A star-studded annual benefit concert, which includes Tibetan music and dance, as well as performances by other outstanding artists, is held in New York each year on March 9, the Tibetan New Year.

This community of Camaldolese Benedictine nuns was licensed to sell its own wines in 1996, an accomplishment of incredible courage and perseverance. St. Benedict Wines are made in four fruit flavors: raspberry, peach, strawberry, and cherry. They also produce red and white table wine, and a Monastery Cellar Blush. Connoisseurs, take note. It's easy to jump in the Cherokee and drive west on Route 17 to Exit 79, then purchase a few cases for those frequent special occasions. There is a well-stocked gift shop where monastery-made fragrances, oils, soaps, local maple syrup, and gift baskets are available.

Every July, usually on the third Sunday of the month, the sisters hold the Field of Dreams Bazaar, which features good food, music, dancing, and wine-tasting. A log-cabin-style guesthouse for private retreatants is on the 100-acre property.

TRANSFIGURATION MONASTERY

◆

701 N.Y. Rte. 79
Windsor, NY 13865
(607) 655-2366

WINE
FRAGRANCES
OILS
FLOWER SPLASHES
SOAP
MAPLE SYRUP
ICONS
FESTIVAL
RETREATS

(JACK KELLY)

(JACK KELLY)

WINE

Winemaking and wine-drinking have a history almost as old as civilization itself. Archaeological findings indicate that the enjoyment of wine is a pastime at least 5,000 years old. Our own continent has a rich history with the grape; Leif Erikson reportedly called the North American continent "Vineland the Good" because of its vast store of grapes. Long an element in the Catholic Communion ritual, the first wine to appear on the West Coast of the United States was sacramental and was made in the early seventeenth century by Spanish mission priests.

Transfiguration Monastery in Windsor, New York, takes advantage of one of the best grape-growing regions in the United States, the Finger Lakes of central New York State. The monastery's St. Benedict Winery buys juice from area growers and produces a variety of fruit and table wines. Most of its customers, we are told, "want wine for a festive meal" or other special event. Of course, many people who know of the monastery's cottage industry are surprised that these monastics sell, of all things, wine. Yet customers buy Transfiguration Monastery's wines in a spirit not of senseless indulgence but of social connection, both with the contemplative sellers and those to whom they will serve the wine. The Romans used to say, *In vino veritas*—in wine there is truth. Perhaps, in this case, truth is not in the product itself but in those who offer it.

◆

For a listing of wines offered by Transfiguration Monastery, phone (607) 655-2366. Calls from area restaurants are especially welcome.

Situated in a former convent near downtown Glens Falls, Wellsprings holds a four-month renewal program for Christian ministers, religious, and laypeople who want to revitalize their calling.

The Bruderhof Communities have been in the United States since 1954. Today they have eight settlements with approximately 2,500 members throughout the world, who attempt to follow Christ and his teachings. They live a simple, rural community life based on church discipline, with the father as the head of the house and the mother at his right hand. All dress simply and reach out to others when there is a crisis, often joining the Red Cross or other groups in disaster relief. Each community has common work, a common purse, and its own schools. They refuse military service and violence of any kind, and will not hold public office or swear oaths. The community left Germany in the 1930s when the government tried to get it to close its schools.

The Woodcrest Bruderhof has several thriving businesses. First there is Community Playthings, the group's main livelihood for the last several decades, which produces solid maple classroom furniture and wooden toys (such as scooters, doll cradles, and wagons) for children. In the workshop, it is immediately apparent that this is not just a factory but a nerve center of the community's daily life. As the men and women who work there say, it's not just a business but a place to

(© COMMUNITY PLAYTHINGS.
USED WITH PERMISSION)

show love—to the children and teachers who will use the equipment, to their own families, who benefit by the sale of the products, and to their coworkers right next to them in the workshop.

Then there is Rifton, a newer branch of the community's work, which consists of a line of therapeutical equipment for children and adults with disabilities, and includes everything from adjustable chairs to therapy rolls (see p. 199).

rolls (see p. 199).

A third line of work, the Plough Publishing House, has been spreading the message of the community through "the mission of the printed word" since 1920. Plough, whose slogan is "breaking the soil for new seeds," puts out a quarterly magazine with news items, human interest stories, reflective pieces, spiritual prose and poetry, and feature articles on social justice issues such as the abolition of the death penalty.

The Bruderhof's publishing house also distributes a catalog of books and music that carries not only its own publications (many of them best-sellers) but also a wide variety of books from other imprints. Selections reflect the New Testament basis of the community, but there are dozens of offerings from other traditions as well, in categories such as community; peace and justice; radical Christianity; culture and issues; classics; and the spiritual life.

In addition to writers from within the community, most notably author Johann Christoph Arnold, authors include Dorothy Day, Leo Tolstoy, Thomas Merton, Mumia Abu-Jamal, Flannery O'Connor, Nathaniel Hawthorne, Henri Nouwen, Dan Berrigan, Rainer Maria Rilke, and Margery Kempe.

THE BEGINNING OF RIFTON EQUIPMENT

Rifton Equipment is a business that was brought to us by one of our friends. One of our communities is located in a town with four homes for children with disabilities. Our young people enjoyed going to these homes to play with the children or help fix things up. It wasn't long before the children, teachers, and therapists at these homes became our friends. The staff knew that we made Community Playthings, high-quality wooden day-care equipment, and they began to bring broken adaptive equipment for us to repair, and to ask our help in improving it. Brothers and sisters in our other communities were experiencing the same thing. Therapists and teachers brought us their problems and their expertise, and together we experimented. The result is Rifton for People with Disabilities.

We realized that we would not be able to supply customized items, so our goal was to make quality products that can be adjusted to meet the needs of as many as possible. Input from therapists and teachers who use our products continues to be an essential part of our design process. We have discovered that equipment which helps normal positioning can open up whole new worlds for children and adults with disabilities.

◆

Woodcrest Bruderhof, Rifton, New York

Rifton Equipment (USED WITH PERMISSION)

YOGA ASANA
CENTER

◆

**297 Third Ave.
New York, NY 10010
(212) 889-8160**

**YOGA INSTRUCTION
POSTURE CHART
COUNTRY LODGE RETREATS**

The sounds of Third Avenue can be faintly heard at this third-floor ashram, but are quickly forgotten when Dharma Mitra begins his yoga classes. A yoga teacher for more than 30 years, Mitra came to New York from Brazil in the 1970s and has changed locations of his teaching and meditation rooms from West 57th Street to Greenwich Village, then to East 12th Street, and now at 23rd and Third, a semicircular journey around Manhattan, like a Pied Piper leading his students to calm, sensitivity, compassion, and health. By photographing himself with a time-release 35-mm camera, he has created a most comprehensive wall chart that shows 908 yogic poses and positions.

This chart, available by mail order, has become so famous it can be seen in yoga centers around the world. The center acquired a lodge and country acres in 1996. Less than two hours by car from New York City, weekend programs and retreats are scheduled there regularly.

This monastery is a monastic Zen training center with a distinctly American approach for men and women of all ages and religious backgrounds. Abbot John Daido Loori is the resident teacher and spiritual leader. He was born in the United States, is active in the daily life of the monastery, and is very accessible to students. His book, *The Eight Gates of Zen,* presents Zen practice as a full-time spiritual discipline and examines meditation, gratitude, personal study, creative process, care of the physical body, Buddhist tradition, work, and compassion as the activities of an awakened mind.

Dharma Communications is the education and publishing arm of the monastery, and offers Buddhist books, videos, a journal *(Mountain Record),* and Buddhist supplies such as zafus, zabutons, travel altars, and hundreds of other items listed in their extensive catalog.

ZEN MOUNTAIN MONASTERY

◆

**P.O. Box 197 PC, South Plank Rd.
Mount Tremper, NY 12457
(914) 688-2228/
688-2415 fax
E-mail:
zmmtrain@mhv.net
(914) 688-7993/
688-7995 fax: Dharma
Communications
E-mail: dharmacom
@zen-mtn.org
Web site:
www.zen-mtn.org**

**INSTRUCTION IN MARTIAL
ARTS, ZEN ARTS, AND
BUDDHIST STUDIES**

BOOKS

VIDEOS

JOURNAL

BUDDHIST SUPPLIES

RETREATS

N
E
W

Y
O
R
K

◈

North Carolina

AVILA RETREAT CENTER

◆

**711 Mason Rd.
Durham, NC 27712
(919) 477-1285**

PHOTOGRAPHS
ART
COOKBOOK
RETREATS

This former Carmelite monastery for cloistered nuns is now an ecumenical retreat center. Built on a sloping 51 acres of woods and meadows, it has a one-mile meditation trail that winds through the property. The original building, designed like a European monastery, serves as a buffer against the outside world, protecting the peaceful inner courtyard of landscaped lawns, bushes, and flowers. Walkways lead back to comfortable cottages built a short distance from the main building, which has a dining room, meeting rooms, and a chapel.

The Catholic sisters who live here offer beautiful photographs and other art for sale, as well as a cookbook, *Sharing Our Best*, which may explain their very good food. Their ecumenism peaked recently when they were invited to be spiritual leaders at another retreat center. One described it: "So here were Catholic nuns giving a retreat to Methodists at a Baptist retreat center!"

Retreats are available throughout the year, and their programs are designed to touch every human need. There are single and double rooms with shared baths for 54 men and women in seven cottages.

With modern greenhouses and 390 sheltered acres, 30 miles north of Asheville, this farm grows organic vegetables for community use and for the market. In addition, it is building unique dome structures for workshops and other gatherings. The emphasis is on spiritual development, learning, self-sufficiency, healing the earth, and respecting native traditions.

K&K ORGANIC HEALTH FARM

◆

Rte. 3, Box K&K
Mars Hill, NC 28754
(704) 689-4998/
689-4999 fax

ORGANIC FARM GARDENS
WORKSHOPS

Secluded in the North Carolina mountains about an hour from Asheville, this center invites teachers from a variety of traditions to give meditation instruction and retreats in a supportive environment acknowledging that spiritual growth is individual, each person's response is unique, and different spiritual paths answer different needs.

In the 1970s, wanting to work at something they believed in and felt was worthwhile, Elizabeth Kent and Melinda Guyol shared the idea of starting a retreat center somewhere in the mountains. They envisioned a place where individuals could come to nurture a sense of peace, uncover the truth within the heart, and study and practice the dharma. The land was acquired in 1978, and five years were spent clearing, building, and remodeling the property, and improving the roads. During that time a few programs were sponsored, and gradually the new retreat center became well known. There are 19 retreats planned for 1998.

A staff of three lives here, maintains the buildings, and prepares for retreatants. Individuals can come for their own spiritual purposes between scheduled groups. There are a few private rooms with shared baths, and a dormitory in a well-constructed main house. The kitchen is off the dining room, where a potbellied stove adds warmth and charm. The meditation hall, with polished wood floors, is nearby.

SOUTHERN DHARMA RETREAT CENTER

◆

1661 West Rd.
Hot Springs, NC 28743
(704) 622-7112 phone/fax

MEDITATION INSTRUCTION
RETREATS

North Dakota

ASSUMPTION ABBEY

◆

P.O. Box A
Richardton, ND 58652
(701) 974-3315/
974-3317 fax

WINE
HONEY
COMMERCIAL PRINTING
RANCHING
RETREATS

For more than 100 years, these Catholic Benedictine monks have adjusted to changing needs, from farming to education to ranching, not to mention the innumerable times they have served as hosts to stranded travelers overwhelmed by winter storms that swoop down from Canada across this western section of the northern Great Plains. They sell excellent Monastery label wines, both regular and altar wines, something they began in the 1960s to generate income. Assumption Abbey's estate-bottled wines include a Sonoma County Pinot Noir, a Russian River Chardonnay, and an Alexander Valley White Zinfandel, in addition to their altar wine, a California *vin rosé*. The wine comes from the Central Coast and Sonoma County regions of California, while the wine labels are printed by their own Abbey Press, which is a commercial printer of books, newsletters, and brochures for local customers. They raise 200 head of cattle for commercial purposes. They also have an apiary and a woodcraft shop. In the summer, monks who have been away teaching return to their home monastery to help with the haying. The gift shop sells books, cards, crafts, honey, and pottery made by one of the brothers. Retreats are available for those interested in examining and experiencing the Benedictine way of life.

The monastery sits on a high point overlooking farm buildings and a small lake, and the prairie stretches away like a sea. The dining room has a wall of windows that

look north across the prairie to the Kildeer Mountains, 40 miles away. When we took a walk down to the lake in the afternoon, the wiry grass tugged at our ankles, and prairie roses bloomed in profusion. That evening, clouds built heavily and thunder rolled and cracked. Rain began in heavy drops, then slanted down fiercely. Lightning danced over the prairie sea. Intermittent lights of an occasional car passing on the road to the west looked like a small boat crossing. We were on a covered porch where we could watch the majesty of the storm. Lightning shot down to the lake where we'd been, then flashed horizontally, over and over. We watched the magnificent storm, close enough to be part of the drama, yet dry and protected.

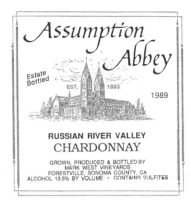

Assumption Abbey

Estate Bottled

EST. 1893 — 1989

RUSSIAN RIVER VALLEY
CHARDONNAY

GROWN, PRODUCED & BOTTLED BY
MARK WEST VINEYARDS
FORESTVILLE, SONOMA COUNTY, CA
ALCOHOL 13.5% BY VOLUME • CONTAINS SULFITES

SACRED HEART MONASTERY HARNESSES THE WIND

On the hills north of Sacred Heart Monastery, two 80-foot-high wind turbines, with 22-foot blades bearing the Benedictine cross painted by one of the sisters, are finally turning, and the Benedictine sisters are producing their own electrical power. After years of research, consultations with experts, and using donations, savings, and pending grants, the sisters purchased the secondhand wind turbines for just over $60,000 each. The monastery's one-year daily turbine monitoring study will provide the public with important alternative energy information. "We should know if it has been a success or a failure by the end of the first year," said Sacred Heart prioress Sister Paula Larson. "We live in a wind tunnel area, so I don't expect it will fail. If it works as well as our coal furnace did, it will be a tremendous savings. It's all a matter of wind on the right day at the right time that will determine the savings," she said.

SACRED HEART MONASTERY

◆

P.O. Box 364
Richardton, ND 58652
(701) 974-2121/
974-2124 fax
E-mail:
sacheart@richardton
.etctel.com

LLAMAS
WORKSHOPS
RETREATS

A few years ago, when these Catholic Benedictine sisters sent out a fund-raising appeal, one of their friends responded by saying, "I don't have any money, but I have a lot of llamas." So the sisters accepted a "gift in kind" of a breeding pair, and by 1997 they had 18 animals. The llama is from South America. It is used as a beast of burden and for a source of meat and milk. Its silky fleece, which is similar to alpaca and vicuña, is light, warm, and sheds moisture. The animals have a gentle nature, and some people keep them as pets.

These creative and resourceful sisters are experimenting with wind power to reduce their electric bills. They have installed two wind turbines, which they hope will cut power costs in half, as well as serving as an example for North Dakotans to use the inexhaustible energy of the wind as an environmentally clean power source. A 1990 study ranked North Dakota as the top state for producing wind power, with the potential to generate 36 percent of all the electrical needs for the lower 48 states. When they are not tending the llamas or monitoring their wind turbines, the sisters host programs at their Spirituality Center for people of all denominations.

After our visit to Sacred Heart Monastery, we took I-94 east to Mandan, then turned south onto State Route 6. It was a perfectly clear morning, the blue sky spread over us and the dry, washed air sparkled. After a few miles, all we could see was the great spread of land, pasture for horses and cattle, no billboards or buildings, but only an occasional dirt road marked by mailboxes. During that hour's drive, we saw only one other vehicle, a pickup that came down for the mail, then turned around and went back. Horses stood in the corner of one field, and the sun shimmered off their powerful shoulders and backs. Cattle grazed contentedly, hardly moving, as we drove through a panorama of solitude, vastness, and quiet.

LLAMAS

The llama, the only beast of burden native to the Western Hemisphere, was first domesticated in South America. Capable of supporting loads of over 100 pounds for hikes of up to 20 miles a day, llamas proved valuable to native South Americans for life in the rugged Andean terrain. In North America, llamas are more prevalent than one might think; currently, 100,000 llamas call North America home. What is to be done with so many llamas? Sandy Mubarak, writing on behalf of the Rocky Mountain Llama and Alpaca Association, explains that the llama "has had a six thousand-year relationship with man providing him with not only meat, transportation of goods, protection of sheep herds, a source of fertilizer and building materials, but most importantly a renewable resource for warm, natural, yet biodegradable fiber for everything from lead ropes, backpacks for carrying belongings, to ponchos, leggings, mittens, hats, clothing, blankets and other shelter from the elements. Today ecologically responsible people are wisely returning to our appreciation of the renewable gifts these creatures continue to offer us." Where some see a humpless camel, prone to fits of angry spitting, Ms. Mubarak sees a companion for the struggle to heal and restore the planet. It is exactly this sort of difference of perception that allows spiritual communities to be models for how we all ought to be stewards of creation.

◆

For more information on llama raising in the United States, visit www.llama.org. Sacred Heart Monastery in Richardton, ND, raises llamas commercially.

Ohio

INSIGHT TRAVEL

◆

**602 S. High St.
Yellow Springs, OH
45387
(800) 688-9851
(937) 767-1102/
767-6469 fax
Web site: www
.insight-travel.com**

TRAVEL TO SACRED PLACES

This small family community with ties to the Yellow Springs Dharma Center practices right livelihood with their Insight Travel pilgrimages to sacred places in India and Nepal. Trips are led by veterans of travel in Asia who hold an intense interest in Asian religions and a deep involvement in the living traditions of those countries. Insight Travel believes that a journey taken with a spiritual focus can be transforming.

JESUIT RETREAT HOUSE

◆

**5629 State Rd.
Cleveland, OH 44134
(216) 884-9300**

**INSTRUCTION
PROGRAMS
RETREATS**

This former seminary is located in an oasis of trees in the Cleveland suburb of Parma. Every year, over an eight-month period, Jesuit priests hold weekly meetings on the Spiritual Exercises of Saint Ignatius of Loyola. Their other retreat programs are designed to fit the spiritual needs of society: days of recollection for seniors, priests, and teachers; programs that encourage spiritual self-expression through poetry, journal-keeping, and autobiography; family-oriented weekends such as Engaged Encounter, Mother-Daughter Retreats, and Couples Night Out. One recent program had an intriguing title: "Strategy: Planning from a Business Perspective with God's Approval."

Oklahoma

The primary product of this ashram, run by Catholic sisters from various congregations, is hospitality. They also make and sell cards with beautiful photographs taken by one of the sisters, and laminated bookmarks with prayer inscriptions. Retreat space is available for those seeking complete solitude.

This property, located 25 miles west of Tulsa, is named after the Osage Indians whose territory it is in. The monastery was founded with the specific purpose of uniting the spiritual traditions of East and West. The chapel has icons and symbols from Native American, Hindu, Jewish, and Buddhist traditions, as well as the lighted candle that marks the resting place of the Holy Eucharist. The community meets here for meditation, prayer services, satsang, and daily Communion.

**OSAGE+
MONASTERY
FOREST OF PEACE**

◆

**18701 W. Monastery Rd.
Sand Springs, OK 74063
(918) 245-2734**

PHOTO CARDS
BOOKMARKS
RETREATS

(SISTER JOSETTA, O.S.B.)

The national headquarters of Light of Christ Community Church and Sancta Sophia Seminary are located on 430 acres in the western Ozarks. An intentional spiritual community of 76 adults and 14 children, it is home to members of various Western and Eastern religions, in addition to the core group of esoteric Christians. They seem to combine "New Age" Christianity with older mystical practices. An architect who is a member of the community has designed buildings of distinction, including the water tower in the form of a cross. The church and seminary sponsor classes and speakers, and guests and visitors are welcome to attend.

**SPARROW HAWK
VILLAGE**

◆

**12 Summit Ridge Dr.
Tahlequah, OK 74464
(918) 456-3421**

SEMINARY
BOOKSTORE

Oregon

ALPHA FARM

◆

Deadwood, OR 97430
(541) 964-5102/
964-3102 fax
E-mail:
alpha@pioneer.net

CAFÉ
CONTRACT MAIL DELIVERY
CONSENSUS WORKSHOPS

ALPHA FARM

I n 1971, four like-minded people set out from Phila-delphia to found a rural, holistic community. The old homestead they purchased in a rural valley, 55 miles northwest of Eugene, had once had a post office and was named Alpha. "How fitting! Alpha, the first letter of the Greek alphabet meaning 'the beginning.'" They live comfortably, though without television, and heat mainly with wood. They have been influenced by Native Americans, Rudolph Steiner, and Findhorn, and they seek to honor and respect the spirit in all people and in nature, and to integrate all aspects of life into a balanced whole. Most community work is in communally owned enterprises and on their farm.

Alpha-Bit is their café/bookstore/gift shop in a nearby town, which has been open for 25 years, a way of participating in the local community and doing business at the same time. Reports state that they have "politically correct" coffee at affordable prices! Their contract with the U.S. Postal Service to deliver mail is one of their most successful businesses. A series of consensus workshops is also held at the farm. The average number of adults in the community varies from 15 to 20 plus children, and their expressions of spirit have been far-ranging, from Quaker meetings to Sufi dancing to Jewish and Christian holidays. They say, "Our group 'spiritual practice' is actually to express, moment by moment in our work and in our relations with others, qualities of cooperation, respect, nurturance, and helpfulness."

Catholic Benedictine sisters have been in this location for more than 100 years, and actively maintain contact with alumni of the academy that was once here. They hold the Shalom Plum Blossom Festival at Easter time, and a fall celebration. The sisters are an especially creative group, and their art and crafts are for sale in the new Little Store at Shalom. The store offers tapes, discs, yarn angels, afghans, lap quilts, herbal scents, caramel corn, pizelles, Benni's mustard, cinnamon rolls, and Sister Immaculata's famous bread.

They recently renovated the monastery (it was extensively damaged by the 1993 earthquake), and have 15 guest rooms in Howard Hall for women only, and another fifteen rooms in a nearby building for men and women seeking a place of prayer and peace. The community of sisters come together for prayer in the chapel three times a day, and guests are welcome. An afternoon mass is celebrated daily. Workshops, conferences, and retreats are ongoing throughout the year.

The 40 acres of monastery grounds are on both sides of South Main Street, and are planted with pin oaks and incense cedars. Horticulturalists can find a bulge-eye catalpa, an American smoke, Kentucky coffee, and linden trees. The orchard contains apple, pear, prune, plum, cherry, and quince trees as well as a grape arbor, a dazzling demonstration of what will grow in this fertile part of Oregon.

BENEDICTINE SISTERS OF MOUNT ANGEL

◆

**840 S. Main St.
Mount Angel, OR 97362
(503) 845-6141
(503) 845-6773: retreats**

**FESTIVALS
ART AND CRAFTS
WORKSHOPS
RETREATS**

BREITENBUSH HOT SPRINGS

◆

P.O. Box 578
Detroit, OR 97342
(503) 854-3314/
854-3819 fax
E-mail: thebush
@teleport.com
Web site:
www.unotes
.com/breitenbush

WORKSHOPS
BOOKS
APPAREL
JEWELRY
CRAFTS
RETREATS

An intentional community of approximately 50 adults and children owns and operates this remote, 86-acre hot springs retreat on the edge of the Mount Jefferson wilderness, surrounded by old-growth temperate rain forest in the Willamette National Forest of the Oregon Cascades. Workshops on ecology are offered, as well as programs on yoga, meditation, dance, and many other topics. The gift shop sells books, apparel, jewelry, and crafts, and there are rustic cabins for retreat.

In the parking area at the edge of the property, you transfer your bags into a cart to reach the snug wooden cabins, all of which have heat and electricity and basic furnishings, but only half of which have plumbing. There are community bathhouses nearby, and several hot pools of different temperature. The electricity for the retreat is provided by an ingenious hydroelectric plant from the rushing waters of the Breitenbush River, which flows through the area. Geothermal energy is taken from the source of the hot springs to heat the buildings and cabins.

One cold night we disrobed and slipped into the hot springs with only the sound of the river flowing, and the outline of the mountains delineated against the clear, star-marked sky.

This valley of 2,500 acres along Dorena Lake, near Eugene, is made up of village, farm, and forest, and a pedestrian solar village is being built here. The community's first manufacturing business is Equinox bicycle trailers, sold throughout the United States. These unique, 19-pound, two-wheel trailers were started as a way for bikers to bring their small children along. Equipped with windowed rain covers and safety belts, they are built to hold two children. Like a boat trailer, they can also haul other small loads. Coca-Cola used 14 of them to transport cases of Coke at the Olympic relighting ceremonies, and local carpenters have been seen hauling their wood behind their bicycles. Cerro Gordo also has a forestry cooperative that produces enough lumber for 25 homes a year. As the village grows, it is planning a lodge, organic agriculture, and small, privately owned businesses. The aim is to create a "life-enhancing community which reintegrates the human community and our inner selves with the larger community of the biosphere—diverse yet mutually supportive."

CERRO GORDO COMMUNITY

◆

**Dorena Lake, Box 569
Cottage Grove, OR 97424
(541) 942-7720
(541) 942-7895: bicycle trailers
E-mail: don_n@efn.org
E-mail: equinox@efn.org
Web site: www.efn
.org/~andrewm/Cerro-
Gordo/Cerro-Gordo.html
Web site:
www.efn.org
/~equinox**

BICYCLE TRAILERS
LUMBER

KUNSAL IMPORT

◆

**Chagdud Gonpa
198 N. River Rd.
Cottage Grove, OR 97427
(541) 942-9253/942-3106
fax (marked: attn. Jigme
Lama at 942-9253)**

**TRADITIONAL BUDDHIST
RITUAL ITEMS AND ARTWORK**

LAMA DANCING

Invited in 1992 by the Tibetan Buddhist Chagdud Gonpa Foundation to teach lama dances in the United States, Jigme Lama and his family have settled at their Dechhen Ling center in Cottage Grove. Born in India, Jigme Lama and his family lived in Orissa, India, at the Tibetan settlement founded by His Holiness Dudjom Rinpoche. Jigme Lama received training at an early age from his father, Lama Dorje Namgyal Rinpoche, who was the head lama for H. H. Dudjom Rinpoche's Dudul Raptenling monastery in Orissa. Jigme Lama completed nine years of traditional studies in the Nyingma lineage of Tibetan Buddhism, which included lama dancing, chanting, musical instrumentation, ritual arts, and shrine keeping. As a guest lama, he continues to teach this traditional style of dancing, chanting, and musical instrumentation.

Jigme Lama and his wife, Kyizom Wangmo, began Kunsal Import to meet the growing need for dharma items among Buddhist practitioners in this country. For those seeking traditional meditation, ritual, and shrine items, artifacts, thangka paintings, statues, and commissioned artwork they have a wide selection. The fine thangkas they carry are detailed tempera paintings on canvas with a traditional brocade fabric border and are usually displayed as wall hangings for meditation practice. These are made by well-known Tibetan and Bhutanese artists living in Nepal.

The exquisite Buddhist statues are of copper with gold-leaf faces and 24-karat plating throughout, with detailed hand-painted features. Paintings and statues depict traditional Buddhist themes. These meditation deities represent the perfect qualities of Buddha and one's own potential for enlightenment. The ornate ritual and meditation items are traditional water bowls, butter lamps, mandala pans, bell and dorje sets, drums, horns, cymbals, brocade sets for thrones, and puja tables, providing a rich part of Tibetan Buddhist culture in the West.

L ichen was established in 1971 as a cooperative land conservancy/trust, and most of its 140 acres is a wildlife refuge and environmental sanctuary. Because of this, it now prohibits domestic animals. "Environmentalism is our nearest approach to a community spirituality, and our philosophy of personal growth is based on the individual's development within the community context, rather than having the community be a hodgepodge of individualized traits." Current businesses include contract services, non-defense electromechanics; field recording, editing, and producing cassette tapes of nature sounds, especially birdsong; and crafts.

LICHEN

◆

**P.O. Box 25
Wolf Creek, OR 97497
(541) 866-2665
(most easily reached
7:00–8:00 A.M.)**

**ELECTROMECHANICAL
MEASURING DEVICES
BIRDCALL TAPES
CRAFTS**

BIRDCALL TAPES

For the Lichen Co-op in Wolf Creek, Oregon, Eleanor Pugh puts together 60- and 90-minute tapes of calls of birds of the entire Western United States. Pugh offers a listing of available cassettes, but the possibilities are not confined to those listed. Tapes are made to order, so that if a customer has two favorite families of birds (such as wrens and warblers or owls and thrushes), Pugh can easily produce a tape to meet the request. One can also order a cassette of calls from a specific habitat. These are the ones that are readily available: Mountain Forest Birds, Birds of Foothill Woodland, Birds of Wetlands, Birds of the High Desert, Birds of the Southwestern Low Deserts, Backyard Bird Songs, Wintering Birds, Owls, Woodpeckers, Flycatchers, Sparrows, Warblers, Four Difficult Flycatchers, Pacific Tidelands and Coastal Birds, Wrens, Thrushes, and Finches and Bunting. There is also a tape of Mammals.

According to Lichen Co-op, some people enjoy the tapes for their instructional value as an aid to getting further acquainted with the sounds and songs of nature. Others like to listen to the tapes in their cars. And some test their knowledge by trying to guess the source of a call, so they will request a tape that identifies the call after it is heard. One can order tapes without narrative, like "Beautiful Bird Songs of the West," for undistracted listening. Special tapes for young people are also available.

◆

*For a listing of available cassettes, call Eleanor Pugh at Lichen, (541) 866-2665.
Between 7:00 A.M. and 8:00 A.M. Pacific Time is best.*

MONASTERY OF OUR LADY OF CONSOLATION

◆

**23300 Walker Ln.
Amity, OR 97101
(503) 835-8080/
835-9662 fax**

CHOCOLATE FUDGE AND
TRUFFLES

CALLIGRAPHY

ROSARIES

RETREATS

These Catholic Brigittine monks moved to this property from California in the 1980s to acquire a permanent home for their cloistered community. They make chocolate confections, reasoning that "everyone likes chocolate," and sell them by mail. Their fudge and truffles are good enough to satisfy the most demanding chocoholic. One resident monk does calligraphy, others make rosaries. There is room for six retreatants to share the life of prayer with the monks who observe the canonical hours.

MOUNT ANGEL ABBEY

◆

**St. Benedict, OR 97373
(503) 845-3030/
845-3594 fax**

SEMINARY AND GRADUATE
SCHOOL

BACH FESTIVAL

RETREATS

This is one of the main Catholic seminaries in the Northwest, run by Benedictine monks who settled here more than 100 years ago. Courses can be taken by laypeople at the Theological Graduate School, which has a 44,000-square-foot library with 250,000 volumes.

The annual Bach Festival is held in the latter part of July. For three evenings in a row, the sacred music of Bach is performed on harp, flute, harpsichord, trumpet, and by a capella singers, solo or together. Each evening's program starts with a Vespers prayer service followed by music, then a break for a picnic supper on the lawn. After the meal, the concert continues in the hall at Damian Center. Hundreds attend for the elegant music and a chance to visit the monastery and college. The Abbey buildings sit on a butte with commanding views of the surrounding lush countryside that stretches for miles, and the snowcapped peak of Mt. Hood hovers in the distance.

The Abbey's annual program of retreats includes weekends for artists, flight attendants, and other professional groups.

PRAYER BEADS/ROSARIES

Similar-sized beads or knotted cords, usually in a continuous circular pattern, are used in many traditions to aid in counting consecutive prayers. The use of prayer beads has long been a custom in Christianity, Hinduism, Buddhism, and Islam.

In Christianity, one source traces the practice of using prayer beads to Eastern Orthodox monks during the third century A.D. The practice evolved through various forms and came to be called the rosary (from the Latin *rosarium,* "rose garden," suggesting a tour through). In its current form, it is a chaplet of 55 beads separated into decades of ten identical beads with one slightly larger bead between. The larger bead represents the "Our Father" prayer and the smaller beads the "Hail Mary," followed by the "Glory be to the Father."

The rosary developed as a substitute for the monastic practice of saying all 150 psalms every week. Instead of the 150 psalms, individuals would say 150 prayers, keeping track with beads. The full rosary is 150-plus prayers divided into three mysteries, each accompanied by a meditation. The Joyful Mysteries focus on Christ's incarnation; the Sorrowful Mysteries on His death; the Glorious Mysteries on His resurrection.

The Eastern Orthodox tradition of Greece and Turkey uses 100 beads of equal size; the Russian Orthodox *chotki,* or chaplet, has 103 beads in irregular sections separated by four larger beads that suggest a ladder. In Islam, three turns of a chaplet of 33 beads represent the 99 names of Allah found in the Koran. The Buddhist mala has 108 beads for counting one's breath or the repetition of a mantra. Counting the beads can also be employed as a simple timing device.

Almost every Christian monastery that has a gift shop sells rosaries, often in very elegant forms. We found one monastery that does rosary repair, and one very large gift shop, attached to a monastery in Georgia, which has an enormous selection in sizes from small to wall-size. The Marian Shrine in West Haverstraw, New York, has an outdoor, mile-long Rosary Way where the fifteen Mysteries of the Rosary are depicted in life-size sculpture groups, each in its own woodland setting.

OUR LADY OF GUADALUPE TRAPPIST ABBEY

◆

9200 N.E. Abbey Rd.
P.O. Box 97
Lafayette, OR 97127
(503) 852-0103/
852-7748 fax
(800) 294-0105:
fruitcake orders

FRUITCAKE
NUT CAKE
BISCOTTI
BOOKBINDING
WINE WAREHOUSING
RETREATS

Trappist monks came to this out-of-the-way region of Oregon in 1953 and are now known for their delicious fruitcake and nut cake, both soaked in bourbon for an exotic flavor, which inspired one writer to compare the flavors to music: "Think of the melding of voices in the Hallelujah chorus or the Phil Spector version of 'White Christmas.'" The monks also make and sell Honey Almond Biscotti and Hazelnut Chocolate Chip Biscotti.

The abbey does book and pamphlet binding for local universities and businesses, and warehouses bottled wine for local wineries. The 1,300 acres of monastery property are a carefully managed forest, which they have extensively replanted and nourished. It provides private retreatants with woodland trails to wander when sharing the prayerful life of the monastery.

J acquelyn Bruni, a psychotherapist, who founded the Rosewood Institute, says, "For as long as I can remember, things Tibetan have sung to me." Ten years ago she began to study Tibetan Buddhism and became acquainted with many Tibetan people and their sacred art, which has traditionally had the ability to transport the practitioners viewing it to greater spiritual heights. The spiritual practice of the artisans is said to be so deep that the objects they create carry within them profound blessings.

Rosewood's purpose is to help make these artifacts available in the West as one way to keep Tibetan culture alive and to provide a market for artists in refugee communities in India and Nepal. These communities are constellated around *gompa*s, Tibetan Buddhist monasteries, with lamas, monks, nuns, and laypeople creating the art. The thangkas are painted on cloth and framed in brocade, and represent compassion in many energies, peaceful and fierce. They help students visualize the qualities desired or needed: Tara for wisdom and compassion; Vajrasattva, who purifies; or Vasadhara, who helps create wealth. Rosewood will custom-order any deity desired. "We are able to provide *zdi* beads, which are found only in high Himalayan streams and have no known origin on this planet.

"Rosewood sells rupas, hollow statues which represent energies in the same manner as the thangkas. Sanctification is done by cleansing the interior and filling the statue with relics and prayers before sealing it tightly." The Institute offers "wealth" vases as well as "earth treasure" vases, whose blessings are said to extend for 15 miles. They contain images and mantras of many divine beings and precious substances like gold, silver, turquoise, rubies, pearls, jade, emeralds, minerals, water, and soil from sacred places, and grains and sacred herbs from around the world. The secret nature of the vases is the increase of goodness and the elimination of evil. The wealth treasure vase contains many precious substances such as gold, silver, jade, amethyst, crystals, shells, grains such as peas, lentils, rice, and pictures and mantras of wealth deities. Its secret nature is the state of a happy and contented mind, the elimination of evil, and the increase of goodness.

ROSEWOOD INSTITUTE OF TIBETAN ART

◆

**130 Helman St.
Ashland, OR 97520
(541) 488-7981
(541) 482-1308 fax
E-mail: jackieb@mind.net**

TIBETAN *ZDI* BEADS

WEALTH AND EARTH
TREASURE VASES

THANGKAS

RUPAS

STATUES

Lama Sonam

OREGON

219

Pennsylvania

◆——◆——◆

COMMUNITY OF CELEBRATION

◆

809 Franklin Ave.
P.O. Box 309
Aliquippa, PA 15001
(412) 375-1510/
375-1138 fax
E-mail: celebrat
@nauticom.net
Web site:
www.nauticom.net/
www/ritters
/celebration.htm

BOOKS
SHEET MUSIC
RECORDINGS
MUSIC AND LITURGY
CONSULTING
CONFERENCES
GUEST ROOMS FOR A
BENEDICTINE COMMUNITY
EXPERIENCE

This Episcopal community of 18 helps support itself through sales of its worship resources consisting of CDs and tapes such as *Let Our Praise Be as Incense, Worship with the Fisherfolk* (scriptural songs), and *How Sweet the Sound* (gospel); books such as *A Pilgrim's Way: A Guide for Building Christian Community* and *I'm Gonna Run, Run, Run,* action songs for children; sheet music which includes *The Celebration Psalter, A Hymn Tunes Mass,* and *Piano Solos;* and videos such as *Leading Worship with the Guitar.* Some members of the community act as consultants for liturgy and music and programs for small churches to enliven their music.

This is a unique community of couples, children, and singles, which welcomes guests for short or long visits who would like to experience a Benedictine lifestyle of stability, conversion, and obedience. It holds conferences on Celtic spirituality and other themes exploring how our eyes may be opened to the presence of God in the ordinary things of life.

The community has more than 200 companions worldwide who share their vows, help with donations, follow a discipline of daily prayer and Scripture reading, attend Holy Eucharist weekly, observe the evangelical virtues of poverty, chastity, and obedience by living simply, pursuing purity of heart in all relationships, taking baptismal and other sacramental vows with utmost seriousness, and participating actively in the life of a local church community. Quite a commitment!

The headquarters of the Institute is located on 400 acres of rolling hills in the Pocono Mountains of northeastern Pennsylvania. Founded by Swami Rama in 1971 to create a bridge between East and West, the Institute is devoted to teaching holistic health, yoga, and meditation as a means to foster personal growth of the individual and the betterment of society. It operates a publishing venture that produces spiritually useful books and tapes on meditation, sacred wisdom and art, healthy and purposeful living, and mindful dying. Its magazine deals with the philosophy of yoga and meditation, and it operates the East West bookstores in New York City, which carry a large selection of spiritual books and tapes. Courses, lectures, programs, and retreats are given regularly in Honesdale and the metropolitan New York area.

HIMALAYAN INTERNATIONAL INSTITUTE OF YOGA SCIENCE AND PHILOSOPHY

◆

RR 1, Box 400
Honesdale, PA 18431
(717) 253-5551/
253-9078 fax
(800) 822-4547
E-mail:
himalaya@epix.net

INSTRUCTION
YOGA ACCESSORIES
BOOKS
TAPES
MAGAZINE
BOOKSTORES
RETREATS

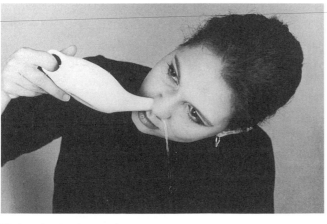

Neti pot for clearing nasal passages

PENDLE HILL

◆

**338 Plush Mill Rd.
Wallingford, PA 19086
(610) 566-4507/
566-3679 fax
(800) 742-3150**

INSTRUCTION
BOOKS
RETREATS

Pendle Hill is a Quaker center for study and contemplation situated on 23 acres in a suburban neighborhood of Philadelphia. The resident community makes it possible for students of all ages to visit and stay for various periods to take courses in Quaker faith and practice, and examine fundamental questions such as "What am I called to do now, and how can I find the place to do it?" and "Who am I becoming?" Since the 1930s, Pendle Hill has published books and pamphlets relating to Quaker philosophy and history, and makes them available through their bookstore catalog. Retreats are scheduled throughout the year.

SAINT BENEDICT CENTER

◆

**355 E. Ninth St.
Erie, PA 16503
(814) 459-7199/
459-8066 fax
(814) 459-5994 orders
E-mail:
benetvision@juno.com
E-mail:
paxchristi@igc.apc.org**

BOOKS
VIDEOS
ART CLASSES FOR CHILDREN
PAX CHRISTI PUBLICATIONS

The Catholic Benedictine sisters who live here describe themselves as "ordinary women with an extraordinary love for life." This is home to the poet and writer Mary Lou Kownacki, O.S.B., and the inspiring and indefatigable speaker and writer Joan Chittister, OSB. In *A Passion for Life: Fragments of the Face of God,* Chittister writes, "Saints are people like ourselves, reachable figures, who have lived well through situations similar to our own, as proof that we too . . . can stretch ourselves to the limits of the best in us." The sisters invited the Erie community to join them in starting the Neighborhood Art House, an art center for inner-city children that gives them a chance to learn music, painting, sculpture, writing, and other art forms. This vibrant place is now a thriving part of the city. Their feeling is expressed in the maxim "To give people welfare allows survival; to give them art develops their soul." This is also the center for Pax Christi USA, an international Catholic organization that publishes books and newsletters speaking out for peace and justice.

5

A soup kitchen regular,
Jim babbles on for hours
in nonstop nonsense.
In eight years,
we never heard him speak
a coherent sentence
until the day
a volunteer brought in her newborn
to the kitchen
and was walking
from table to table,
showing baby Joel to the guests.
When Jim beheld the child,
the baffled look
disappeared from his eyes
and he announced
in a loud and clear voice:
"I was like that once.
I'd like to be like that again."
A five-second sentence,
then Jim's eyes clouded over
and he babbled on.

Is this not a miracle?

◆

From The Blue Heron and Thirty-seven Other Miracles *by Mary Lou Kownacki, O.S.B.,*
published by Benetvision, 355 E. 9th St., Erie, PA 16503. (814) 459-0314. Reprinted with permission.

Rhode Island

PORTSMOUTH ABBEY

◆

Portsmouth, RI 02871
(401) 683-2000

PREP SCHOOL
PROGRAMS

These Catholic Benedictine monks run a coeducational prep school on 500 acres of shorefront just seven miles north of Newport. The more than 300 students are taught to meet the challenges and responsibilities of life in the Christian tradition. Eighty percent of the students are Catholic, and all go on to college. During the summer, programs are offered for visitors who stay in the dormitories. Monks sing the canonical hours in the octagonal chapel, which has a gold crucifix suspended over the altar by a multitude of fine wires radiating out like beams of light.

THE ELECTION OF A PRIORESS/ABBOT

In choosing a prioress/abbot, the guiding principle should always be that the one placed in the office be the one selected either by the whole community acting unanimously out of reverence for God, or by some part of the community, no matter how small, which possesses sounder judgment. Goodness of life and wisdom in teaching must be the criteria for choosing the one to be made prioress/abbot even if s/he is the last in community rank.

May God forbid that a whole community should conspire to elect a prioress/abbot who goes along with its own evil ways. But if it does, and if the bishop of the diocese or any Benedictine leaders or other Christians in the area come to know of these evil ways to any extent, they must block the success of this wicked conspiracy, and set a worthy person in charge of God's house. They may be sure that they will receive a generous reward for this, if they do it with pure motives and zeal for God's honor. Conversely, they may be equally sure that to neglect to do so is sinful.

◆

Chapter 64, A Reader's Version of the Rule of Saint Benedict in Inclusive Language

South Carolina

Since 1949, when Trappist monks were given this former plantation by Henry and Clare Booth Luce, they have worked as cattle ranchers and corn, wheat, and soybean farmers; have raised hogs; and—the latest and most successful endeavor—are raising chickens for eggs that they sell to local institutions and businesses.

The monks discovered that 40,000 chickens create a by-product that has to be dealt with on a regular basis, and they were able to create a silk purse out of chicken droppings. One of the brothers attended compost school to learn scientific procedures, while another tested the mixtures on garden plots, and success began to materialize. The product name was an inspiration during a radio talk show while one of the monks was being interviewed, and *Earth Healer* was born. The hen manure is mixed with kiln-dried white pine shavings, and the combination replenishes soil with natural microorganisms that foster healthy root systems. The soil is healed organically in an ecologically safe way, and the process recycles animal waste and timber at the same time. Each step of the mix formulation is done by the monks, and no chemicals are used.

The monastery offers a program for men interested in examining Trappist life, to live and work with the community for varying periods of time. There are a few rooms for retreatants, and, naturally, eggs are served at meals at least once a day.

MEPKIN ABBEY

◆

1098 Mepkin Abbey Rd.
Moncks Corner, SC 29461
(803) 761-8509/
761-6719 fax

EGGS
COMPOST FERTILIZER
RETREATS

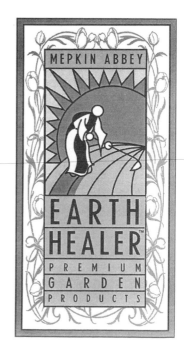

MONASTERY OF
ST. CLARE

◆

**1916 N. Pleasantburg Dr.
Greenville, SC 29609
(864) 244-4514/
268-9379 fax
E-mail:
abrgreenville@prodigy.net**

ALTAR BREAD

VESTMENTS

POTTERY

CARDS

ROSARY REPAIR

RETREATS FOR WOMEN AND
PRIESTS

Invited by the local Catholic bishop, Poor Clare sisters came to Greenville in 1954 to establish an island of prayer in this distinctly Southern city. Reportedly, the bishop said their arrival "would get a pincer's movement on the devil." The metaphor is an unlikely one, since the sisters are anything but combative. They rise early and spend their day in a prayer cycle, living a life where, as one writer described it, "riches are found in poverty, freedom in sequestration, and intimacy in chastity." Each sister performs work to contribute to products that support the community's modest lifestyle. The main product is altar bread. Other sisters create handwoven liturgical vestments, pottery, and note cards, and one unusual service offered is rosary repair. Retreats are available for women and priests. One woman, a writer, came for a weekend retreat 25 years ago, joined the community, and has been there ever since.

ST. CHRISTOPHER
CAMP AND
CONFERENCE
CENTER

◆

**2810 Seabrook Island Rd.
Johns Island, SC 29455
(803) 768-0429**

RETREATS

LOCAL ART

T-SHIRTS

This Episcopal retreat has 308 acres of shorefront where dolphins swim within twenty feet of the land, and old oaks and palmettos grace the area. The natural wood buildings blend into the low country 25 miles south of Charleston, and the staff offers family retreats for Thanksgiving, Advent, and Lent, attracting families who return year after year. Local art and printed T-shirts are available in the gift shop.

ALTAR BREAD

For Christians, the symbolic eating of bread or wafers as part of a service commemorates the Last Supper, when Jesus took bread, broke it, and said, "Take ye and eat, for this is my body . . . do this in remembrance of me." Many communities make bread for their own use at a service.

However, when congregations are large, it is more efficient to have the bread or wafers already prepared in a flat, light, circular form known as the host, for ease of distribution. Some communities make or provide hosts as an ongoing business.

The Poor Clares of Greenville, South Carolina, report they have been supplying altar bread since 1954, and this involvement is a form of sacred work. It is required that the hosts be made of unleavened bread, a tradition traced to the Book of Exodus, which describes the Jews leaving Egypt in such haste that there was no time to allow the bread to rise. The sisters believe this requirement is upheld today because there is a purity about bread made simply, without preservatives, especially bread that will ultimately be transformed spiritually into the Body of Jesus during the Eucharist service.

The Poor Clares are contemplative sisters who attempt to keep the spirit of prayer alive in any work they do. Making altar bread is a quiet and prayerful activity that adds a dimension to their contemplative life, and it can be produced in the confines of the monastery. They sell to Catholic as well as Episcopalian, Methodist, and Presbyterian churches.

Managed by a group of Catholic sisters from various congregations, the programs center on the power of creative energy and the importance of spiritual, mental, and physical health. Part of a huge plantation, this retreat has 65 acres of its own in a secluded, remote setting amid the indigenous vegetation of South Carolina: live oaks, Spanish moss, flowering bushes. Courses throughout the year are taught by skilled potters, basket weavers, and other art and craft teachers, with a focus on tapping the inner spirit.

SPRINGBANK RETREAT CENTER

◆

**Rte. 2, Box 180
Kingstree, SC 29556
(803) 382-9778**

ART INSTRUCTION

PROGRAMS

RETREATS

S
O
U
T
H

C
A
R
O
L
I
N
A

◈

South Dakota

◆ ◆ ◆

MANNA MINISTRY CENTER

◆

27213 473rd Ave.
Sioux Falls, SD 57108
(605) 743-2228

SOD

MEDIATION CENTER

SPIRITUAL DIRECTION

RETREATS AND
CONFERENCES

FESTIVAL

The newsletter *Manna from Manna* gives the essence of this evangelical group, whose center is on fourteen acres in rural South Dakota: "The Lord has blessed the sod business again this year. In the past this is what has enabled us to keep moving Manna ahead. However, we are now at a point . . . when we will begin needing help with the financial support of other ministries. Manna has had to broaden its base so it can begin helping new, small ministries in this area. They are doing what no one else has been able to do. For example, Paul is working with the teens in the inner city. Regan is a chaplain in the prison. Paul speaks in the public schools. Trinity Corrections is teaching prisoners how to work. Tom is training teens in mission work and taking them to missions abroad."

In addition, "a good number of memorials were received and several churches had their baptismal services at Lake Manna. The Harvest Festival will include raffles, hayrides, booths, games, supper. Please bring a treat for the Sioux Falls Food Pantry."

The center can serve up to 120 people for meals, and has beds for up to 40 overnight, and a variety of groups come for conferences and retreats.

They also offer "Mediation: The Christian Alternative for Dispute Resolution," in association with the South Dakota Center for Conflict Resolution. Their mediation "emphasizes commonalities, connectedness, and mutuality of people. It focuses on the future, not the past, [and] does not find fault with any party, but focuses on solutions to the dispute and reopening lines of communication."

Tennessee

◆——————◆——————◆

Founded by Stephen Gaskin in 1971, this intentional community of families and friends lives on three square miles in the southern part of central Tennessee. The community is based on honesty, meaningful work, compassion, and love. As one writer says, "It is not what we are doing, [but] rather *how* we are currently doing it . . . it is a process rather than an end result."

Over the years, The Farm has published books, magazines, and newsletters, and has developed a number of products, available by mail order, that reflect the growing consciousness of right livelihood and proper nourishment. Among the many products available are: tofu, yogurt, soy milk, tempeh, supplies for gourmet mushroom growers, and Radiation Alert, a handheld radiation monitor used by laboratories, hospitals, schools, and homes. The Midwife School, started by Ina May Gaskin, author of *Spiritual Midwifery,* is still active here, and many babies are delivered yearly. One of their videos is *Birthing for Midwives.* The construction company does remodeling and log cabins. Each Labor Day weekend, The Farm's annual harvest festival welcomes thousands to workshops and demonstrations. And in April there's a three-day Unity Fest. People come to the festival for live music, good food, and fun for all.

**THE FARM
COMMUNITY**

◆

**34 The Farm
Summertown, TN 38483
(615) 964-3574/
964-3518 fax
(800) 695-2241:
books and products
Web site:
www.org.thefarm**

◆

**THE MAIL ORDER
CATALOG
P.O. Box 180
Summertown, TN 38483
E-mail: catalog@usit.net
Web site:
www.vege.com**

BOOKS

VIDEOS

TOFU

YOGURT

MUSHROOMS

RADIATION MONITORS

MIDWIFE SCHOOL

CONSTRUCTION

FESTIVALS

MUSHROOMS

Noted poison, hallucinogen, and pizza topping, the mushroom appears in many forms and species in the meadows and forests of the world. Although most mushrooms are safe and edible, one must be extremely cautious when dealing with these versatile fungi. Known to be a good source of vitamin B, edible mushrooms may have other, lesser-known health benefits. For example, The Farm community in Summertown, Tennessee, offers the shiitake mushroom, which appears to be a virtual panacea. Loaded with "immune-boosting action," the shiitake also is reputed to be antiviral, to reduce serum cholesterol in the body, to regulate blood pressure, to counteract fatigue, and even to improve the complexion.

◆

Interested in growing your own shiitake mushrooms? Contact The Farm and ask for MushroomPeople, their suppliers for mushroom growers.

SOYBEANS AND SOY PRODUCTS

An integral part of the Chinese diet for over 4,000 years, the soybean has only in the last century worked its way into the American diet, its agriculture, and its industry. Yet despite its infancy in the West, this annual summer legume appears to be here to stay. Soy milk, tofu, and soy meat substitutes are widely consumed (especially by those who are lactose intolerant), and soybean oil, according to the *Encyclopedia Americana,* accounts for 34 percent of the total production of edible fats and oils in the United States and about 60 percent of edible vegetable oils. Furthermore, soybean meal enjoys widespread use in industry (for adhesives and plastics, among other products) and as feed for poultry and livestock.

What makes soy such an attractive dietary and agricultural option? As a source of energy and protein, it's tough to beat. One has to eat five pounds of meat to obtain the same amount of protein that is in just two pounds of soy flour. In addition to its nutritive value, it has proven its ability to grow in different climates and on different continents. As one of its cottage industries, The Farm in Summertown, Tennessee, offers various soy products, including tofu and TVP—textured vegetable protein—a meat substitute that is low in fat and has no cholesterol. Producers at The Farm have seen how soy can contribute to meeting the vast food needs of the world, and their Farm Soy Company is furthering the exploration of alternative methods of food production and distribution.

◆

For information on TVP and TVP cookbooks, call The Farm's mail-order line at (800) 695-2241.

Short Mountain Sanctuary (SMS) is a community of gay men and lesbian "womyn," families, and friends. It operates programs in sustainable agriculture, holistic forestry, low-cost shelter, and alternative energy. The working farm includes goats, an organic garden and fruit trees, chickens, and beehives. Income is derived from annual dues of $75 and registration fees for two nine-day gatherings in May and October. SMS is also home to *RFD: A Country Journal for Gay Men Everywhere*, "for and about radical faeries."

Texas

CORPUS CHRISTI ABBEY

◆

HCR 2, Box 6300
Sandia, TX 78383
(512) 547-3257/
547-5184 fax
(800) 395-8057
food supplements
E-mail: ccabbey@aol.com

FESTIVAL
FRUITCAKES
FOOD SUPPLEMENTS
RETREATS

This monastery has 110 acres on the shores of Lake Corpus Christi, about 50 miles northwest of Corpus Christi. The Catholic Benedictine monks host the annual Abbeyfest on the last full weekend of October, which offers plenty to eat and drink, bingo, an auction, and dancing. Fruitcakes are available during the holiday season, and the gift shop sells religious items, books, and art objects made by the monks and oblates of the community. Powdered organic Barleygreen, carrots, and other items are available by mail. The monks welcome anyone for retreats, regardless of race, color, or national origin. There is a large charismatic group that meets at the Abbey regularly.

The Order of St. Clare, also called the Poor Clares, was founded by Clare of Assisi, who was inspired to follow in the footsteps of her brother, Saint Francis, to lead a life dedicated entirely to contemplation. "We seek to re-experience the original Franciscan community in which all loved, served, and nourished one another. By our mutual love we offer ourselves to the world as disciples of Christ, joyfully journeying toward the communion of eternal happiness. Our poverty goes far beyond the giving up of earthly possessions. It is an expression of the complete confidence of children who entrust themselves wholly to their Father."

Although these nuns are cloistered contemplatives, they need more than alms to survive, so they have turned to "the work of our hands" in unusual ways. Since 1981 they have raised and sold miniature horses, bred to be under 34 inches in height and as small as 25 inches at maturity. Miniature horses were all but unheard of until about 20 years ago, earliest legends placing them in the courts of royalty, where they were "unique and fanciful gifts and playthings for the young lords and ladies of the palace. It is reported that Empress Eugenie, wife of Napoleon III, began a fad in the mid-1800s as she used miniatures to pull her carriage around the streets of Paris." These tiny creatures are intelligent, affectionate, eager to please, and easy to train. Enthusiasm and interest in them has spread, and in 1978 the American Miniature Horse Association was formed, recognizing them as a breed and setting forth breed standards and height limits. The Franciscan Poor Clares of Brenham currently have sixty miniature horses, which sell for $3,000–$5,000 each.

The sisters got into the horse business quite by chance. For years they raised parakeets and coped with the constant cleaning and continual chirping of their many charges. Because their customers were pet shops all over the United States, they spent a great deal of time packing the birds up and taking them to the airport for shipment. Then they decided to raise Persian and Himalayan long-haired cats. The sisters loved the cats,

MONASTERY OF ST. CLARE

◆

**Rte. 7, Box 7504
Brenham, TX 77833
(409) 836-2444/836-9652
fax/answering machine
E-mail:
chandler@phoenix.net**

MINIATURE HORSES
GUIDED TOURS
CERAMICS
ARTS AND CRAFTS
ALTAR BREAD
AUCTIONS

and the business was profitable, but after a while the strain of caring for 100 kittens that needed brushing, playing with, vaccinating, and worming was more than the small community could cope with. At just about this time, a friend offered them a miniature horse. The gift was an immediate sensation, with a story eventually appearing in *National Geographic* in March 1985, which drew attention from around the world. The horses are sweet and friendly. They require two daily feedings and periodic care of their hooves, which is done by a specialist, and this leaves much more time for the nuns to pray. Their 98 acres of hills and woods, ponds and meadows, trees and wildflowers, and the moderate local climate is a perfect location for this venture.

Located halfway between Austin and Houston, the monastery opens its grounds to visitors daily from 2:00 to 4:00 P.M. for self-guided tours of the horses, the Art Barn gift shop, and the chapel. Guided tours are available by reservation. The Sister Bernadette Memorial Auction is held each May and September, where you can buy the monastery's miniature horses or those on consignment, sent by breeders across the United States.

In addition, the sisters offer 3,000 to 4,000 ceramic molds and other arts and crafts of horses, nativity sets, tree ornaments, angels, and other decorative items, which are for sale in their gift shop. The sisters also make altar breads for the Austin and Corpus Christi dioceses, which they find very satisfying as it allows them to participate in the Eucharist in a very personal way.

ENTRANCE PROCEDURE

If you feel you might be called to our way of life, we will help you in the discernment process by means of correspondence, visits, etc. (We have a guesthouse available for overnight stays.) If, after a time of mutual discernment, it seems you might have a vocation, the next step would be to fill out an application form and get the necessary paperwork begun. We do require a medical and dental checkup as well as our interview with you.

FORMATION PROCESS

If you are accepted, you will spend six years in formation before taking final vows in the religious life. The first year covers the postulancy, in which the discernment process continues as you adjust to life in our community. The second and third years are spent in the novitiate, and mark the true beginning of religious life. You will live the final three years of formation as a Sister in temporary vows of poverty, chastity, obedience, and enclosure before making the decision to commit to them for the rest of your life.

Who is eligible?

We are presently accepting as candidates young women between 21 and 38 years of age. One must be

- ◆ a practicing Catholic
- ◆ single
- ◆ of good health in mind and body
- ◆ at least a high school graduate

and have a capacity and willingness to grow in the spiritual life through life in community.

If you meet these qualifications and desire to give yourself entirely to Jesus in the Franciscan way of life, if you can cry out with Francis, "This is what I wish, this is what I seek, this is what I long to do with all my heart," call or write today for an appointment.

◆

Monastery of St. Clare, Franciscan Poor Clare Nuns, Rte. 7, Box 7504, Brenham, Texas 77833; (409) 836-2444/9652 fax

Utah

ABBEY OF OUR LADY OF THE HOLY TRINITY

◆

1250 S. 9500 E.
Huntsville, UT 84317
(801) 745-3784

LIQUID AND CREAMED HONEY

GRAIN

RETREATS

Trappist monks have been in this secluded valley, 18 miles east of Ogden, since 1947. The liquid and creamed honey, which is available by mail order, comes from their hives used to pollinate the 750 acres of alfalfa, barley, and wheat raised commercially. Male retreatants can sample the whole-wheat and raisin bread made by the monastery from its own wheat.

Writing in *The Waters of Siloe,* Thomas Merton described how a Trappist scout discovered this region for a new foundation of monks from Gethsemani, Kentucky: "After a long climb through Ogden canyon, the valley opened out into a mile-wide bowl between mountains. The clean air of high altitudes breathed silently over these fields. Not a home was in sight. The snowy ridge of Mount Ogden stood up stark against the sky, as if it were the sentinel of this wilderness. Eastward was a no-man's-land of snow and sagebrush, and there were deer tracks in the snow. There were 1,600 acres of land with good springs . . . the very silence of the place cried out for Trappists."

Vermont

Part of a network of communities with the same philosophy and beliefs, Community in Island Pond started in 1978 and was once home to 350 people in 14 community houses. In 1992 they began to send families out to begin new communities, and Island Pond now has one house and 30 people. Their business is Simon the Tanner, a retail store selling and repairing shoes and other items listed in the margin. In describing their purpose, they say, "We have not tried to reform something old but rather to restore what was begun but soon lost by the early church in the first century—communities of believers who surrendered all to live together in faith." The store is closed Saturdays in observance of the Sabbath.

COMMUNITY IN RUTLAND NEW SOCIAL ORDER IN MESSIAH

◆

115 Lincoln Ave.
Rutland, VT 05701
(802) 747-7217/
773-0582/747-7538 fax

SOAP

An outgrowth of the Island Pond community in Vermont, like the Trappist monks who send members off to form new "foundations," they moved their Common Sense Soap Factory here to begin another community, made up of about 80 people in two households. The soap is sold to retail stores throughout the United States and to individuals via mail order.

KARMÊ-CHÖLING

◆

Barnet, VT 05821
(802) 633-2384
(1:00–5:30 P.M.)/
633-3012 fax
(800) 331-7751
E-mail: karmecholing
@shambhala.org
Web site: www.kel
.shambhala.org

INSTRUCTION
PROGRAMS
MEDITATION SUPPLIES
RETREATS

This Tibetan Buddhist meditation center was founded in the 1970s by Chögyam Trungpa, Rinpoche, and has 540 acres in northern Vermont. Instruction and guidance in meditation, from beginner to advanced, through a full series of programs, which include traditional Japanese archery, is offered throughout the year. Samadhi cushions are made here and sold by mail. The gomden, zafu, zabuton mat, and support cushion have been specially designed so that sitting meditation can be comfortable, something the Western mind appreciates and expects. Retreats combined with meditation practice are held regularly.

SOAPMAKING

Making soap is more an art than a science. You don't need to be a chemist to make good soap, either. The soapmaking process, called saponification (from the Latin *saponaria*—a plant which the Romans used for washing), is one of the oldest chemical reactions known and the basis of most modern soapmaking is still the simple process it was centuries ago, with a few refinements.

Soap is actually a salt, the result of an acid reacting with an alkali or base, the acid being a weak organic acid in the form of rendered animal fats or vegetable oils and the base being either sodium hydroxide, which produces a hard soap, or potassium hydroxide, which produces a softer soap. The result of this reaction is a molecule that is attracted to water at one end and oil at the other. Soap cleans by causing greasy dirt, which does not mix well with water, to mix with water and be removed from clothes or hands.

Our soap begins with pure vegetable oils into which we blend a solution of sodium hydroxide and water. Near the end of the saponification process, we add pure essential oil blends for fragrance. The result is a hard soap that is mild and nice-smelling.

We never intended to form a community around soapmaking. We began making soap and other natural body-care products because we wanted to use pure and safe natural ingredients to make products we would use ourselves, and we wanted to include our children in the practical outworking of the life we'd been living for the past 25 years.

For us, people of all ages, races, cultural, and intellectual distinctions living and working together in unity is not an elusive dream. It's a practical reality that comes about from surrendering our individual lives to the Creator of heaven and earth, not living for our own self-advancement, or merely to have a pleasant place to live, but rather to demonstrate the love He has given us in our life together.

◆

David Woodward, Common Sense Soap Shop, Community in Rutland, Rutland, Vermont

BUDDHIST MEDITATION CUSHIONS

The journey of Buddhism to the West has been markedly successful, but the trip has not left original sitting practice unmodified. Western would-be practitioners have realized that Western joints, accustomed to chairs, often undergo excruciating strain in the normal meditation position. Eastern practitioners were anxious to continue to build a spiritual bridge between East and West, however, and accommodations were quickly made. Out of the demand for a comfortable way for westerners to meditate arose a market for meditation cushions. Several varieties are currently available. For example, Karmê-Chöling in Barnet, Vermont, offers a gomden cushion (18 by 12.5 by 6 inches high) for reduction of knee, leg, and back strain; a zafu (14 inches in diameter by 10 inches high) filled with resilient kapok fiber; a zabuton mat (34 by 30 by 5 inches), which cushions the legs and ankles; and a support cushion (15 inches square or 18 by 12 inches, both 4 inches thick) for extra height or relief of a sore knee. Shasta Abbey in Mount Shasta, California, offers a portable meditation (seiza) bench and a foam meditation wedge, which, when placed on a chair, gives the practitioner the proper angle for meditation. All of these products are designed to help the westerner meditate with fewer physical hindrances. Explaining the importance of body position in meditation, the Shasta Abbey Buddhist Supplies Catalog notes, "Correct posture is essential to the right attitude of mind in meditation practice. When the body is comfortable and relaxed, with the weight centered and the back straight, the mind can be calm and bright."

◆

Shasta Abbey's mail-order line is (800) 653-3315. Karmê-Chöling can be reached at (802) 633-2384.

MILAREPA CENTER

◆

Barnet Mountain
Barnet, VT 05821
(802) 633-4136/
633-3808 fax

FESTIVALS
RETREATS

Buddhist festivals are celebrated at this rustic Buddhist retreat, the location of the famous "Monk Xing" sign, in July, August, and December. Retreats are scheduled throughout the year.

(JACK KELLY)

BUDDHIST FESTIVALS

Many of the Buddhist communities in the United States hold special festivals. Shasta Abbey, in Mount Shasta, California, offers traditional festival ceremonies in which "the community of trainees express their reverence to the Buddhas, Bodhisattvas, and Ancestors who are the symbols of our religious aspiration." Milarepa Center in Barnet, Vermont, conducts four ceremonies annually: three of purification (Buddha's Descent from God Realms; Buddha's Birth, Death, and Enlightenment; Buddha's First Teaching) and one of offering (the Dalai Lama's birthday). Purification ceremonies involve prostration, visualization, mantras, and fasting. Tara Enterprises International, in Poolesville, Maryland, hosts a less formal sort of festival in late October called "Arts for the Park," whose proceeds help support its meditation park. Through these festivals, Buddhist communities of the United States both honor their communal faith and open themselves to larger social communities.

◆

To find out more about various Buddhist festivals held throughout the year, call Shasta Abbey at (916) 926-0428; Tara Enterprises at (301) 407-0499; or Milarepa Center at (802) 633-4136. Shasta Abbey invites "our congregation and all fellow Buddhists to join us for any of these ceremonies."

MONASTERY OF THE IMMACULATE HEART OF MARY

◆

**HCR 13, Box 11
Westfield, VT 05874
(802) 744-6525**

ALTAR BREAD

WATERCOLORS

BOOKS

WOODEN ONE-DECADE AND
15-DECADE ROSARIES

DOLOMIE STATUES

BYZANTINE WOOLEN BEADS

HOST CUTTINGS

TAPES

PLAQUES

CARDS

MEDALS

BIBLES

MISSALS

ICONS

GUEST ROOMS FOR WOMEN

This monastery of contemplative nuns is located in northern Vermont, less than an hour from the Canadian border. The resident chaplain, Father Guy-Marie Oury, is a gifted painter, and his lovely watercolors of the Vermont countryside and his native France are for sale in the monastery gift shop at very reasonable prices. He has also written more than 60 books on monasticism, theology, and early Christianity in Canada, many of which are available in the gift shop in several languages.

The gift shop has a large and interesting variety of religious offerings, including Douai and Revised Standard Version Catholic Bibles, Daily Roman Missals, and a wide variety of books from many publishers; exquisite reconstituted stone Dolomie statues from the Sisters of Bethlehem in France; boxwood and olivewood rosaries in many colors, as well as knotted nylon cord rosaries, wooden 15-decade rosaries, one-decade rosaries, and Chotki or Byzantine woolen beads; miraculous medals; crosses and medals of Saint Benedict and other saints; icons mounted on wood; a wide variety of cards for different occasions, including icons, illuminations, and great masters; cassettes of Gregorian chant; small plaques; and host cuttings. Host cuttings are the pieces of bread left after the altar bread that the nuns make is cut into rounds. These unconsecrated pieces are sold to the local natural foods store, which has developed a series of recipes for them. "We often crisp them in the oven like waffles—they're delicious!"

The altar bread business is the main source of income for the monastery. They offer a variety of sizes: $1\frac{1}{8}$ inch for communion, a $2\frac{1}{2}$-inch priest's host, and a $4\frac{1}{2}$-inch size for concelebrations. They sell to religious institutions all over the country.

For women only, there is a four-bedroom guesthouse adjoining the monastery.

This community of Catholic Benedictine monks has 500 acres adjoining the Green Mountain National Forest, four miles north of Weston. They are known primarily for their recordings of music that grew out of the prayer and life experiences of the monks. The songs are from Scripture or from poetic expressions that celebrate creation, life's journey, our care for the world, and new pathways to freedom. The cassettes and CDs are exceptional, and are presented beautifully in a color catalog and brochures. Song and organ books accompany the recordings. Some of the monks are fine artists, and their work is displayed in a gallery at the monastery. Private retreatants can stay in priory guesthouses. The monks arrange retreats to Mexico to experience the historical, social, and cultural context of Mexican life, under the guidance of Mexican nuns who work with the poor.

WESTON PRIORY

◆

**58 Priory Hill Rd.
Weston, VT 05161
(802) 824-5409/
824-3573 fax**

AUDIOCASSETTES AND CDS

SONG AND ORGAN BOOKS

ARTWORK

GALLERY

RETREATS HERE AND IN
MEXICO

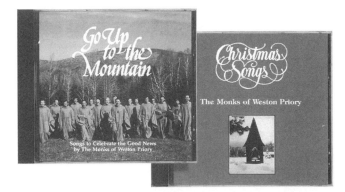

PILGRIMAGES

Pilgrimage has a long history in the religions of the world. Perhaps the most universally known are those of the Islamic faith; the annual pilgrimage to Mecca is one of the "five pillars" of Islam. As the anthropologist Alan Morinis explains in his book *Sacred Journeys,* "Pilgrimage is born of desire and belief. The desire is for solutions of all kinds that arise within the human situation. The belief is that somewhere beyond the known world there exists a power that can make right the difficulties that appear so insoluble and intractable here and now. All one must do is journey."

Weston Priory in Vermont offers a unique pilgrimage experience called the Guadalupe Retreat, or a "Retreat/Hospitality Experience in Latin American Context." Anyone is welcome to join as long as there is room (each of the 11 retreats per year accommodates 16 people). A community of Mexican Benedictine sisters hosts the retreat in Chiapas, the poorest state in Mexico. Weston Priory's brochure notes, "In the context of prayer, discussion, recreation, and reflection, the Sisters seek to introduce participants to the present-day reality of the Mexican people and to give some understanding of life and faith as lived in Latin America." Sound more like a service project than a pilgrimage? Weston Priory adds, "The journey of the retreat is a pilgrimage not to a shrine, but to the temple of the living God in the heart of a people."

◆

For information on Weston Priory's Guadalupe Retreat call (802) 824-5409. For information on Shasta Abbey's Buddhist pilgrimage to the 33 shrines of the Bodhisattva Avalokiteshwara, call (916) 926-4208.

MISSION IN MEXICO

Our Mexican Benedictine Sisters have a mission in northern Chiapas—in the heart of the conflictive zone, among the beleaguered Maya. In the town of Sabanilla, surrounded by incredible natural beauty, four of our sisters work. Living in the old parish center (from which the priest has been recently expelled by the Mexican authorities), the sisters do pastoral work in the town and in the many scattered settlements in the area. The pretext of security, following the recent uprising in Chiapas, has meant a heavy and intimidating military presence in the area.

It is with great love and courage that the sisters daily go out to the isolated hamlets in the mountains. There they encounter a terrified and destitute people, without food, medicine, housing. Many are refugees forced out of their villages, unable to return, some with death threats over their heads. Again and again we heard, "Help our children."

Under suspicion themselves and with little means, the sisters can only hope to rally the hope and gentleness of the people and encourage them to press ahead. Perhaps it is the willingness of the sisters to stay, sharing the hardships and sorrow of the people, that is the greatest witness. Perhaps hope is awakened too, when visitors come, who can bring the story out to the wider world and share as fully as possible the reality they encounter.

◆

Weston Priory Bulletin, Spring/Summer 1997, Weston, Vermont

Virginia

◆ — ◆ — ◆

ABUNDANT DAWN

◆

Rte. 3, Box 51D
Floyd, VA 24091
(540) 745-5853
(540) 745-5835: Tekiah

PORTABLE SAWMILL

HAMMOCKS

**COMMUNITY SUPPORTED
AGRICULTURE (CSA)**

This group of experienced communitarians have created a number of cooperative and communal households that have a commitment to "clear communication and self-awareness, Earth stewardship, and self-realization through service." One of the sub-communities, called Tekiah, subcontracts hammocks for the Twin Oaks community, using polyester yarn rope made from recycled pop bottles. Community members love to work with this rope, and say its fibers make "the softest, prettiest hammocks" of all.

One member of the group has a portable bandsaw, and takes jobs locally as part of an effort to do sustainable harvesting of local woods. The group aims to get a kiln to dry the lumber and sell it locally. They're also intrigued with the possibility of an electric kiln using wind power.

Some of the members are part of a growing movement called Community Supported Agriculture (CSA). This is how it works: A local farmer gets a group of customers to become fee-paying subscribers for the growing season. The fee entitles each customer to a certain amount of produce, and gives them a real connection to their food and the farm; at the same time, it gives the farmer a stronger economic base. It's a way of "investing in the farm" that is of benefit to all concerned.

Located on 72 acres bordering the South Anna River, the Acorn community has close ties with Twin Oaks Community nearby, and earns money from the manufacture and sale of hammocks and tofu. It is also developing crafts businesses, and operates a tinnery, where lampshades are made out of old tin cans. The community is committed to a cooperative, ecologically sustainable lifestyle flexible enough to meet the varied needs of members of all ages and interests. "We take great pleasure living together on the land; work and play are often intertwined. Gathering to swim in the river, sing folk songs, or soaking outside in our wood-fired hot tub are just a few of the things we do to relax and enjoy ourselves."

ACORN

◆

**1259-D6 Indian Creek Rd.
Mineral, VA 23117
(540) 894-0595
E-mail:
AcornFarm@aol.com
Web site:
www.ic.org/acorn**

TINNERY
HAMMOCKS
TOFU

KITCHEN WISH LIST

Kitchen helpers needed

Dessert makers for open house

Jam/jelly makers year-round

Breadmakers

Prepare lunch for a hungry garden crew in June,
    July, August, September, pick your day to cook!

ORGANIC GARDEN AND ANIMAL WISH LIST

Square straw bales for bedding

Sunflower seeds for birds

Oats for llamas

Cost of starter flock of free-range chickens

Hay or alfalfa

Fencing

Donations to organic cash crop expenses

Used, old farm equipment (call for details)

◆

The Bridge Between… Retreat Center, 4471 Flaherty Dr., Denmark, WI 54208; (920) 864-7230

HOLY CROSS ABBEY

◆

Rte. 2, Box 3870
Berryville, VA 22611
(540) 955-3124/
955-4006 fax
E-mail: fruitcak
@globalcom.net
Web site:
www.presstar.com/
fruitcake.html

FRUITCAKE
ELECTRONIC SCRIPTORIUM
PHOTOGRAPHS
CREAMED HONEY
NUT SPREADS
RETREATS

*S*ixty miles from Washington, D.C., this Trappist monastery sits on 1,200 acres of farmland that was the site of the Civil War Battle of Cool Spring. It is now an oasis of quiet and serenity. The main source of its income is the sale of Monastery Fruit Cake, which is an old-fashioned Southern recipe using choice fruits and nuts in a brandy-laced batter. The monks guarantee it's the best you'll ever eat, or your money back. They must be doing something right, since they sell more than 28,000 cakes each year.

In the early 1990s, when cake orders rose tenfold, the monks computerized their fulfillment system and kept the business flowing. That led to an alliance with Electronic Scriptorium, which uses the intelligent, well-educated, and dedicated monks to do catalog entries for libraries, universities, and many other clients by using the computers they already have. Since the Middle Ages, monks working in monasteries have been the keepers of knowledge, much to the benefit of civilization, and this seems to continue the tradition.

There is a limited-edition portfolio for sale of 12 photographs, titled *Conversatio: Cistercian Monastic Life,* which capture the beauty and grace of the Cistercian life. The gift shop has religious items, spiritual books, and monastery products. Additional food items were introduced in 1998, including creamed honeys in three flavors (cinnamon, almond, and brandy), as well as natural peanut butter and walnut and pecan spreads. Private retreatants stay in the guesthouse, where they can sample Trappist hospitality, a gift in itself.

(BONNIE JACOBS)

Openway is a center for healing and education that promotes the process of self-healing. It teaches the Integral Healing Method, a synthesis of psychology, channeling energy for transformation, and an ongoing process of self-discovery and self-healing. The method presumes an existing energy field (aura) and energy centers (chakras) as guides to seven levels of consciousness that lead to the soul. By progressive awakening of every center, the student begins to know and understand each one and how it manifests in daily life. The goal is freedom of the spirit. Courses are taught in a series of workshops that can be taken separately. Two books are available by Openway's founder, Graciela Damewood: *The Soul of Healing: An Autobiography* and *The Psychosynthesis Manual.*

OPENWAY

◆

**206 Broad Axe Rd.
Charlottesville, VA 22903
(804) 293-3245/979-4606
fax (call first)
E-mail: Openway
@compuserve.com**

INSTRUCTION
WORKSHOPS
BOOKS

Delicious Gouda cheese is made by Trappistine sisters in batches of 750 pounds, using fresh pasteurized milk from healthy cows in the nearby Shenandoah Valley. The milk is heated and cultures added to produce curds, which are hand-cut, packed in forms, then pressed. No color or preservatives are added. The finished cheeses are immersed in salt brine and cured in a refrigeration room where the sisters turn and inspect them daily. A special rind is hand-painted on each cheese, which allows it to breathe as it ages. Prior to shipping, each cheese is dipped in a protective wax coating. Two- and five-pound wheels are available by mail. When the sisters acquired this rural property on the eastern slope of the Blue Ridge Mountains, there was already a cheese-making facility on it, and the previous owners were making Gouda. "The decision was made for us," one sister noted, "and it has worked out well, thanks be to God."

OUR LADY OF THE ANGELS MONASTERY

◆

**3365 Monastery Dr.
Crozet, VA 22932
(804) 823-1452/
823-6379 fax
Web site:
www.esinet.net
/angels.html**

GOUDA CHEESE

CHEESE

Techniques for cheesemaking evolved over centuries before refrigeration as a way to store and preserve the nutritional values of milk. Cheese products vary according to the selection and treatment of the milk. Cow's milk is one main source, but milk from goats, sheep, buffalo, llamas, camels, and yaks can be and is used, depending on what animals are available and willing to contribute. Cheese is an excellent source of high-quality complete protein; it provides sufficient amounts of essential amino acids, is moderate to high in cholesterol (depending on variety), and varies in fat content according to cheese type.

Mild, creamy Port Salut was first made by Trappist monks in the French monastery of Port-du-Salut. It has many variations, but is characterized by a distinctive, rich taste that cheese lovers appreciate. Developed in the early 1800s, the formula has been a closely guarded secret. When the cheese was first introduced in Paris in 1875, it was immediately successful and others began to imitate it. After legal wrangling, the name "Port Salut" was assigned for monks' use only. As demand increased in the 1900s, the monks were hard-pressed to meet it, so they developed partnerships with commercial cheesemakers. In the meantime, imitators have developed their own style, and the taste and flavor of Port Salut can be found in many countries, with different names. Denmark makes a cheese known as Esrom, suspiciously close to Port Salut, but it stands on its own merit.

The Trappist monks at Gethsemani, Kentucky, got their recipe from Canadian Trappists who brought it from France. They make three versions: mild, which is young and delicate; aged, which tastes like a strong Esrom; and smoked. The cheese will keep for several months under refrigeration, but for best taste it should be brought to room temperature. It is especially good for dessert with apples and tea.

Gouda cheese, which originated in Holland, is a mild, smooth, pale yellow cheese, perfect for snacks. Gouda is made with a little more butterfat than is Edam. The Trappistine sisters at Our Lady of the Angels Monastery, Crozet, Virginia, make two- and five-pound wheels, which the sisters inspect daily while curing. Each cheese is dipped in a protective wax coating before shipping. Room temperature yields the best taste. The wrapped cheese, if stored in the vegetable bin to avoid extreme cold, should keep for weeks. If mold forms, scrape it away; the rest of the cheese will be fine.

The grand design of this ashram is ecumenism, which is the guiding principle of its founder, Swami Satchidananda. Yogaville occupies 750 acres in central Virginia. The community that lives here runs Shakticom, which produces audio- and videotapes on yoga, including the classic *Integral Yoga Hatha* by Satchidananda—a simple, clear, and well-illustrated guide to more than 80 postures, breathing practices, relaxation, cleansing, and concentration techniques. Their catalog lists books and tapes from many sources on hatha yoga, meditation, relaxation, holistic health, and spiritual guidance, including instruction books from their own Integral Yoga Publications. There is a Tape-of-the-Month Club that allows Satchidananda devotees to keep up on his talks.

One recent discourse states: "Who is responsible for our bondage? Position, power, and possessions don't hold us, we hold them. To free ourselves, we must learn to let go." Programs, which include yoga teacher training, seminars, and retreats, are held throughout the year.

The Light of Truth Universal Shrine, or LOTUS, is one of the outstanding features on the property. The shrine, in a beautiful natural setting, celebrates the unity behind all religious beliefs. The main building, approached through arched gates, is constructed in the shape of the lotus flower, a symbol for enlightenment. Inside are 12 altars, each one dedicated to a major spiritual belief: Native American, African, Sikhism, Islam, Christianity, Buddhism, Taoism, Shinto, Judaism, Hinduism, Other Known Religions, and Those Still Unknown. Daily group meditation is held here.

SATCHIDANANDA ASHRAM– YOGAVILLE

◆

Buckingham, VA 23921
(804) 969-3121
(800) 476-1347 orders

INSTRUCTION
BOOKS
AUDIO- AND VIDEOTAPES
PROGRAMS
RETREATS

TWIN OAKS

◆

138 Twin Oaks Rd.
Louisa, VA 23093
(540) 894-5126/
894-4112 fax
(800) 688-8946:
hammocks
E-mail: TwinOaks
@mcimail.com;
twinoaks@ic.org *and*
hammocks@twinoaks.org
Web sites:
www.twinoaks.org
/hammocks.htm *and*
www.ic.org
/twinoaks

HAMMOCKS
FURNITURE
BOOK-INDEXING
COMPUTER WORK
TOFU/SOY

ounded in 1967 and inspired by B. F. Skinner's novel *Walden Two,* this thriving community of a hundred people aims to be a model social system of human-scale solutions to problems of land use, food production, energy conservation, and appropriate use of technology. They value cooperation, nonviolence, and equality, and try to relate to each other with gentleness and tolerance. They use a trust-based labor system in which all work is valued equally and is considered an enjoyable part of their lives.

They support themselves through the manufacture of handcrafted hammocks and chairs, a book-indexing business, a database fulfillment for magazines and directories, and a tofu and soy-food business. Sales to a large chain helped make the hammock and casual furniture business profitable. They make about a ton of excellent tofu a week, and are experimenting with a variety of unusual flavors. Each member works about 46 hours a week, including domestic chores, which are valued as "real work," from child care to milking the cows. They run two excellent conferences every year: "Women— Celebrating Our Creativity" occurs each summer, and in the fall they host a "Communities Conference," which is a very useful way to network for those now living in communities or considering it.

HAMMOCKS

Tales of many lands and cultures are woven into the history of hammocks. The hammock, like many a good story or beautiful custom, has appeared in multiple places and has left an obscure trail. Many theories have circulated about the hammock's origins, and historians of the Yucatán Peninsula (one of the world's most prominent regions for hammock production) have failed to arrive at a consensus. *Hammock* is believed to be a Haitian word for "tree," suggesting perhaps its position (slung between two trees) or its composition—Spanish conquerors noted hammocks in the Antilles and described them as rough nets made with arboreal fibers. Some say that the hammock is Polynesian in origin and was brought to the Americas by Polynesian explorers. Others argue for the thesis of independent creation, asserting that the hammock was invented by the Polynesians and the inhabitants of the Yucatán independently of one another. All agree that the hammock has been on the Yucatán since at least the sixteenth century, and this region continues to produce hammocks, not only for the Yucatán, but for the United States as well. Known for centuries to be cool and relaxing, the hammock picked up an important modern cultural endorsement when the *Journal of the American Medical Association* praised the back support and stress relief that woven cotton hammocks offer. A well-woven hammock points to the care and focus demanded for its construction, and the relaxation it offers frees the mind from the shackles of the mundane.

The Twin Oaks and East Wind communities produce hammocks to help cover community expenses. However, helping others to reduce stress doesn't take the community away from its primary objectives. Twin Oaks representatives write, "Still, less than half of our work goes into these income-producing activities; the balance goes into a variety of tasks that benefit our quality of life—including milking cows, gardening, cooking and childcare."

◆

For more information on hammocks, visit the Web pages for promotion of Yucatán culture at
www.expo-yucatan.com, *Ramona's Hammocks at* www.ds.net/~mikejim,
or Twin Oaks at www.twinoaks.org.

Washington

CHINOOK LEARNING CENTER

◆

P.O. Box 57
Clinton, WA 98236
(360) 221-3153

TRAINING PROGRAMS
COURSES
WORKSHOPS
CONFERENCES
RETREATS

The center has 72 acres on Whidby Island, a 20-minute ferry ride from mainland Washington, about an hour north of Seattle. There are year-round programs, courses, and workshops on religion, ecology, gardening, psychology, and cultural change. The founders, Vivienne and Fritz Hull, acquired the property in the early 1970s for use as a place to examine the basic questions of why we are here. Inspired by the sixth-century Celtic Christian monastic school on Iona, an island off the coast of Scotland, they see Chinook as a center for study and teaching to create an understanding of the meaning and purpose of life, linking humanity and the earth to concomitant spiritual values. Private retreatants are accommodated according to space available.

CLOUD MOUNTAIN RETREAT CENTER

◆

373 Agren Rd.,
P.O. Box 807
Castle Rock, WA 98611
(360) 274-4859

BUDDHIST INSTRUCTION
RETREATS

Since 1984 the Center has been available for Buddhist groups, regardless of tradition or sect, to use the facilities for classes, sittings, special events, and retreats, which are scheduled throughout the year in conjunction with the Northwest Dharma Association. The rustic center is on five acres of sloping, forested land, and the hand-crafted buildings have been sited according to the earth's energy flow.

EARTH CYCLE FARM

◆

Rte. 1, Box 9-C
Waukon, WA 99008
(509) 236-2265

ORGANIC FARMING

The 80 acres of Earth Cycle Farm are used to develop and demonstrate diverse sustainable agriculture practices. The community engages in organic farming, cover cropping, permaculture, and reforestation, and the farm is an education center for these things. Alternative technologies include windmills, solar electricity, draft animal power, and use of indigenous building materials. People who have a desire to live in harmony with the land and each other are welcome.

SOLAR POWER

In American spiritual communities we consistently find commentary on, and alternatives to, the religious, political, economic, and industrial status quo. Using solar energy is one way in which several communities reject energy uses that are more common and more costly, both in terms of money and the environment. Realizing that the United States' dependence on fossil fuels is inefficient and harmful to the environment, these communities use alternative forms of energy in the hope that others will follow.

The Stelle Group, in Stelle, Illinois, operates its community telephone network on solar power and is dedicated to instructing others about solar power's uses and benefits. According to Mark W. Williamson, president of the Stelle Area Chamber of Commerce, "The Stelle experience could be duplicated anywhere, and we are willing to help facilitate the efforts of like-minded groups to build their own communities."

Earth Cycle Farm, in Waukon, Washington, offers educational services dealing with food production and renewable energy. Opening themselves to the larger community for the improvement of humanity and the environment, Earth Cycle Farm especially enjoys teaching children in the surrounding area.

◆

To contact the Stelle Area Chamber of Commerce, phone (815) 256-2212. Earth Cycle Farm can be reached at (509) 236-2265.

GAIAN CONTEMPLATIVE COMMUNITY

◆

**Church of God at
Vision Mountain
P.O. Box 1147
Tum Tum, WA 99034
(509) 258-9148/
258-9149 fax
E-mail:
Trishuwa@aol.com**

BOOKS
INSTRUCTION
HERBAL PRODUCTS
MEDICINE POUCHES
EQUINOX AND SOLSTICE
CELEBRATIONS
SWEAT LODGES
PIPE CEREMONIES

The Gaian Contemplative Community is an order of earth-centered practitioners. The community was formed in the fall of 1995 under the auspices of the Church of Gaia: Council of Six Directions. Their products reflect their interests and lifestyle, and include such books as *Sacred Plant Medicine* and *One Spirit, Many Peoples: A Manifesto for Earth Spirituality* by Stephen Buhner, an ordained practitioner. There is also a correspondence course by Trishuwa, a ceremonialist for Vision Mountain, called *Ceremony as a Way of Life,* earth astrology charts, and taped readings combining the teaching of the medicine wheel and the zodiac, as well as suggested personal healing ceremonies.

The community also sells beaded leather medicine pouches, herbal tinctures and salves, massage oil, and herbal mosquito repellent. The earth-centered classes include sacred plant medicine, vision quests, and medicine ceremonial programs. Except for the vision quest, programs are available for sponsorship in other parts of the country. In addition to monthly sweat lodges and pipe circles, the community celebrates the equinoxes and summer and winter solstices with special events.

HOLDEN VILLAGE

◆

Chelan, WA 98816

SABBATICALS
PROGRAMS
RETREATS

This former mining settlement is located at the base of Copper Mountain deep in the Cascade Mountains—reached by a 16-mile ferry ride to Holden's dock, then a schoolbus that takes visitors the last 12 miles to the village. A community of 70 men, women, and children live here year-round and make it possible for people of all races, cultures, and beliefs to spend a few months or a year in a spiritual environment to evaluate where they are and where they are going. During the summer, programs are offered on specific spiritual topics, and many come for retreats throughout the year. The gift shop carries books and mementos as well as necessary items one often forgets while traveling. From here, the corner store is not easy to get to.

The Theosophical Society acquired this remote 76-acre retreat on Orcas Island in 1927 as a place where members and friends could come to study and investigate nature, science, and comparative religions. Seminars, workshops, and retreats are held regularly at this quiet, charming, waterfront location where eagles, loons, and otters are frequently seen. There was a resident lama, and a colony of rabbits inhabiting the center of the great lawn when we visited.

(JACK KELLY)

Our Lady of the Rock Priory, a Benedictine foundation of the Abbey of Regina Laudis in Bethlehem, Connecticut, has a unique location, on a small island off the coast of Washington with a population of 125 year-round residents, a few of whom are nuns from a Franciscan order.

In addition to a small guesthouse, the seven nuns run a working farm with two sets of pigs each year, dairy and beef cows, sheep for wool and meat, and llamas for breeding. Their gardens yield the herbs for their vinegars, which include a Melissa vinegar, a light white vinegar that contains lemon balm, bronze fennel, and borage; a basil garlic vinegar, and others depending on the garden that season. They also produce an all-purpose herb seasoning "that can be used on everything but dessert!" Mother Prisca's Hot Mustard is a local favorite, as is their Squaw Bay Herb Tea, made with chamomile, bee balm, peppermint, and other available garden herbs.

These products are sold only at the Franciscan Store on Shaw Island at the Anacordes ferry landing, which is open every day from 9:15 A.M. to 5:00 P.M. except Sunday. During the winter it closes earlier on Tuesday and Thursday.

W
A
S
H
I
N
G
T
O
N
◈

ST. MARTIN'S
ABBEY

◆

**5300 Pacific Ave. SE
Lacey, WA 98503
(360) 491-4700/
438-4387 fax
E-mail:
admissions@stmartin.edu**

COLLEGE
FESTIVAL
EVENTS
PROGRAMS
RETREATS

Catholic Benedictine monks founded St. Martin's College in 1895, and it is the only Benedictine college in the western United States. The abbey and college campus share 380 acres a few miles outside Olympia, the capital city of Washington. The monks seek to imbue Benedictine values of hospitality, graciousness, and tolerance in the education curriculum. They hold the annual Capital Food and Wine Festival, usually the last Saturday in October, which features music, wine tasting, and food and cooking demonstrations. The Abbey Church Events are a series of concerts and lectures, one each month, from October to April. The Spiritual Life Institute holds summer programs that provide continuing theological education, ministerial formation, and personal enrichment. A recent book, *This Place Called Saint Martin's 1895–1995,* by John C. Scott, O.S.B., is the centennial history of the Abbey and college. Private retreatants stay at the guesthouse near the church where the monks pass through the sculptured gates and gather to sing morning, noon, and evening prayer.

"Single parents, retirees, gifted kids (human and animal), and dreamers from 8 to 76 are pioneering a woodsy community, seeking saner social systems, practicing nearly lost crafts, and exploring holistic relationships involved in living close to the land in a sustainable lifestyle." This is a nonprofit co-op, now in its nineteenth year, operated by consensus, which owns the land while its 12 to 21 members retain their own assets and organize projects that suit them. Each pays $380 a month dues, so the organization remains dependent on the members, instead of the members leaning on the organization. There are three community mottoes: "Better off with you than without you"; "Say what you mean and mean what you say"; "Take it seriously or take it elsewhere." They are setting up three "chairs," like a university, in fiber arts, herbal arts, and wild arts, and strive to create value from their work. Some work as shepherds and goatherds. They try to make their presence on the land invisible, with earth-based houses and underground wires. Simplicity, thrift, self-reliance, character, courage, and commitment are important values to them.

Notes from Windward is a journal that covers their theory and practice of life—8 issues a year for $15; $3 for a sample issue. Every June, from the third through the fourth weekend, the community holds a ten-day Festival of Saint Hildegard, a Middle Ages fair featuring educational arts and crafts. Attendees learn how to make cheese, bread, or pottery, or how to weave, starting with shearing the sheep and working until they have their own wool hats.

WINDWARD FOUNDATION

◆

55 Windward Lane
Klickitat, WA 98628
(509) 369-2000
E-mail:
windward@gorge.net

FARM
"THINK TANK"
DAIRY
JOURNAL
APPRENTICESHIP IN FIBER,
HERBAL, AND WILD ARTS
MIDDLE AGES FESTIVAL

West Virginia

BHAVANA SOCIETY

◆

Rte. 1, Box 218-3
High View, WV 26808
(304) 856-3241/
856-2111 fax
E-mail:
bhavanasoc@aol.com

INSTRUCTION
BOOKS
TAPES
RETREATS
NEWSLETTER

In the 1980s, this monastery was founded by Bhante Gunaratana, who came from Sri Lanka in 1968. He found land deep in the West Virginia woods, a two-hour drive from Washington, D.C., and began to build a place to teach meditation and found a community. Since 1985, programs have been given to teach Vipassana or Insight Meditation, a practice that emphasizes a calm, centered awareness of mind and body and enables individuals to transcend personal conflict, confusion, and mental and physical suffering. As one writer described the process, "Vipassana meditators focus on what is ordinary rather than on what is new. We do not focus on what is exciting or attractive, stirring up craving, aversion, or delusion, but on that which is simple, ordinary, and neutral."

Books on meditation including *Mindfulness in Plain English* by Bhante Gunaratana and tapes of talks given at retreats held here are available by mail. The society publishes a quarterly newsletter that reports on past and future events and gives members a chance to articulate their experiences. A recent article described an exercise to learn greater detachment from the body and overcome lust by witnessing an autopsy. The writer concluded, "One thing is for sure, there is no self in the body."

Wisconsin

This lively community of Sinsinawa Dominican sisters is a wonderful example of how a dream of having a community grows and unfolds. The sisters began to pray, read, and listen in 1977 and finally, in 1984, their vision of a network of ministering became a reality. As more retreatants came, they joined in the building, and ideas like a granary, responsible stewardship, and environmental concerns, including an agriculture scholarship for a local high school student, became the focus of the sisters. A holy day for local farmers was organized, and a cookbook became a reality. They began to raise llamas, and were thrilled when one, Ali Babba, was sold for the high price of $5,000. Llama prices are much lower now. Constant hard work, focus, planning, and prayer help the community to thrive.

Today, The Bridge Between seems to have hit its stride. According to their newsletter, "The commitment we have for The Bridge is never ending. We greet strangers and friends with open arms, have a shoulder or two for the tears of life and death, get dirt under our fingernails while tending the organic garden, herb and flower plots. We gain strong backs working with the animals and their care. What a joy it is to be so needed and to give back so much. We love the saying we have here about tending 'soil and soul.' By helping you, we are refreshed and renewed. Our immediate needs are simple but necessary. Staff needs to be paid, we need heat for the winter months, we look forward to the garden work in spring and for a tractor and implements to make it easier."

Their calendar of events is bursting at the seams: On Open House/Craft Day in November, the Forget-

THE BRIDGE BETWEEN . . . RETREAT CENTER

◆

4471 Flaherty Dr. Denmark, WI 54208 (920) 864-7230

LLAMAS

ORGANIC GARDEN

SOAP

COOKBOOK

YEAR-ROUND SPECIAL EVENTS

AGRICULTURE SCHOLARSHIP

RETREATS

Me-Not Shop in their 1890 Granary Lodge is filled with crafts, herbs, baskets, preserves, wreaths, stencils, hats, gloves, mittens, their own cookbook, and lots of delicious food to eat there and take away for gifts. In December they have a live llama Nativity scene in the cathedral barn, with carol singing and readings of the season. January brings soap- and salve-making classes, and in February they teach breadmaking and gardening, and so on throughout the winter. May brings a special "Overnight for Mom," and lessons in bookbinding; and August is the Annual Harvest Festival. And when do they have time for prayer? It seems that living life to its fullest is a prayer in itself.

DEKOVEN CENTER

◆

**600 21st St.
Racine, WI 53403
(414) 633-6401**

**PROGRAMS
NOTE CARDS
ANGLICAN PRAYER BEADS
CERAMIC CROSSES
WORKSHOPS
NEWSLETTER
RETREATS**

Since 1852, DeKoven Center has been a place for learning in a spiritual atmosphere. The 34-acre property is owned by the Episcopal Diocese of Milwaukee, and all the buildings are listed on the National Register of Historic Places. DeKoven offers a full line of note cards from birth through death; *Reflections,* a newsletter; Anglican prayer beads made by Sr. Bridget, solitary of DeKoven, and ceramic crosses made by pastor Chuck Ruehle. A series of programs, workshops, and retreats are given each year, all of which have a perspective of prayer, spirituality, and theological reflection.

An ecological learning center made up of two properties, which grew out of an intentional community, High Wind concentrates on demonstrations of sustainable living. It holds classes and seminars, and publishes *Windwatch,* a semiannual journal that "details its activities, evolution toward a sustainable village, and the relationship between alternative models and mainstream culture." It operates a major alternative bookstore in Milwaukee and holds many seminars in conjunction with the University of Wisconsin.

Silver Springs is a 144-acre private retreat center with chalets for visitors, known for its spring-fed organic trout for fishing and dining pleasure in their restaurant.

O GOD of all the living, we thank thee for the happy memories of those whom thou hast called out of this transitory life into the eternal joy of thy Presence. Thine they were upon earth, and thine they are still. We thank thee for their lives of devoted service, for the happy days spent in their companionship, for the example of their faith and patience, the inspiration of their words and deeds, and for their share in heaven's new opportunities of service. Help us so to live that they may welcome us with joy when thou shalt call us to thyself.   Amen.

Prayer used by Bishop Ingley

Condolence card, Dekoven Center, Racine (opposite)

PLYMOUTH INSTITUTE HIGH WIND ASSOCIATION

◆

W7136 County Rd. U Plymouth, WI 53073 (920) 528-8488 or 7212 E-mail: bhplhp@mail.tcbi.com

SILVER SPRINGS CONFERENCE AND RETREAT CENTER

◆

N4683 Silver Springs Ln. Plymouth, WI 53073 (800) 377-7513; (920) 893-0969: conference and retreat center (920) 332-8288: High Wind Books (920) 892-4856: Springdale Farm

EDUCATION

SEMINARS

JOURNAL

DEMONSTRATION PROJECT FOR SUSTAINABLE DEVELOPMENT

FISH HATCHERY

FISHING

RETREATS

CONFERENCES

W
I
S
C
O
N
S
I
N

◈

SIENA CENTER

◆

**5635 Erie St.
Racine, WI 53402
(414) 639-4100**

**LECTURES
WORKSHOPS
MEETINGS
RETREATS**

The Catholic Dominican sisters have been at this center on the shores of Lake Michigan since 1960, and have a well-organized program of lectures, workshops, meetings, and retreats that draw on the gospels, lives of saints, and the Dominican pursuit of truth and dedication to justice for all.

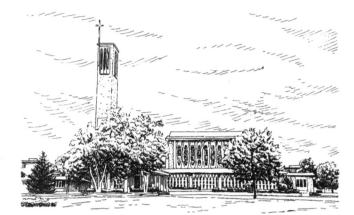

THE PORTER OF THE MONASTERY

At the door of the monastery place a sensible person who knows how to take a message and deliver a reply, and whose wisdom keeps her/him from roaming about. This porter will need a room near the entrance so that visitors will always find her/him there to answer them. As soon as anyone knocks, or a poor person calls out, s/he replies, "Thanks be to God" or "Your blessing, please," then, with all the gentleness that comes from reverence of God, s/he provides a prompt answer with the warmth of love. Let the porter be given one of the younger members if s/he needs help.

The monastery should, if possible, be so constructed that within it all necessities, such as water, mill and garden are contained, and the various crafts are practiced. Then there will be no need for the members to roam outside, because this is not at all good for their souls.

We wish this rule to be read often in the community, so that none of the members can offer the excuse of ignorance.

◆

Chapter 66, A Reader's Version of the Rule of Saint Benedict in Inclusive Language

Wyoming

◆——◆——◆

This is the most recent foundation of the Catholic Benedictine Sisters of Perpetual Adoration, whose home base is in St. Louis, Missouri. In 1980, their research showed little spiritual presence in the great state of Wyoming, so they located about ten miles west of Sheridan in the little town of Dayton, on the road to Billings, Montana. They redistribute altar bread made by one of their sister houses in Clyde, Missouri, and create and sell photo cards and handmade soap. The six sisters who live here are available for spiritual direction and host conferences in a small building on the property.

SAN BENITO MONASTERY

◆

**P.O. Box 520
Dayton, WY 82836
(307) 655-9013**

**ALTAR BREAD
PHOTO CARDS
SOAP
SPIRITUAL DIRECTION
CONFERENCES**

ASSIGNMENT OF IMPOSSIBLE TASKS

A member may be assigned a burdensome task or something s/he cannot do. If so, s/he should, with complete gentleness and obedience, accept the order given her/him. Should s/he see, however, that the weight of the burden is altogether too much for her/his strength, then s/he should choose the appropriate moment and explain patiently to the prioress/abbot the reasons why s/he cannot perform the task. This s/he ought to do without pride, obstinacy or refusal. If after the explanation the prioress/abbot is still determined to hold to her/his original order, then the junior must recognize that this is best for her/him. Trusting in God's help, s/he must in love obey.

◆

Chapter 68, A Reader's Version of the Rule of Saint Benedict in Inclusive Language

Canada

◆━━━◆━━━◆

ABBAYE SAINT-BENOIT

◆

Saint-Benoit-du-Lac
Quebec JOB 2MO
Canada
(819) 843-4080/
868-1861 fax
Fromagerie:
(819) 843-4336/3199 fax

CHEESE

APPLE CIDER

APPLESAUCE

RECORDINGS

RETREATS

For many years the abbey sold a variety of its cheeses to Hickory Farms in the United States, but as milk prices rose, this became unprofitable. Its Mont St. Benoit, Le Moine, Ricotta St. Benoit, and Ermite blue cheese are all fine cheeses available in the gift shop or small orders may be filled by mail. The monks have 800 apple trees and their apple cider (7–8 percent alcohol content) is a major monastery product. The cider and some applesauce are available in the abbey shop.

Many of the 54 members of the community have fine voices and 25 recordings of the monks singing and playing organ and harpsichord are offered for sale.

Accommodations for 50 men are available at the abbey, and 15 women can stay in the nearby Villa Sainte-Scholastique ([819] 843-2340).

ABBAYE SAINTE-MARIE-DES-DEUX-MONTAGNES

◆

2803 Chemin d'Oka
Ste.-Marthe-sur-le-Lac
Quebec JON 1PO
Canada
(514) 473-7278/
473-9833 fax

BOOKBINDING

CDS AND CASSETTES OF
GREGORIAN CHANT

RETREATS

The 50 nuns in this community that began in 1936 have developed a fine bookbinding business. They do luxurious binding with beautiful colors and paper or just simple binding and repair for churches, universities, schools, and individuals—a perfect occupation for a community that rarely leaves the property and is immersed in prayer. Gregorian chant is used in their church and their CD and cassette recordings are available in their gift shop and by mail.

The abbey has rooms for women retreatants here and at their foundation, Monastery of the Immaculate Heart of Mary in Westfield, Vermont (see page 242); women who are considering a religious life are encouraged to visit and experience traditional monastery life.

CEEDS (Community Enhancement & Economic Development) still thinks of itself as part of the hippie "back-to-the-land" movement. The members of the community started out camping in a meadow, and now rent and operate four small farms in the South Cariboo, where they raise and breed cattle, pigs, workhorses, sheep, goats, a variety of poultry, and honeybees. Surplus organic meat and vegetables are sold at farmer's markets and at the gates of their farms but not by mail. Their experiments with sheep have proved that the animals are a viable weed-control alternative to spraying herbicides. Life in this community includes horse-logging and training apprentices in organic farming, in addition to providing a home and a meaningful lifestyle for street people. They contend that agribusiness is destroying the soil with its chemicals, is killing the birds, and is reducing the market and variety of seeds and animal breeds. Thus, CEEDS raises rare Red Duroc pigs, beautiful in their conformation and weight, and the Cariboo potato, a red-and-white tuber that agribusiness dropped because its vines tangled the machinery. And their spiritual focus? "Nature," said one community member, "the great outdoors!"

The name of the town, 100 Mile House, dates back to the gold rush days in the 1860s when prospectors had to walk to the gold territory from the drop-off point in Lillooet. They had to count the miles in order to know where they were. There is still a 12 Mile House (a bar) and towns called 108 Mile House and 150 Mile House, as well as 100 Mile House.

CEEDS

◆

C-184, Horse Lake Site
R.R. 1, Lone Butte
100 Mile House
British Columbia
VOK 1X0
Canada
(250) 395-4225 or 3580:
phone/fax

LIVESTOCK
HONEYBEES
MEATS
ORGANIC VEGETABLES

COMMUNITY
ALTERNATIVES
CO-OP

◆

**1937 West 2nd Ave.
Vancouver, British
Columbia V6J 1J2
Canada
(604) 681-8816/
733-3744 fax**

RESTAURANT

GARNISH AND SALAD
COMPANY

MUFFIN BAKERY

COMMUNITY IN
WINNIPEG
NEW SOCIAL
ORDER IN
MESSIAH

◆

**484 Wardlaw Ave.
Winnipeg, Manitoba
R3L OK3
Canada
(204) 475-3362/
783-0874 fax
(204) 284-4445: café
(204) 783-0357:
candle shop**

SOAP

CANDLES

SHAMPOO

SALVES

HAND CREAM

TOOTHPASTE

CAFÉ

This cooperative community in Vancouver, British Columbia, has 43 members who have initiated such projects as a cooperative restaurant called Isadora's, the Glorious Garnish and Seasonal Salad Company, and a retail/wholesale muffin bakery, the Muffin Works, that trains mentally disabled people of all ages. They also have a ten-acre farm outside the city. Although some of the cooperative communities that are included in this book have no stated "spiritual" focus, such an orientation seems implicit in their choice of lifestyle, their special projects, and their intention to live peacefully and helpfully together and with those in the surrounding communities. Perhaps the term *cooperative* speaks clearly to this issue.

Like its sister communities in the United States, this community aims to share everything, "like the first community in Acts 2 and 4 in the New Testament." Its Sabbath is on Saturday, and its Common Ground Café closes at 3:00 P.M. on Friday. The café, in the Osborne Village section of Winnipeg, serves a wide array of food, including lasagna, spaghetti, spicy chicken on rice, and chicken in a burrito. Rich desserts seem a specialty; a Double Delicious Hot Fudge Cake is a favorite. Vinegar and oil dressings with herbs from their farm are sold at the café. Another community business is Northern Lights Candles, all in votive size and 29 varieties—for example, fruit, flowers, berries (blueberry, cranberry, apricot, plum), citrus (grapefruit, lemon-lime, orange), botanicals (balsam, eucalyptus, tulip, lavender), herbs and spices (yarrow, oak moss, myrtle, thyme, cardamom)—which they sell around the world. Soap comes in 6- or 16-ounce bars, in almond, orange, lavender, wintergreen, and peppermint fragrance. They are also making toothpastes in a variety of flavors, plus shampoos, salves, and hand creams.

L'Arche Daybreak is part of a worldwide network of L'Arche communities founded in 1964 by Jean Vanier, son of a Governor General of Canada. These Christian-based communities grew out of Vanier's own attempt to help two mentally handicapped people in his neighborhood in France by inviting them to live in his house. Eventually others joined him, and as they realized that no one was filling the need of providing homes for the developmentally handicapped, people around the world were moved and inspired to follow this lead and open more houses. There are now more than 100 L'Arche ("the Ark, that unwieldy boat in which Noah sheltered such a motley collection of God's creatures") houses in many countries, with assistants and persons with a disability living together in the same household. "We believe that each person, whether handicapped or not, has a unique and mysterious value," reads their charter. "The handicapped person is a complete human being and as such has the right to life, to care, to education, and to work . . . and we believe that God loves them in a special way because of this poverty."

Daybreak Publications is a thriving company that publishes and sells a variety of spiritually useful books, including Jean Vanier's detailed descriptions of these communities, their philosophy, and how they operate, and *An Ark for the Poor: The Story of L'Arche,* which contains a complete listing of L'Arche communities worldwide. They carry a variety of gift-shop items, too, such as cards, T-shirts, and trivets.

They also sell books by the late Henri J. M. Nouwen, a priest who gave up his active intellectual pursuits to live in this community and help care for others. His *Genesee Diary* recounts his time living with the Trappist monks at the Abbey of the Genesee and the insights he gained that perhaps helped lead to his decision to join the people of L'Arche. *The Road to Daybreak: A Spiritual Journey* details his inner and outer struggle during this time of change.

**L'ARCHE
DAYBREAK**

◆

**11339 Younge St. N.
Richmond Hill
Ontario L4C 4X7
Canada
(905) 884-3454**

BOOKS
CARDS
TRIVETS
T-SHIRTS

C
A
N
A
D
A

◈

WREATHS

Over the years, members of the Dragonfly Farm community, in Lake St. Peter, Ontario, have been involved in a holiday wreath-making business. Depending on the number of residents, it has been a major source of income during the holidays. And selling wholesale to disarmament or AIDS research groups helps with fund-raising for good causes in which they are glad to participate. Over the last few years the wreath-making has taken on a more relaxed character, providing activity to individual community members who feel moved to make a few wreaths and sell them.

The process begins in November, when they roam the farm's own 250 acres, looking for materials. They take along a grain sack and a pair of scissors or a little knife, and as they pass balsams, cedars, and pines with beautiful tips, they snip five to seven inches off and put them in the sack. Watching for interesting ground cover, they collect a few feet here and there. Each person has an individual style, some picking up pinecones, others adding twigs that catch their eye, or things like pearly everlastings, as they enjoy their stroll through the woods. Fluffy red sumac flowers are a favorite with others, and they carefully add those to their growing collection.

In the evening, after dinner, the wreath-making activity begins when someone empties these treasures onto the hearth before the fireplace. Coat hangers are wrapped in a hoop with stovepipe wire, little bundles are made of the pine tips, which are wrapped on the frame, then red ribbon is tied into a bow and added to the wreath. Each one is finished in less than an hour, then put outside again to keep it fresh. The wreaths will last well into January as long as they are kept outside. They are sold for $13–$15 wholesale, and $20–$25 retail ($30 for especially beautiful or unique wreaths.)

"It's a nice walk out in the forest this time of year," reports one community member, "except if there are ice storms! The wreaths smell great when you are building them, and it gets you in the mood for the season."

◆

Dragonfly Farm, (613) 338-2709

In its commercial greenhouse, the community grows a large variety of flowers, both rare and common, and organic vegetable and herb starts. They have a mobile sawmill with which they cut logs to order. Their holiday wreaths, made of frozen balsam, cedar, and pine fir tips, are sold wholesale at co-ops in Toronto and other cities. The small group of people who live on Dragonfly Farm's 250 acres, "in a rather severe climate," welcome visitors who want to experience life in rural Canada and a very primitive lifestyle with no indoor running water. "This is a magical place," says one community member. "Except for the blackflies right now, which I keep away with a geranium and lavender oil potion made by a neighbor, this is a wonderful place to live on the land. Here at Dragonfly the politics of anarchy rule within a sense of communal individualism. A unique kind of spirituality is present."

Most of Dragonfly Farm's sales are local, but seeds and dried herbs can be mailed.

DRAGONFLY FARM

◆

Mink Lake Rd.
Lake Saint Peter, Ontario
KOL 2KO
Canada
(613) 338-2709 or
338-3316

FLOWERS AND SEEDS

VEGETABLE AND HERB STARTS

DRIED HERBS

WREATHS

MOBILE SAWMILL AND CUSTOM WOODWORKING

Philoxians, or Lovable Strangers, was a name given survivors of an ancient pre-continent called Mu, which sank in the Pacific 14,000 years ago. Today's Philoxians, a family community, have published three popular books: *From Grits to Gourmet; The Pheylonian Odyssey;* and *Alpha, Mu, Omega.* The last two of these tell the story of Mu, and recount the adventures of the community. In addition, Iilaz and Tawlia Chickalo operate a beeswax candle business based on Iilaz's Ukrainian grandmother's formula. They make the wicks by hand from Polynesian hemp and use 100 percent beeswax, from which they produce 18,000 pounds or 20,000 to 30,000 candles a year.

PHILOXIA

◆

RR1, P.O. Box 56
Marlbank, Ontario
K0K 2L0
Canada
(613) 478-6070/5410 fax

BOOKS
BEESWAX CANDLES

SALT SPRING CENTRE

◆

355 Blackburn Rd.
Salt Spring Island, British
Columbia V8K 2B8
Canada
(250) 537-2326/
537-2311 fax

ARTS AND CRAFTS
COOKBOOK
ORGANIC GARDENS
CHRISTMAS CRAFTS FAIR
SCHOOL
YOGA RETREAT IN AUGUST
PROGRAMS AND RETREATS

Guided by Baba Hari Dass of Mount Madonna, this spiritual community practices Ashtanga Yoga, which includes ethical principles, yoga postures, breathing exercises, and meditation. Its members supplement their income with a Christmas crafts fair, which sells crafts from their artists-in-residence; an annual yoga retreat; a cookbook called *Salt Spring Island Cooking;* and the sale of produce from their organic gardens. During their retreats they offer massage, reflexology, sauna, and herbal steambox. They sometimes offer their property to local groups, such as a men's drumming group that met one evening when we were there. The people who live here have a substantial commitment to yoga and selfless service.

YASODHARA ASHRAM

◆

Box 9
Kootenay Bay, British
Columbia V0B 1X0
Canada
(250) 227-9224
(800) 661-8711

CLASSES
WORKSHOPS
BOOKS
TAPES
JOURNAL
FARMING

Based on ancient yogic teachings that have been adapted for westerners by the late Swami Radha over more than 35 years, this ashram, which varies in size from 20 to 100 residents, depending on the time of year, offers courses in hatha yoga and a grounded method of working with kundalini energy. In addition, they offer mantra instruction as a way to interpret dreams. The community grows much of its own produce on this 140-acre property on the shores of Kootenay Lake, and publishes a journal called *Ascent* that helps explain its way of life. The bookstore at the center offers works of the founder, such as *Kundalini Yoga for the West* and *Mantra Words of Power,* and also distributes the books throughout Canada.

Instructional tapes of the teachings of Swami Radha, like *Relaxation and Divine Light Invocation,* are also offered for sale in the bookstore and wholesale. They have a center in Spokane, Washington, (800) 251-9273, which sells the books and tapes in the United States and internationally. There are also centers in Mexico and Great Britain.

Mexico

Based on the scientific principles of B. F. Skinner's *Walden Two,* rather than on the ideas or personal beliefs of any one individual, this community encourages every member to participate in decision making in an organizational structure they call Person-ocracy. They are very interested in personal growth and interpersonal behavior, and are a self-sufficient and eco-logical pacificist community that has shared or commu-nal property. They have organic gardens and orchards, communal child-rearing, and their own school. Income is derived from the sale of natural food products such as yogurt and granola, from their summer camps, and from consulting work with other cooperatives. They welcome new members interested in agricultural research, animal farming, ecology, and cooperative life.

LOS HORCONES

◆

**Apartado Postal 372
Hermosillo, Sonora
Mexico 83000
011 (52) (62) 147219
(7 A.M.–7 P.M.
Monday–Saturday)
E-mail: walden
@imparcial.com.mx
Web site:
www.loshorcones
.org.mx**

YOGURT
GRANOLA
CHEESE
HONEY
SUMMER CAMPS
TEACHING
SCHOOL
CONSULTING

France

◆━━━◆━━━◆

Many products that we're all familiar with are made by monks and nuns around the world. Things like Benedictine brandy, Chartreuse, and other liqueurs have been mainstays of monastery income for centuries. We had planned to share with you some of the products made by international monasteries today, with information on how to order them. It turns out, however, that import/export laws make it very difficult for many of the monasteries to send things abroad for sale, so instead we'll give you a glimpse of some of the European products for which arrangements have already made for purchase from abroad.

In an upcoming book, we plan to include details of the places that have great products so that when you visit Europe, you'll be able to purchase them—including in England, pewter, fishing flies, chocolate, honey, tonic wines, mead, hot-cross buns, vestments, and altar bread; and in France, Belgium, Luxembourg, or the Netherlands, fruit preserves and syrups, jelly bears, mints, almonds, hard candy, chocolate, honey, ewe-milk cheese, special breads, shortbread, cakes, cookies, madeleines, meringues, butter, table wines, beer, liqueurs, pasta, cereal, instant coffee, cocoa, yeast tablets, soap, shampoo, bath foam, face and hand cream, sachets, and other toiletries, beeswax candles, candleholders, dishes, plant food, liturgical music tapes, liturgical vestments, banners, religious tiles, statues, figurines, crèches, weaving, embroidery, bookbinding, and stained glass.

Since arrangements have been made to order bottled holy water from Lourdes by credit card, some products from a monastery of cloistered Dominican nuns in France, and Zen Buddhist products from Paris, we include those specifics here.

ASSOCIATION ZEN INTERNATIONALE

◆

175 rue de Tolbiac
75013 Paris, France
33 (0)1 53 80 19 19/
14 33 fax
E-mail: zen-mail
@zen-azi.org
Web site:
www.zen-azi.org

BOOKS BY FOUNDER ZEN
MASTER TAISEN DESHIMARU
INCENSE
ZEN CLOTHING
GONGS
CALLIGRAPHY
PHOTOGRAPHS
POSTCARDS
T-SHIRTS
AUDIO- AND VIDEO-
CASSETTES

DOMINIQUE & BERNADETTE MONASTÈRE DES DOMINICAINES

◆

Route de Pontacq
65100 Lourdes, France
33 55 62 91 12 43/
62 94 89 76 fax

CANDLES
POTPOURRI
ROSARIES
ABOVE-AVERAGE-SIZE ICONS

IMAGES & RÉSEAUX/MBO

◆

127, rue Amelot
75011 Paris, France
Web site:
www.religion-
store.com/cde.htm

LOURDES WATER
VIRGIN MARY STATUETTES
BRACELETS
ROSARIES
MEDALS
KEY RINGS
(VISA, MASTERCARD, AND
AMERICAN EXPRESS
ACCEPTED VIA MAIL OR
INTERNET ORDERS. ORDER
FORM ON WEB SITE.)

F
R
A
N
C
E

◈

Festivals

◆ ◆ ◆

We have listed these by date and then alphabetical order (except where it makes more sense not to). However, we suggest checking with each place to ascertain actual dates, which may vary from year to year.

JANUARY
◆

New Year's: New Year Sesshin, New Orleans Zen Center, New Orleans, La.

January 7: Festival, Monastery of the Resurrection of Christ, Fridley, Minn.

10-Day World Peace Day Celebration in Bodh Gaya, India, with simultaneous chanting at Nyingma Institute, Berkeley, Calif.

Barbershop Chorus Celebration and Benefit, Mount St. Scholastica, Atchison, Kans.

FEBRUARY
◆

Taizé Retreat, Mercy Center, Burlingame, Calif.

MARCH
◆

Equinox Celebration, Gaian Contemplative Community, Tum Tum, Wash.

Equinox Celebration, Upland Hills Ecological Awareness Center, Oxford, Miss.

Lenten Family Retreat, St. Christopher Camp and Conference Center, Johns Island, S.C.

Spring Festival, Short Mountain Sanctuary, Liberty, Tenn.

Tibetan New Year Concert, Tibet House, New York, N.Y.

Fourth Sunday in March: Maine Maple Sunday, Notre Dame Spiritual Center, Alfred, Maine

Second Sunday after Easter: Myrrhbearers Sunday, Holy Myrrhbearers Monastery, Otego, N.Y.

APRIL
◆

Dance Festival, Kalani Honua Oceanside Eco-Resorts, Pahoa-Kehena Beach, Hawaii

Easter: Healing Center of Arizona, Sedona, Ariz.

Plum Blossom Festival, Benedictine Sisters of Mt. Angel, Mt. Angel, Ore.

MAY
◆

Cultural Festival, Chautauqua Institution, Chautauqua, N.Y.

Gilbert and Sullivan: First two weekends in May, Arden Village, Wilmington, Del.

Festival, Mission San Luis Rey, San Luis Rey, Calif.

Mother's Day: Fiesta de la Primavera, Holy Trinity Monastery, St. David's, Ariz.

Ramayana Festival, Mount Madonna Center, Watsonville, Calif.

Sister Bernadette Memorial Auction of Miniature Horses, Monastery of St. Clare, Brenham, Texas

Summer Social, Monastery Immaculate Conception, Ferdinand, Ind.

Taizé Celebrations, Mercy Center, Burlingame, Calif.

JUNE
◆

June 3–4 weekend, 10-day Festival of Saint Hildegard, Windward Foundation, Klickitat, Wash.

Crafts Festival, Rochester Folk Art Guild, Middlesex, N.Y.

JUNE
(cont'd)

Shakespeare Festival, Arden Village, Wilmington, Del.

Solstice Celebration, Gaian Contemplative Community, Tum Tum, Wash.

Solstice Celebration, Upland Hills Ecological Awareness Center, Oxford, Miss.

Strawberry Festival, Common Place Land Cooperative, Truxton, N.Y.

JULY
◆

Buddhist Festival, Milarepa Center, Barnet, Vt.

Festival, Mission San Luis Rey, San Luis Rey, Calif.

July 4, approximately: "Art and the Spirit" Week, Quaker Center, Ben Lomond, Calif.

Fourth of July Celebration, Community of Jesus, Orleans, Mass.

Fourth of July Cornerstone Music Festival, Jesus People U.S.A., Chicago, Ill.

2nd Sunday in July: Chicken Dinner, Mount St. Scholastica, Atchison, Kans.

3rd Sunday in July: Field of Dreams Bazaar, Transfiguration Monastery, Windsor, N.Y.

July 24: Anniversary Celebration, Healing Center of Arizona, Sedona, Ariz.

Last Wed.–Fri. in July: Bach Festival, Mount Angel Abbey, St. Benedict, Ore.

Shakespeare Festival, Arden Village, Wilmington, Del.

AUGUST
◆

Ashtanga Yoga Retreat, Salt Spring Centre, Salt Spring Island, British Columbia, Canada

Buddhist Festival, Milarepa Center, Barnet, Vt.

Summer Festival, Camphill Village USA, Copake, N.Y.

Dance Festival, Kalani Honua Oceanside Eco-Resorts, Pahoa-Kehena Beach, Hawaii

Feast of the Dormition of the Mother of God, Dormition of the Mother of God Orthodox Monastery, Rives Junction, Mich.

Festival, Mission San Luis Rey, San Luis Rey, Calif.

Summer Gathering, Common Place Land Cooperative, Truxton, N.Y.

Women: Celebrating Our Creativity, Twin Oaks Community, Louisa, Va.

August 15, Sunday on or before: Feast of the Assumption Pilgrimage, St. Mary's Villa, Sloatsburg, N.Y.

Barbecue/Wine Auction, Carmelite House of Prayer, Oakville, Calif.

Communities Conference, Twin Oaks Community, Louisa, Va.

Crafts Festival, Rochester Folk Art Guild, Middlesex, N.Y.

Equinox Celebration, Gaian Contemplative Community, Tum Tum, Wash.

Equinox Celebration, Upland Hills Ecological Awareness Center, Oxford, Miss.

Fall Celebration, Benedictine Sisters of Mount Angel, Mount Angel, Ore.

Fall Festival, St. Andrew's Abbey, Valyermo, Calif.

Festival, Mission San Luis Rey, San Luis Rey, Calif.

Oktoberfest, Sacred Heart Retreat House, Ipswich, Mass.

Sister Bernadette Memorial Auction of Miniature Horses, Monastery of St. Clare, Brenham, Texas

Labor Day Saturday: Arden Fair, Arden Village, Wilmington, Del.

Labor Day Weekend Farm Harvest Fest, The Farm, Summertown, Tenn.

Labor Day Weekend: Campout, Camp Webb, Milwaukee, Wisc.

Labor Day Weekend: Pignic, rock 'n' roll concert, Black Oak Ranch, Laytonville, Calif.

SEPTEMBER

◆

F
E
S
T
I
V
A
L
S

◈

Weekend after Labor Day: Oktoberfest, Benedictine Sisters of Mount Angel, Mount Angel, Ore.

Sunday after Labor Day: The Faire, The Common, Peterborough, N.H.

OCTOBER
◆

Last full weekend in October: Abbey Fest, Corpus Christi Abbey, Sandia, Texas

Arts for the Park, Tara Enterprises, International, Poolesville, Md.

Fall Festival, Short Mountain Sanctuary, Liberty, Tenn.

Food and Wine Festival, St. Martin's Abbey, Lacey, Wash.

Open House, Padanaram Settlement, Williams, Ind.

Patrons' Party, St. Joseph Abbey, St. Benedict, La.

Pilgrimage, Holy Myrrhbearers Monastery, Otego, N.Y.

NOVEMBER
◆

Coury House Annual Bazaar, Subiaco Abbey, Subiaco, Ariz.

Craft Show: Thanksgiving Sunday, Arden Village, Wilmington, Del.

Festival, Holy Trinity Monastery, St. David's, Ariz.

Native American Corn Fest, St. Hilda's country retreat, St. Cuthbert's Retreat House, Brewster, N.Y.

Kansas Thomas Merton Conference, Mount St. Scholastica, Kans.

3rd weekend in November: Craft and Bread Sale, Mount St. Scholastica, Atchison, Kans.

Thanksgiving: Family Retreat, St. Christopher Camp and Conference Center, Johns Island, S.C.

DECEMBER
◆

Buddhist Festival, Tara Enterprises, International, Poolesville, Md.

Buddhist Festival, Milarepa Center, Barnet, Vt.

Crafts Fair, Salt Spring Centre, Salt Spring Island, British Columbia, Canada

Dance Festival, Kalani Honua Oceanside Eco-Resorts, Pahoa-Kehena Beach, Hawaii

Solstice Celebration, Gaian Contemplative Community, Tum Tum, Wash.

Solstice Celebration, Upland Hills Ecological Awareness Center, Oxford, Miss.

Christmas Festival, Healing Center of Arizona, Sedona, Ariz.

Christmas Festival, Monastery of the Resurrection of Christ, Fridley, Minn.

Christmas Village—House Tour, Community of Jesus, Orleans, Mass.

New Year's Eve: Chanting, Nyingma Institute, Berkeley, Calif.

Buddhist Festivals and Celebrations: Shasta Abbey, Mt. Shasta, Calif., and Aryaloka Buddhist Center, Newmarket, N.H.

Retreat/Hospitality Experience in Latin-American Context: Weston Priory, Weston, Vt.

Christian Pilgrimages, early May to mid-October: Montfort Retreat Center, Litchfield, Conn.

Seasonal Festivals: Chinook Learning Center, Clinton, Wash.

Vision Quests: Gaian Contemplative Community, Tum Tum, Wash.

FESTIVALS HELD THROUGHOUT THE YEAR

◆

BIBLIOGRAPHY

◆

Ashworth, William. *The Encyclopedia of Environmental Studies.* New York: Facts on File, 1991.

Attwater, Donald G., ed. *The Catholic Encyclopædic Dictionary.* New York: The Macmillan Company, 1931.

Beinert, Frederica. "Jelly and Jam." Entry in *Encyclopedia Americana.* 1993 edition.

Blue Evening Star. "The Expanding Circle." *Communities,* Spring 1997: 34–36.

Bulman, Jan. "'I Own Isadora's Restaurant'." *Communities,* Spring 1997: 42–44.

Christian, Diana Leafe. "Straw into Gold: Creating Value-Added Products." *Communities,* Spring 1997: 37.

Communities Directory: A Guide to Cooperative Living. 1996 edition. Rutledge, Mo.: Fellowship for Intentional Community, 1995.

"Fruitcake History and Facts." Web site: www.tesla. csuhayward.edu (17 June 1997).

"The Hammock." *Web Pages for the Promotion of Yucatán Culture.* Web site: www.expo-yucatan.com (17 June 1997).

Janzen, David. *Fire, Salt, and Peace.* Evanston, Ill.: Shalom Mission Communities, 1996.

Johnson, Herbert W. "Soybean." Entry in *Encyclopedia Americana.* 1994 edition.

Kelly, Jack and Marcia Kelly. *Sanctuaries, The Northeast: A Guide to Lodgings in Monasteries, Abbeys, and Retreats.* New York: Bell Tower, 1991.

———. *Sanctuaries. The West Coast and Southwest: A Guide to Lodgings in Monasteries, Abbeys, and Retreats.* New York: Bell Tower, 1992.

———. *Sanctuaries. The Complete United States: A Guide to Lodgings in Monasteries, Abbeys, and Retreats.* New York: Bell Tower, 1996.

Miller's Honey Company. "How Honey Is Made." Web site: www.millershoney.com (17 June 1997).

Morinis, Alan ed. *Sacred Journeys.* Westport, Conn.: Greenwood Press, 1992.

Mubarak, Sandy. "Wool Basics." *Rocky Mountain Llama and Alpaca Association.* Web site: www.llama.org (17 June 1997).

Schauble, Sister Marilyn, and Sister Barbara Wojciak, eds. *A Reader's Version of the Rule of St. Benedict in Inclusive Language.* Erie, Pa.: Benedictine Sisters of Erie, Inc., 1989.

Stein, Edith C. *The Environmental Sourcebook.* New York: Lyons and Burford, 1992.

Thurston, Herbert. "Chasuble." Entry in *The Catholic Encyclopedia.* New York: Robert Appleton Company, 1908.

West, Edward N. "Icon." Entry in *Encyclopedia Americana.* 1994 edition.

Young, Anna. "Boss? What Boss?" *Communities,* Spring 1997: 30–33.

PERMISSIONS

❖

The authors gratefully acknowledge the *Communities Directory* for pointing them to the following communities: Abundant Dawn (Floyd, Va.); Acorn (Mineral, Va.); Alpha Farm (Deadwood, Ore.); Aquarian Concepts (West Sedona, Ariz.); Arden Village (Wilmington, Del.); Cerro Gordo Community (Cottage Grove, Ore.); Clearview Center for the Celebration of Life (Moriah, N.Y.); Common Place Land Cooperative (Truxton, N.Y.); Community in Buffalo (Lakeview, N.Y.); Community in Island Pond (Island Pond, Vt.); Community in Rutland (Rutland, Vt.); Earth Cycle Farm (Waukon, Wash.); East Wind Community (Tecumseh, Mo.); Four Winds Village (Tiger, Ga.); Gaian Contemplative Community (Tum Tum, Wash.); Ion Exchange Village (Harpers Ferry, Iowa); Koinonia Partners (Americus, Ga.); Lichen (Wolf Creek, Ore.); Madre Grande Monastery of the Paracelsian Order (Dulzura, Calif.); Open Way (Charlottesville, Va.); Padanaram Settlement (Williams, Ind.); Sandhill Farm (Rutledge, Mo.); Shepherdsfield (Fulton, Mo.); Shiloh Community (Sulphur Springs, Ark.); Short Mountain Sanctuary, Inc. (Liberty, Tenn.); Sikh Dharma/3HO Foundation (Los Angeles, Calif.); Sparrow Hawk Village (Tahlequah, Okla.); The Stelle Group (Stelle, Ill.); Twin Oaks (Louisa, Va.); and Windward Foundation (Klickitat, Wash.).

Illustrations on page 36 reprinted with permission from the Corita Art Center Immaculate Heart Community.

INDEX OF PLACE NAMES

◆

INDEX OF PRODUCTS AND SERVICES

◆

ABOUT THE AUTHORS

(ROBERT T. COBB)

Marcia and Jack Kelly are writers who live in New York. Over the years they have chosen monasteries and retreats as their stopping places in their travels, and have now visited more than 250 such places. Their first book, *Sanctuaries: The Northeast,* was published in 1991. *Sanctuaries: The West Coast and Southwest* followed in 1993, and *Sanctuaries: The Complete United States* appeared in 1996. They have also edited *One Hundred Graces,* a collection of mealtime blessings gathered along the way. Marcia Kelly is also the author of *Heavenly Feasts: Memorable Meals from Monasteries, Abbeys, and Retreats.*

QUESTIONNAIRE

❖

If you know of a community, product, art, or service not yet included in our book, please make a photocopy of this page and ask a community representative to complete this form and return it to Marcia and Jack Kelly, c/o Bell Tower, 201 East 50th Street, New York, NY 10022, so that we have a chance to add this new information to the next edition of this book. We also welcome any updating of existing entries.

THE WHOLE HEAVEN CATALOG

Community Name:

Address:

City: State: Zip Code:

Telephone: Fax: E-mail:

Contact: Web site:

1. List and describe your main products, arts, and/or services, including price range:

2. Annual festivals, bazaars, special holiday events (include dates, location, activities, and other relevant details):

3. Special classes and offerings you'd like people to know about:

4. Stories, anecdotes, history of your business and products:

5. Photos/drawings of your products, buildings, and staff: We'd like to illustrate as many products as possible, to give readers a real flavor of each place and product.